ALSO BY THE EDITORS AT AMERICA'S TEST KITCHEN

The Complete Slow Cooker

The Complete Make-Ahead Cookbook

The Complete Mediterranean Cookbook

The Complete Vegetarian Cookbook

The Complete Cooking for Two Cookbook

Cooking at Home with Bridget and Julia

What Good Cooks Know

Cook's Science

The Science of Good Cooking

The Perfect Cookie

Bread Illustrated

Master of the Grill

Kitchen Smarts

Kitchen Hacks

100 Recipes: The Absolute Best Ways to Make the
True Essentials

The New Family Cookbook

The America's Test Kitchen Cooking School Cookbook

The Cook's Illustrated Meat Book

The Cook's Illustrated Baking Book

The Cook's Illustrated Cookbook

The New Best Recipe

Soups, Stews, and Chilis

The America's Test Kitchen Quick Family Cookbook

The America's Test Kitchen Healthy Family Cookbook

The America's Test Kitchen Family Baking Book

The Best of America's Test Kitchen (2007–2018 Editions)

The Complete America's Test Kitchen TV Show
Cookbook 2001–2018

Food Processor Perfection

Pressure Cooker Perfection

Vegan for Everybody

Naturally Sweet

Foolproof Preserving

Paleo Perfected

The How Can It Be Gluten-Free Cookbook: Volume 2

The How Can It Be Gluten-Free Cookbook

The Best Mexican Recipes

Slow Cooker Revolution Volume 2: The Easy-Prep Edition

Slow Cooker Revolution

The Six-Ingredient Solution

The America's Test Kitchen D.I.Y. Cookbook

Pasta Revolution

THE COOK'S ILLUSTRATED ALL-TIME BEST SERIES

All-Time Best Sunday Suppers

All-Time Best Holiday Entertaining

All-Time Best Appetizers

All-Time Best Soups

COOK'S COUNTRY TITLES

One-Pan Wonders

Cook It in Cast Iron

Cook's Country Eats Local

The Complete Cook's Country TV Show Cookbook

FOR A FULL LISTING OF ALL OUR BOOKS

CooksIllustrated.com

AmericasTestKitchen.com

PRAISE FOR OTHER AMERICA'S TEST KITCHEN TITLES

"The editors at America's Test Kitchen, known for their meticulous recipe testing and development, are back at it again. This time, they've trained their laser-eyed focus on reduced-sugar baking. . . . Cooks with a powerful sweet tooth should scoop up this well-researched recipe book for healthier takes on classic sweet treats."
BOOKLIST ON *NATURALLY SWEET*

Selected as the Cookbook Award Winner of 2017 in the Baking Category
INTERNATIONAL ASSOCIATION OF CULINARY PROFESSIONALS (IACP) ON *BREAD ILLUSTRATED*

"With 1,000 photos and the expertise of the America's Test Kitchen editors, this title might be the definitive book on bread baking."
PUBLISHERS WEEKLY ON *BREAD ILLUSTRATED*

Selected as one of Amazon's Best Books of 2015 in the Cookbooks and Food Writing Category
AMAZON ON *THE COMPLETE VEGETARIAN COOKBOOK*

"The sum total of exhaustive experimentation . . . anyone interested in gluten-free cookery simply shouldn't be without it."
NIGELLA LAWSON ON *THE HOW CAN IT BE GLUTEN-FREE COOKBOOK*

"The 21st-century *Fannie Farmer Cookbook* or *The Joy of Cooking*. If you had to have one cookbook and that's all you could have, this one would do it."
CBS SAN FRANCISCO ON *THE NEW FAMILY COOKBOOK*

"A one-volume kitchen seminar, addressing in one smart chapter after another the sometimes surprising whys behind a cook's best practices. . . . You get the myth, the theory, the science, and the proof, all rigorously interrogated as only America's Test Kitchen can do."
NPR ON *THE SCIENCE OF GOOD COOKING*

"The perfect kitchen home companion. . . . The practical side of things is very much on display . . . cook-friendly and kitchen-oriented, illuminating the process of preparing food instead of mystifying it."
THE WALL STREET JOURNAL ON *THE COOK'S ILLUSTRATED COOKBOOK*

"Another winning cookbook from ATK. . . . The folks at America's Test Kitchen apply their rigorous experiments to determine the facts about these pans."
BOOKLIST ON *COOK IT IN CAST IRON*

"Some 2,500 photos walk readers through 600 painstakingly tested recipes, leaving little room for error."
ASSOCIATED PRESS ON *THE AMERICA'S TEST KITCHEN COOKING SCHOOL COOKBOOK*

"An exceptional resource for novice canners, though preserving veterans will find plenty here to love as well."
LIBRARY JOURNAL (STARRED REVIEW) ON *FOOLPROOF PRESERVING*

"A terrifically accessible and useful guide to grilling in all its forms that sets a new bar for its competitors."
PUBLISHERS WEEKLY (STARRED REVIEW) ON *MASTER OF THE GRILL*

"This book is a comprehensive, no-nonsense guide . . . a well-thought-out, clearly explained primer for every aspect of home baking."
THE WALL STREET JOURNAL ON *THE COOK'S ILLUSTRATED BAKING BOOK*

"This encyclopedia of meat cookery would feel completely overwhelming if it weren't so meticulously organized and artfully designed. This is *Cook's Illustrated* at its finest."
THE KITCHN ON *THE COOK'S ILLUSTRATED MEAT BOOK*

"The go-to gift book for newlyweds, small families, or empty nesters."
ORLANDO SENTINEL ON *THE COMPLETE COOKING FOR TWO COOKBOOK*

"There are pasta books . . . and then there's this pasta book. Flip your carbohydrate dreams upside down and strain them through this sieve of revolutionary, creative, and also traditional recipes."
SAN FRANCISCO BOOK REVIEW ON *PASTA REVOLUTION*

"Further proof that practice makes perfect, if not transcendent. . . . If an intermediate cook follows the directions exactly, the results will be better than takeout or Mom's."
THE NEW YORK TIMES ON *THE NEW BEST RECIPE*

nutritious
DELICIOUS

turbocharge your favorite recipes
with 50 everyday superfoods

the editors at America's Test Kitchen WITHDRAWN

Library of Congress Cataloging-in-Publication Data

Names: America's Test Kitchen (Firm)
Title: Nutritious delicious : turbocharge your favorite
    recipes with 50 everyday superfoods / the editors at
    America's Test Kitchen.
Description: Boston, MA : America's Test Kitchen, [2017] |
    Includes index.
Identifiers: LCCN 2017030625 | ISBN 9781945256110
Subjects: LCSH: Natural foods. | Cooking (Natural foods) |
    LCGFT: Cookbooks.
Classification: LCC TX741 .N88 2017 | DDC 641.3/02--dc23
LC record available at https://lccn.loc.gov/2017030625

AMERICA'S TEST KITCHEN
21 Drydock Avenue, Suite 210E, Boston, MA 02210
Manufactured in the United States of America

10 9 8 7 6 5 4 3 2 1

Distributed by Penguin Random House Publisher Services
Tel: 800-733-3000

CHIEF CREATIVE OFFICER Jack Bishop

EDITORIAL DIRECTOR, BOOKS Elizabeth Carduff

EXECUTIVE EDITOR Julia Collin Davison

EXECUTIVE EDITOR Adam Kowit

EXECUTIVE FOOD EDITOR Suzannah McFerran

SENIOR EDITORS Stephanie Pixley and Anne Wolf

ASSOCIATE EDITORS Leah Colins, Nicole Konstantinakos,
and Russell Selander

TEST COOKS Kathryn Callahan and Afton Cyrus

ASSISTANT TEST COOK Esther Reynolds

EDITORIAL ASSISTANT Alyssa Langer

CONSULTING NUTRITIONIST Alicia Romano, MS, RD, LDN

DESIGN DIRECTOR, BOOKS Carole Goodman

DEPUTY ART DIRECTOR Allison Boales

DESIGNER Katie Barranger

PRODUCTION DESIGNER Reinaldo Cruz

PHOTOGRAPHY DIRECTOR Julie Bozzo Cote

PHOTOGRAPHY PRODUCER Mary Ball

SENIOR STAFF PHOTOGRAPHER Daniel J. van Ackere

STAFF PHOTOGRAPHERS Steve Klise and Kevin White

ADDITIONAL PHOTOGRAPHY Keller + Keller and Carl Tremblay

FOOD STYLING Catrine Kelty, Kendra McKnight, Marie Piraino,
Elle Simone Scott, and Sally Staub

PHOTOSHOOT KITCHEN TEAM

    MANAGER Timothy McQuinn

    TEST COOK Daniel Cellucci

    ASSISTANT TEST COOKS Mady Nichas and Jessica Rudolph

PRODUCTION DIRECTOR Guy Rochford

SENIOR PRODUCTION MANAGER Jessica Lindheimer Quirk

PRODUCTION MANAGER Christine Walsh

IMAGING MANAGER Lauren Robbins

PRODUCTION AND IMAGING SPECIALISTS Heather Dube,
Dennis Noble, and Jessica Voas

COPY EDITOR Deri Reed

PROOFREADER Ann-Marie Imbornoni

INDEXER Elizabeth Parson

CONTENTS

ix Welcome to America's Test Kitchen

x A Better Way to Eat

39 Breakfast

81 Lunch

135 Main Dishes

201 Vegetables and Sides

255 Snacks

283 Dessert

302 Conversions and Equivalents

304 Index

WELCOME TO AMERICA'S TEST KITCHEN

This book has been tested, written, and edited by the folks at America's Test Kitchen. Located in Boston's Seaport District in the historic Innovation and Design Building, it features 15,000 square feet of kitchen space including multiple photography and video studios. It is the home of *Cook's Illustrated* magazine and *Cook's Country* magazine and is the workday destination for more than 60 test cooks, editors, and cookware specialists. Our mission is to test recipes over and over again until we understand how and why they work and until we arrive at the best version.

We start the process of testing a recipe with a complete lack of preconceptions, which means that we accept no claim, no technique, and no recipe at face value. We simply assemble as many variations as possible, test a half-dozen of the most promising, and taste the results blind. We then construct our own recipe and continue to test it, varying ingredients, techniques, and cooking times until we reach a consensus. As we like to say in the test kitchen, "We make the mistakes so you don't have to." The result, we hope, is the best version of a particular recipe, but we realize that only you can be the final judge of our success (or failure). We use the same rigorous approach when we test equipment and taste ingredients.

All of this would not be possible without a belief that good cooking, much like good music, is based on a foundation of objective technique. Some people like spicy foods and others don't, but there is a right way to sauté, there is a best way to cook a pot roast, and there are measurable scientific principles involved in producing perfectly beaten, stable egg whites. Our ultimate goal is to investigate the fundamental principles of cooking to give you the techniques, tools, and ingredients you need to become a better cook. It is as simple as that.

To see what goes on behind the scenes at America's Test Kitchen, check out our social media channels for kitchen snapshots, exclusive content, video tips, and much more. You can watch us work (in our actual test kitchen) by tuning in to *America's Test Kitchen* or *Cook's Country from America's Test Kitchen* on public television or on our websites. Listen in to test kitchen experts on public radio (SplendidTable.org) to hear insights that illuminate the truth about real home cooking. Want to hone your cooking skills or finally learn how to bake—with an America's Test Kitchen test cook? Enroll in one of our online cooking classes. However you choose to visit us, we welcome you into our kitchen, where you can stand by our side as we test our way to the best recipes in America.

FACEBOOK.COM/AMERICASTESTKITCHEN
TWITTER.COM/TESTKITCHEN
YOUTUBE.COM/AMERICASTESTKITCHEN
INSTAGRAM.COM/TESTKITCHEN
PINTEREST.COM/TESTKITCHEN
GOOGLE.COM/+AMERICASTESTKITCHEN

AMERICASTESTKITCHEN.COM
COOKSILLUSTRATED.COM
COOKSCOUNTRY.COM
ONLINECOOKINGSCHOOL.COM

A BETTER WAY TO EAT

2 Building a More Nutritious Recipe

4 Vitamins, Minerals, and You

6 Decoding Phytonutrients

8 50 Superfoods to Turbocharge Everyday Cooking

32 Flavor, Flour, and Fat: Building a Nutrient-Dense Pantry

For many years, a dish was considered healthy based not on what it contained, but on what it didn't—notably, fat, calories, sugar, and salt. This way of eating sets up expectations for disappointment, which are often confirmed upon first bite. Not a winning formula for long-term success, nor a way to ensure you're getting proper nutrition. So we've been happy to see a shift in how people think about healthy eating that focuses more on the nutrients that go into our food. This is no doubt aided by the surge of interest in the health benefits of various ingredients, in particular, the so-called superfoods, an undefined category of items at the high end of the nutritional spectrum. A more accurate term might be "nutrient-dense," which refers to foods that contain a significant amount of vitamins, minerals, and other healthful substances with respect to their calories, and are not "diluted" by added sugars, solid fats, and refined starches.

The notion of amping up the nutritional value of our daily meals sounded a lot better to us than a diet based on elimination. And focusing recipes on nutrient-dense ingredients seemed like a great way to do it. Rather than counting calories, we could make every calorie count. A dietitian would call this approach "crowding out" not-so-healthy ingredients with healthier ones. Getting the most out of what we eat fills our bodies with essential nutrients and can prevent overindulging, since we are not left with cravings that send us back to the fridge.

Our goal was to build recipes that utilized the most nutrient-dense foods that are widely available and easily incorporated into everyday cooking. We weren't going to get there by relying on blueberries alone. We needed a full basket of ingredients that could constitute a new lineup of staples. Fortunately, many of the most nutrient-dense foods can be found right in your own backyard (or local market). With guidance from a registered dietitian, we compiled a list of 50 high-nutrient superfoods across fruits, vegetables, legumes, grains, and proteins, selecting foods based on what we knew could get plenty of use in the kitchen and constitute a significant part of a meal. We also assembled a pantry of nutritious seasonings, flours, and fats. Every item listed is super in its own way and deserves a place in your grocery cart and on your plate.

BUILDING A MORE NUTRITIOUS RECIPE

If we were to build a truly nutrient-dense recipe, we couldn't just select salmon or spinach as our main ingredient and then treat it any old way. Adding a butter sauce to salmon or drenching spinach in cream would nullify the benefits. We were going to have to rethink our habits, yet we wanted meals we would be happy to eat on a regular basis.

So we delved into updating the nutritional framework of the dishes we loved in order to make them nutrient-dense through and through. Rather than deny ourselves macaroni and cheese, we used whole-wheat pasta and incorporated a bunch of Swiss chard, yielding a dish with a significantly healthier profile. We partnered eggs with greens on the breakfast plate, folded creamy butternut squash into polenta, and whipped buttery avocado into a chocolate pudding. We pushed ourselves to bring as much nutrient-density as possible into every recipe, which often involved a thorough reworking.

The more we tested, the more we found creative, healthier ways to great flavor. We achieved smokiness without bacon, creaminess without cream, and richness without butter. These recipes also shifted the balance of the ingredients we consumed, with more emphasis on vegetables and fish. Nuts and seeds played a bigger role, too, as did whole grains and plant-based protein sources such as beans and tofu. Lean red meat, while nutrient dense, became an occasional option (which is why we only feature it three times in the book). We traded refined grains for whole as much as possible, and even found ways to reduce added sugar while celebrating the natural sweetness of fruit.

EATING THE RAINBOW

Eating nutritiously means eating a variety of foods across and within various groups. Preparing quinoa as your only grain is therefore not a shining example of healthy eating. A mix of grains offers more diverse benefits. Different fruits and vegetables have varying nutrient profiles, depending on their type, their color, and even whether you eat them raw or cooked.

While you are probably familiar with most of the ingredients in the book, they may not all get regular use in your kitchen. We hope these recipes will encourage you to branch out and try something new, and hopefully find a new go-to for mealtime.

KEEP AN EYE OUT FOR "EXCELLENT SOURCE OF"

To highlight the many essential nutrients found in our recipes, in addition to general nutrition information, we indicate when a recipe is an "Excellent Source" of protein, fiber, and key vitamins and minerals. This means a single serving provides 20 percent or more of the Daily Value (DV) of a nutrient as set by the Food and Drug Administration (FDA) for adults and children over 4 years of age. Note that only some nutrients have established Daily Values (others, such as phytonutrients, do not have quantifiable standards at this time). All the recipes are "Excellent" in at least one nutrient and many are "Excellent" in far more.

NUTRIENT-DENSE EATING IN A NUTSHELL

1 Consume more vegetables in a variety of colors and types (see pages 12–22).

2 Consume more fruits, primarily whole fruits, limiting fruit products with added sugars (see pages 8–11).

3 Ensure at least 50 percent of your grains are whole grains (see pages 29–30).

4 Vary your protein routine, drawing from seafood, eggs, lean poultry and beef, and plant-based sources such as legumes, nuts, and seeds (see pages 23–28).

5 Focus on healthy fats. Limit saturated fat to less than 10 percent of calories per day (see page 35).

6 Limit added sugars to less than 10 percent of calories per day (see page 35).

SIX SIMPLE SWAPS

BACON For meaty, smoky flavor without the saturated fat and sodium, we combined portobello mushrooms with smoked paprika in our MLT sandwich (page 83).

MAYONNAISE A 2:1 ratio of yogurt to mayonnaise still provided plenty of richness in our Turmeric Chicken Salad Sandwiches (page 85). Elsewhere, we mashed avocado and lemon juice to create a creamy dressing for our Broccoli Salad with Almonds and Cranberries (page 211).

BUTTER Heart-healthy canola oil worked surprisingly well in our baking instead of butter. When more richness was needed in our Cranberry-Orange Oat Muffins, we added low-fat yogurt (page 60).

REGULAR PASTA To enjoy pasta without the refined grains, using whole-wheat pasta was just the starting point. We also traded white pasta for toothsome farro in our Pesto Farro Salad (page 117) and for spiralized vegetables in our Raw Beet and Carrot Noodle Salad with Almond-Sesame Dressing (page 122).

WHITE BREAD Opting for 100 percent whole-wheat bread in place of white was an easy swap that went a long way in reducing the need for refined white flour. In developing these recipes, we used 100 percent whole-wheat versions of sandwich bread, rustic loaves, burger buns, and even panko bread crumbs.

ICEBERG LETTUCE For a crisp salad green that brought more nutritional punch than run-of-the-mill iceberg lettuce, we tossed nutrient-dense napa cabbage into our Chinese Chicken Salad (page 124) and employed sparkling, mildly bitter escarole as a base for our Quinoa Taco Salad (page 120).

For a healthy twist on a BLT, our MLT uses nutrient-dense mushrooms instead of bacon, whole-wheat bread instead of white, arugula instead of iceberg/Bibb lettuce, and avocado instead of mayo.

VITAMINS, MINERALS, AND YOU

We all know vitamins and minerals are essential for our bodies to function, but what do they actually do? Here is a snapshot of their key roles, and some of the best food sources of each.

VITAMIN	KEY FUNCTIONS AND BENEFITS	COMMONLY FOUND IN
A	• Immune function • Healthy vision • Organ maintenance and cell growth	Cherries, grapefruit, figs, dates, dark leafy greens, red cabbage, sweet potatoes, winter squash, carrots, tomatoes, red bell peppers, legumes, sardines, eggs
B1 THIAMINE	• Energy production • Nervous system support	Legumes, nuts, sunflower seeds, oats, barley
B2 RIBOFLAVIN	• Energy production • Antioxidant protection	Dark leafy greens, avocado, asparagus, mushrooms, soybeans, tempeh, eggs, poultry, almonds, milk products
B3 NIACIN	• Heart and skin health • Brain function • May help improve joint mobility and arthritis symptoms	Mushrooms, legumes, fish, tempeh, poultry, beef, seeds
B5 PANTOTHENIC ACID	• Energy metabolism • Essential for breaking down nutrients for fuel and fat storage	Pomegranates, broccoli, sweet potatoes, avocado, corn, mushrooms, lentils, salmon, poultry, yogurt
B6	• Brain development and function • Hormone production (serotonin, norepinephrine, melatonin)	Spinach, kale, cauliflower, butternut squash, carrots, avocado, bananas, legumes, fish, eggs, poultry, sunflower seeds, whole grains
B7 BIOTIN	• Hair and skin health	Avocado, legumes, salmon, sardines, eggs, organ meats, almonds, yeast
B9 FOLIC ACID/FOLATE	• DNA synthesis and repair • Cell growth • Fetal development (prevention of neural tube defects) • Heart health	Grapefruit, dark leafy greens, broccoli, cauliflower, Brussels sprouts, eggplant, avocado, asparagus, legumes, seeds
B12	• Nerve and blood cell health • Metabolism	Fish, eggs, poultry, beef, milk products
C	• Immune function • Protein metabolism and wound healing • Collagen production • Absorption of plant-based iron • Antioxidant properties • Possible role in delaying certain cancers and heart disease	Berries, cherries, pomegranates, apples, citrus, dark leafy greens, broccoli, cauliflower, Brussels sprouts, red cabbage, sweet potatoes, butternut squash, carrots, eggplant, avocado, tomatoes, red bell peppers, artichokes, asparagus, onions, green beans, edamame

VITAMIN	KEY FUNCTIONS AND BENEFITS	COMMONLY FOUND IN
D	• Bone growth and remodeling • Neuromuscular and immune function • Calcium absorption • May protect against diabetes	Fortified milk products (milk, yogurt, kefir), certain mushrooms (see page 21), salmon (especially canned), white fish, eggs, cod liver oil
E	• Immune function • Antioxidant activity • May help prevent or delay cancer and heart disease	Figs, dark leafy greens, broccoli, avocado, asparagus, eggs, nuts, seeds, vegetable oils
K	• Blood clotting • Bone metabolism	Figs, dates, dark leafy greens, broccoli, cauliflower, Brussels sprouts, cabbage, avocado, red bell peppers, artichokes, asparagus, legumes, eggs

MINERAL	KEY FUNCTIONS AND BENEFITS	COMMONLY FOUND IN
CALCIUM	• Bone growth and maintenance • Required by heart, muscles, and nerves • May help protect against cancer, diabetes, and high blood pressure	Milk products, oranges, figs, dates, dark leafy greens, broccoli, sweet potatoes, legumes, salmon (especially canned), sardines, trout, fortified soy products, almonds
COPPER	• Building strong tissue • Maintaining blood volume • Energy production • Facilitating some antioxidant activity	Figs, avocado, asparagus, mushrooms, legumes, trout, tempeh, eggs, nuts (especially almonds and cashews), sunflower seeds, dark chocolate
IRON	• Hemoglobin and red blood cell production (to prevent anemia) • Protein metabolism	Figs, dates, dark leafy greens, Brussels sprouts, mushrooms, legumes, trout, tofu, eggs, poultry, beef, whole grains
MAGNESIUM	• Protein synthesis and nerve function • Blood pressure regulation • Energy metabolism	Oranges, figs, dates, dark leafy greens, sweet potatoes, butternut squash, eggplant, avocado, artichokes, legumes, tofu, almonds, pepitas, milk products, raw cacao
MANGANESE	• Bone health • Antioxidant properties	Berries, dark leafy greens, sweet potatoes, legumes, trout, fortified soy products, nuts, oats, pepitas, whole grains, brown rice
PHOSPHORUS	• Helps build strong bones and teeth • Involved in metabolism and the conversion of food into energy	Legumes, fish, tofu, poultry, beef, nuts, whole grains, milk products
POTASSIUM	• Blood pressure regulation • Electrolyte balance and fluid regulation • Muscle function (helps muscles contract) • May lower stroke and heart disease risk	Cherries, watermelon, citrus, figs, dates, potatoes, dark leafy greens, cauliflower, Brussels sprouts, sweet potatoes, winter squash, carrots, eggplant, avocado, tomatoes, beets, mushrooms, legumes, salmon, white fish, whole grains, milk products
SELENIUM	• DNA synthesis and thyroid metabolism repair • Anti-inflammatory and antioxidant properties • May reduce risk of cancer and heart disease	Mushrooms, fish and shellfish, poultry, beef, Brazil nuts, seeds
ZINC	• Cell metabolism • Immune function • Protein synthesis • Wound healing	Legumes, shellfish (especially oysters), eggs, beef, pepitas, milk products, raw cacao

DECODING PHYTONUTRIENTS

Vitamins and minerals may have proven functions in our bodies. But they are the tip of the iceberg when it comes to the molecules in food that may benefit our health. There is another world of phytonutrients, or biologically active chemicals found in plants, and they are over 100,000 strong.

Many act as antioxidants and may be associated with health benefits ranging from preventing disease to slowing brain degeneration. (While animals use their muscles to fight or flee danger, plants evolved chemicals to protect themselves. When we eat these powerful chemicals, the thinking goes, they may offer us protection, too.) While you may not know phytonutrients by name, you have seen, tasted, and smelled them, because many are the very compounds that give plants their colors, flavors, and aromas. The pigment in a red apple's skin, the peppery flavor in arugula, and the warm aroma of cinnamon are all produced by phytonutrients that may benefit us in a variety of ways.

So do they work, and which should we eat? Hundreds of studies explore how we absorb and utilize phytonutrients, and while it can be difficult to draw definitive conclusions, evidence points to links between some of them and reduced risk of chronic diseases. The USDA recommends that we "eat a rainbow," in order to obtain a broad variety of nutrients. Different colors of fruits and vegetables—including white—often connote different nutritional profiles. Orange, for example, typically indicates beta-carotene, while anthocyanins provide the deep purple and red hue in many plants. There are many classes of phytonutrients, including flavonoids, the largest class, with over 5,000 nutrients spread across the plant kingdom. The chart at right highlights some of the most studied phytonutrients.

WHAT IS AN ANTIOXIDANT?
Antioxidants are molecular scavengers that find and neutralize free radicals (formed during the natural oxidation that occurs in our bodies) that otherwise can damage our cells and DNA, putting us at higher risk for chronic diseases. Many phytonutrients act as antioxidants, but some vitamins do too, such as vitamins C and E.

PHYTONUTRIENT	POSSIBLE BENEFITS	COMMONLY FOUND IN
ALLICIN A sulfur-containing compound that produces a pungent aroma	• Various detoxifying powers	Onions, leeks, shallots, garlic
ANTHOCYANIN A flavonoid pigment that provides red, purple, and blue colors. Anthocyanin-rich plant mixtures such as dried leaves, berries, roots, and seeds have played a role in many traditional medicines	• May be associated with slowing the aging process • May protect against heart disease, diabetes, tumors • May prevent blood clots and inflammation	Blueberries, raspberries, blackberries; cherries; red apples (with skin); blood oranges; red and purple grapes; purple cauliflower; red cabbage; purple sweet potatoes; eggplant; purple asparagus; red wine
BETA-CAROTENE An antioxidant that provides yellow-orange hues to fruits and vegetables. The more intense the color, the more beta-carotene it likely contains	• Converts in our bodies to vitamin A, which is important for vision, skin, and immune system • Antioxidant properties	Cherries, grapefruit, cantaloupe, dark leafy greens, broccoli, sweet potatoes, winter squash, carrots
BETALAIN A class of antioxidants, including betacyanin, that provides beets with their deep purple color	• Various detoxifying powers • Anti-inflammatory properties may help fight chronic diseases such as obesity, cancer, and heart disease	Chard, beets
GLUCOSINOLATES Sulfur-containing compounds in cruciferous vegetables which react with enzymes to provide the vegetables' familiar peppery or bitter flavor	• Converts during chopping, cooking, or chewing to chemicals (isothiocyanates and indoles) studied for their role in detoxifying the body and preventing cancer and heart disease	Dark and bitter leafy greens, broccoli, cauliflower, Brussels sprouts, cabbage, horseradish, radishes, rutabaga, turnips, wasabi
ISOFLAVONES A class of phytoestrogens (compounds found in plants that have estrogenic properties) found primarily in legumes	• May reduce risk factors for heart disease and hormone-related cancers	Soybeans and other soy products
LIGNANS A class of phytoestrogens	• Can balance hormones and may reduce risk of certain cancers, osteoporosis, and heart disease	Berries, apricots, kale, cabbage, seeds, whole grains
LUTEIN AND ZEAXANTHIN Red-yellow pigments that may protect plants by absorbing sunlight	• May help prevent macular (eye) degeneration and cataracts • Has antioxidant properties • May reduce risk of heart disease and breast cancer	Dark leafy greens, avocado, golden yellow beets, beet greens, egg yolks, goji berries
LYCOPENE A red pigment that becomes more absorbable when cooked	• A potent antioxidant that may be associated with cancer prevention, especially prostate cancer • May lower risk of heart disease and age-related eye disorders	Red and pink grapefruit, watermelon, guava, red cabbage, tomatoes, red bell peppers
PHENOLIC ACIDS Aromatic compounds that give scent to spices, heat to chiles, and astringency to tea, coffee, and red wine	• May be associated with lowered risk of degenerative brain disease • Various antioxidant properties	Berries, cherries, citrus, mangoes, plums, kiwis, onions, chiles, whole grains, spices, tea, coffee, red wine
RESVERATROL A phenolic compound that plants produce as a response to stress, ultraviolent radiation, or infection	• Has antioxidant and anti-inflammatory properties • May help prevent cancer and heart disease	Blueberries, cranberries, red and purple grapes, peanuts, pistachios, red wine

50 SUPERFOODS TO TURBOCHARGE EVERYDAY COOKING

There are a lot of healthy foods out there, so how to pick the best? To make it onto our list, nutrient density was key, but we also focused on ingredients that we could cook with often and in significant amounts. These 50 foods, selected with the guidance of a registered dietitian, are jam-packed with vitamins and minerals, protein and fiber, healthy fats, and phytonutrients. Our goal was to incorporate these nutritional powerhouses as much as possible into our recipes, keeping in mind the importance of variety along the way.

BLUEBERRIES

SUBSTITUTE
Strawberries, raspberries, blackberries

Plump, juicy, and boasting a slight dusty sheen (or "bloom"), blueberries are loaded with anthocyanins, the antioxidant compound that gives them their unique hue and may be associated with everything from heart health to slowing the aging process. The same can be said for other berries, such as raspberries, strawberries, and blackberries, all of which also boast deep red, blue, or purple skin, though each has its own unique nutritional qualities. Blueberries especially seem to appear on every superfood list you'll find—and for good reason, as they're also full of fiber, vitamin C, and manganese. You can find them fresh, frozen, or dried. If buying frozen or dried berries, make sure to look for the unsweetened variety. We incorporated as many blueberries as possible into our Whole-Wheat Blueberry-Almond Muffins (page 58) and Blueberry-Oat Pancakes (page 52), where the blue-purple jewels studded our breakfasts with juicy bursts of natural sweetness.

CRANBERRIES

Cranberries deserve more time in the spotlight (other than at Thanksgiving) thanks to their wide range of impressive health benefits. The deep red berries are loaded with proanthocyanidins (PACs), compounds that have been linked to improved urinary, digestive, and dental health, as well as inhibiting cancer growth and decreasing inflammation. As with other berries, they are also an easy way to incorporate more fiber, vitamin C, and manganese into your diet. In this book, we came to appreciate their tart flavor in both fresh and dried forms, using a modest amount of sugar to balance their tartness in our Cranberry-Orange Oat Muffins (page 60), and pairing them with naturally sweet fruits like apples in our Cranberry-Apple Crisp (page 293).

CHERRIES

Cherries pack a super-nutritional punch for their small size. They're rich in phytonutrients, including anthocyanin, beta-carotene, and phenolic acids, and also offer potassium and vitamins A and C. Tart cherries are an especially good source of vitamin A, while sweet cherries provide three times more anthocyanins due to their darker hue. Cherries have also been shown to reduce uric acid in the body, which can cause inflammation, and therefore may play a role in pain reduction in osteoarthritis and even gout. Similarly, the antioxidants in cherries may also help relieve postexercise muscle soreness and aid in muscle recovery, making them a great snack for athletes. Tart cherries may help as a natural sleep aid, as they are one of few natural sources of melatonin, a hormone that helps regulate sleep-wake cycles. No matter the type, cherries are a great choice and can be found fresh, dried, frozen, or juiced; be sure to look for unsweetened varieties. (In general, dried fruit contains similar nutritional qualities as fresh, but in more concentrated amounts; however, heat used during drying may decrease heat-sensitive nutrients such as vitamin C.) We incorporated dried tart cherries into our Sunflower Seed, Hazelnut, and Cherry Muesli (page 40) and Chocolate Bark with Almonds and Cherries (page 301), where they provided chewy texture and tart flavor to contrast with the crunchy nuts and seeds.

POMEGRANATES

Eating a pomegranate may be a labor of love, but they are well worth the effort. Native to the Middle East and India, the dark red fruit famed for its high antioxidant levels has grown rapidly in popularity and is now readily available in most grocery stores. True to reputation, pomegranate seeds contain a large number of phytonutrients (up to 122 have been cited). They are also rich in vitamin C and pantothenic acid, which may help ease muscle cramping and reduce joint pain and inflammation. Shoppers can often find the edible seeds (called "arils") prescooped and packaged (the rest of the pulp is not edible). Though this is certainly convenient, the longer the seeds have been removed from the whole fruit and exposed to light or air, the more the vitamins will degrade. You can also find pomegranate juice in stores; look for 100 percent pomegranate juice with no added sugar. For our Super Guacamole (page 258), we added pomegranate seeds to bring pops of juicy sweetness and a nutritional boost in a fun twist on the traditional dip.

APPLES

Though it really takes more than just an apple a day to keep the doctor away, the expression does hold some truth, as apples are a very healthful addition to the diet. Apples are a good source of dietary fiber, including soluble fiber such as pectin (associated with lowering cholesterol levels and controlling blood sugar), and insoluble fiber (which aids in digestive health). They're readily available year-round, budget-friendly, and super portable. There are thousands of different varieties of apples (100 grown commercially within the United States alone) with varying skin colors, tartness, and crispness, but nutritionally speaking, the redder, the better. Red-skinned apples, such as Rome, Fuji, and Braeburn, contain the highest concentration of anthocyanins and may provide more antioxidant benefits. Be sure to eat the skin: In addition to antioxidants, it contains much of the fruit's vitamin C and insoluble fiber. We used apples in savory and sweet applications: In our Fennel and Apple Salad with Smoked Trout (page 130), its fresh, bright flavor contrasted nicely with the rich, smoky fish; and in our Skillet-Roasted Apples with Dried Figs, Walnuts, and Maple Yogurt (page 294), apple's natural sweetness was balanced by crunchy nuts in place of buttery pastry.

ORANGES

SUBSTITUTE
Clementines, tangerines

Citrus fruits have an interesting historical past; though scurvy had been first described by the ancient Egyptians and Greeks and wreaked havoc on long-distance travelers (on land and at sea) who lacked fresh produce, it was not discovered until the 18th century that citrus fruits, such as oranges, could cure the deficiency, and then another two centuries passed before vitamin C was specifically identified as the cure. Now we recognize the importance of this vitamin—it enables the body to efficiently use carbohydrates, fats, and protein, is required for collagen formation, has a key role in iron regulation, and acts as an antioxidant. It should be noted that processing and cooking may degrade vitamin C. But oranges offer more than just their vitamin C; they're also full of fiber, potassium, calcium, magnesium, and more. Like all citrus fruits, they may help lower heart disease and stroke risk and seem to have anti-carcinogenic effects. There are many different types of oranges, with varying hues of vibrant orange to deep reddish-purple. To capture their fiber along with the other nutrients, we incorporated fresh orange segments into our Beets with Orange and Walnuts (page 207) and Chinese Chicken Salad (page 124).

GRAPEFRUIT
(RED AND PINK)

SUBSTITUTE
White grapefruit

Named for the way they grow in grape-like clusters, grapefruits are slightly mysterious, as their skin color does not typically give away the interior flesh color. Similar to oranges, grapefruits are quite high in vitamin C, with just half of one providing 100 percent of your daily value. Though white grapefruits are certainly a healthy choice, we opted for red or pink grapefruits in these recipes as, in addition to being sweeter, they contain more lycopene and beta-carotene than their white counterparts. These carotenoids act as antioxidants and may reduce cancer risk, improve bone density, and slow down bone loss. No matter the color, all grapefruits have cholesterol-lowering potential thanks to their soluble fiber, which may help reduce total cholesterol, LDL cholesterol, and potentially triglycerides; this may be enhanced by flavonoids also present in the fruit. The large citrus is also high potassium, folate, and more. We took advantage of red grapefruit's sweetness and bright acidity by incorporating whole segments into Salmon, Avocado, Grapefruit, and Watercress Salad (page 129).

FIGS

Despite popular belief, figs are actually more flower than fruit; they bloom inward, hiding their tiny blossoms and seeds within. Native to the Middle East and Mediterranean, figs may be small, but they contain a large number of health benefits. They are high in fiber, thanks to the edible seeds within their delicate flesh. They're also rich in vitamins A, E, and K, and potassium, copper, and iron. You can find both fresh and dried figs; though they have similar nutritional qualities, dried figs contain less vitamin A and lose some B vitamins during processing. We liked the floral quality fresh figs gave our Chicken and Arugula Salad with Figs and Warm Spices (page 127).

DATES

Cultivated as early as 4000 B.C., dates are famous for their low moisture content and resulting wrinkly, shiny brown exteriors, chewy texture, and candy-like sweetness. Along with that sweetness comes plenty of fiber, which can help lower cholesterol, as well as vitamins A and K, potassium, and magnesium, which helps make them one of the most nutrient-dense fruits. As a great source of whole-fruit sweetness, dates starred in our Whole-Wheat Date-Nut Bread (page 63). We also liked their chewy texture in our hearty Brown Rice Pilaf with Dates and Pistachios (page 250).

SPINACH

Dark leafy greens—a group that includes spinach, kale, collards, and Swiss chard—are some of the most nutrient-dense foods out there. They're packed full of chlorophyll, fiber, calcium, antioxidants, vitamins A, C, E, K, and some B vitamins like folate, important for heart health and preventing certain birth defects of the brain and spinal cord (neural tube defects). All this while being low in carbohydrates, sodium, and calories, so you get serious nutritional bang for your calorie buck. Among dark greens, spinach is one of the most accessible for its mild flavor and tender texture. Full of beta-carotene (whose orange hue is masked by the chlorophyll), spinach is also a great vegetable source of iron, which plays a large role in the function of red blood cells. (Note that the iron found in plants may be more absorbable in the presence of vitamin C, such as in lemon juice.) Spinach is a good example of a vegetable that offers different levels of nutrients depending on whether it is eaten raw or cooked, so switching up your preparation methods is a good idea. When cooking spinach, avoid boiling, which will leach out many of the water-soluble vitamins. Prewashed baby spinach is an especially convenient way to bring a nutritious boost to your meals; we added it by the handful to several soups and sandwiches in this book. But sturdier curly-leaf spinach stands up better to sautéing, which made it the perfect choice for our Sautéed Spinach with Yogurt and Dukkah (page 232).

KALE

SUBSTITUTE
Collard greens

The new "it" vegetable, kale is fairly comparable to spinach nutritionally, but edges it out in terms of vitamin and mineral content. Just 1 cup of the hearty greens has over 100 percent of the daily value of vitamins A and C (gram for gram, kale contains more than twice the vitamin C as an orange). It's also packed with potassium, calcium, and vitamins K and B6. Similar to alliums like onions and garlic, which are odorless until sliced, the particular flavor of cruciferous plants such as kale comes into existence only after being chopped, massaged, or chewed. These actions break down the cell structure to bring out the pungent, bitter taste. On the other hand, blanching kale breaks apart the bitter compounds, resulting in a less assertive flavor. Soaking kale in a hot water bath, like we do for our Kale Caesar Salad (page 108), works in the same way, albeit more mildly, as well as tenderizes the leaves. But our uses for kale went far beyond salad: We stirred it into soup, pureed it into pesto, and roasted it. And, as many kale chips on the market are laden with salt and fat, we also opted to make our own Kale Chips (page 269), which are perfect for snacking.

SWISS CHARD

SUBSTITUTE
Mustard greens, turnip and beet greens

Despite its misleading name, Swiss chard is native to Sicily. Like other dark leafy greens, it is a good source of magnesium, manganese, potassium, iron, and vitamins A, C, E, and especially K (a 1-cup serving of chard provides over 700 percent of your daily value). But the green also shares nutritional qualities with beets, a relative, including high levels of nitrates, which may help lower blood pressure and enhance athletic performance; and betalains, which offer anti-inflammatory and detoxification support. Look for colorful rainbow chard; the vibrant stems owe their hues to different types of betalains. All of these nutrients, combined with a hearty texture and earthy flavor, ensured the vegetable got plenty of play in our recipes, from a stir-in for mac and cheese (page 185) to a partner for eggs at breakfast (page 67). Be sure to not discard the stems, which are edible and delicious; they need only a brief head start in the pan to soften before adding the greens.

WATERCRESS

SUBSTITUTE
Arugula, escarole, dandelion greens

Watercress doesn't always get the credit it deserves and is often overshadowed by the more-popular kale and spinach. But in a CDC ranking that analyzed 47 fruits' and vegetables' nutrient densities, watercress topped the list. The reason? Watercress is packed full of vitamins A, C, and K. It also contains plenty of fiber, potassium, and calcium. Add to that the sulfur-containing compounds that give cruciferous vegetables like watercress their bitter, peppery bite, which may help fight cancer. We liked the bite it added to our Egg Salad Sandwiches with Radishes and Watercress (page 86).

OUR FAVORITE NUTRIENT-DENSE SALAD GREENS

KALE An ideal base for hearty salads; a soak in warm water relaxes the sturdy leaves, making them tender, not chewy (see Super Cobb Salad, page 112).

WATERCRESS Its peppery punch complements rich or sweet components (see Salmon, Avocado, Grapefruit, and Watercress Salad, page 129). Use alone or mix with other greens.

SPINACH A mild, tender dark green; a handful can lighten richer salads (see Turmeric Chicken Salad Sandwiches, page 85).

ARUGULA Prewashed leaves make a nutritious base for all kinds of simple salads (see Three-Bean Salad with Arugula, page 119).

ESCAROLE Contributes a subtle bitterness and more character than lettuce (see Mediterranean Chopped Salad, page 111).

a better way to eat

BROCCOLI

One of the oldest cultivated varieties of wild cabbage (others include cauliflower, kale, collards, and Brussels sprouts), broccoli belongs to a larger family known as cruciferous vegetables. These vegetables are nutritionally distinct in that they are rich sources of glucosinolates, sulfur-containing phytonutrients that, upon being chopped or chewed, form pungent compounds called isothiocyanates, which deliver the vegetables' aroma and bitter flavor. These same compounds may also be associated with preventing certain types of cancer. Overcooking destroys the enzyme that breaks down glucosinolates, so to ensure you get all the health benefits, cook broccoli briefly (such as by steaming, sautéing, or grilling) or simply eat it raw. In addition to powerful glucosinolates, broccoli is a great source of vitamins A, C, E, K, and fiber and folate. We steamed broccoli florets and stalks before adding a creamy avocado dressing in our Broccoli Salad with Almonds and Cranberries (page 211). We also brought broccoli to the breakfast table in our Frittata with Broccoli and Turmeric (page 72).

SUBSTITUTE
Broccoli rabe, Chinese broccoli

CAULIFLOWER

Though we typically associate brightly colored foods with nutrient density, cauliflower is a notable exception. The less colorful relative of broccoli is a rich source of vitamins B6 and C and potassium. Cauliflower also has the second-highest concentration of glucosinolates within the cruciferous family, providing pungency and health benefits. (All that said, if you do find one of the colorful varieties of cauliflower, it will offer a slight antioxidant edge: Purple cauliflower is rich in anthocyanins, orange cauliflower contains beta-carotene, and green cauliflower gets its hue from vitamin C–containing chloroplasts.) But what makes cauliflower a real nutritional hero is its kitchen versatility, which makes it easy to enjoy myriad ways. We cut large cross-sections for our Cauliflower Steaks (page 194), pureed it into a silken topping for shepherd's pie (page 164), blitzed florets to make a stand-in for rice (page 223), and even transformed it into a savory pizza crust (page 198).

BRUSSELS SPROUTS

Good things certainly do come in small packages when it comes to Brussels sprouts. Though they have a notoriously smelly reputation, their sulfuric odor only occurs when overcooked (once they've transformed from bright green to muted green). The little sprouts are packed with fiber that helps promote colon health and lower cholesterol, plus folate, potassium, vitamins C and K, B vitamins, iron, and glucosinolates. Brussels sprouts are delicious both raw and cooked, so we put them to use both ways, shredding them for our Brussels Sprout, Red Cabbage, and Pomegranate Slaw (page 214), and roasting them to get a crisp, caramelized exterior in our Roasted Brussels Sprouts with Walnuts and Lemon (page 213).

RED CABBAGE

SUBSTITUTE
**Green cabbage, bok choy,
napa cabbage**

Red cabbage gets its stunning red-purple color from anthocyanins, the same antioxidant compounds found in blueberries and cherries. This red variety also stands out due to its higher concentration of vitamins A and C (10 times the vitamin A and almost 30 percent more vitamin C than green cabbage). No matter the color, all cabbages contain glucosinolates. When shopping, opt for whole heads of cabbage rather than pre-shredded, as preshredded bags may have lost some vitamin C over time. Because overcooking can destroy many of its nutrients, we opted to keep the cabbage raw in our slaws, which also lent fantastic texture to our dishes. Red cabbage provided vibrant color and pleasant crunch to our Salmon Tacos with Super Slaw (page 139) and Pulled BBQ Turkey with Red Cabbage Slaw (page 170).

8 EASY WAYS TO UP YOUR EATING GAME

1 **TRY VEGETABLES FOR BREAKFAST**
Why wait until lunch to get your first daily dose of veggies? Make our Frittata with Broccoli and Turmeric (page 72).

2 **SAVE YOUR STEMS**
Broccoli and Swiss chard stems taste great and offer valuable nutrition. We use both stems and leaves in Pomegranate Roasted Salmon with Lentils and Chard (page 140).

3 **DOUBLE UP ON HERBS**
A hefty amount of cilantro gives Tofu Rancheros (page 74) a pop of green color and boost of vitamins.

4 **DIP INTO YOUR SPICE RACK**
Spices add nutrients in concentrate form; Red Lentil Soup with North African Spices (page 101) uses six different kinds.

5 **DON'T FREEZE OUT FROZEN OR CANNED**
Convenient canned pumpkin provided richness and a boost of vitamin A to our Pumpkin Turkey Chili (page 169).

6 **THINK TWICE BEFORE PEELING**
If washed properly, there's often no reason to skip the skin. Apple skin added fiber to Cranberry-Apple Crisp (page 293).

7 **SCATTER ON SOME SEEDS OR NUTS**
Flax, sesame, and chia seeds contributed healthy fats and fiber to our Whole-Wheat Seeded Crackers (page 273).

8 **EAT FRUIT (AND VEGETABLES!) FOR DESSERT**
Pureed beets gave our Beet-Chocolate Cupcakes (page 288) plenty of nutrients and acted as a natural food dye.

SWEET POTATOES

Though we appreciate regular white spuds for their versatility, when compared side by side, sweet potatoes pack a stronger nutritional punch than their white counterparts. Their bright orange flesh indicates their wealth of vitamin A: Just one potato provides about 400 percent of your recommended daily value—important for eye health. They also contain more fiber, calcium, and manganese than white potatoes. Like white potatoes, they're a great source of potassium and magnesium, which help regulate blood pressure. Note that sweet potatoes are different than yams and contain many more nutrients, so read signs carefully when shopping. Sweet potatoes can be found in a variety of colors, including white, yellow, orange, and even purple. Though purple sweet potatoes are not widely available in America, if you can find them, they contain the most anthocyanins of these varieties. Orange-fleshed sweet potatoes contain more beta-carotene (converted in the body to vitamin A) than white or yellow, so the brighter the better. Make sure to eat the skin, which contains much of the spud's fiber. We prefer baking to boiling, as boiling leaches the vitamins into the cooking water. Our Sweet Potato and Swiss Chard Gratin (page 238) is a lighter, brighter, vitamin- and fiber-rich alternative to the classically heavy dish.

BUTTERNUT SQUASH

SUBSTITUTE
Acorn squash, delicata squash

In the kitchen, we love butternut squash for how its hearty-but-not-starchy yellow-orange flesh turns sweet when roasted and silky smooth when steamed and pureed. But, like sweet potatoes, that vibrant interior also speaks to bountiful stores of vitamin A; just 1 cup of cubed butternut squash provides nearly 300 percent of your daily value, but it also contains vitamins C and B6, plus potassium, magnesium, fiber, and even some omega-3 fatty acids. Other bright orange winter squash have similar nutritional profiles. Though often discarded, a butternut's seeds are excellent when roasted; they're rich in protein, healthy fats, and zinc. When kept in a cool, dry place, many whole winter squash can keep for three to six months (depending on the variety), so you don't have to worry about them spoiling. Though we prefer fresh squash, you can find frozen pureed squash, as well as canned pumpkin puree (which is often partly squash), all of which offer nutritious alternatives and convenience in a time crunch. We stirred soft roasted squash into polenta (page 247) for a luscious and nutritious update on the rustic side dish. And we took advantage of canned pumpkin to add body and a vitamin boost to our Pumpkin Turkey Chili (page 169).

CARROTS

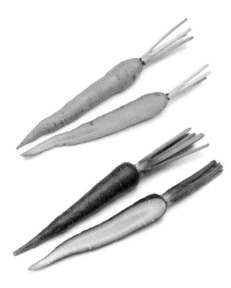

It's no coincidence that "carrot" sounds like "beta-carotene"; the phytonutrient's name is derived from the Latin name for carrot. (The compound was discovered in 1826 during the chemical analysis of carrot juice.) In our bodies, beta-carotene is converted to vitamin A; just one medium carrot yields 210 percent of the recommended daily value of the vitamin. Overall, carrots have a similar nutritional profile to sweet potatoes and butternut squash, boasting fiber, potassium, and vitamins C and B6. While they are certainly nutritious raw, some health benefits may improve with cooking, as phytonutrient levels may increase. Though most commonly found orange, carrots can be purple, yellow, and white, each with its own antioxidant profile, though all contain beta-carotene (look for mixed bags of different colors). Such a nutritional superstar needed more uses than roasting and snacking on raw: We called on its sweet-earthy flavor to supercharge our morning oatmeal (Steel-Cut Oatmeal with Carrots and Cherries, page 46), ground it into a vegetable take on tabbouleh (Carrot "Tabbouleh" with Mint, Pistachios, and Pomegranate Seeds, page 216), and simmered it gently to preserve nutrients and let its flavor shine through (Slow-Cooked Whole Carrots with Pine Nut Relish, page 218).

EGGPLANT

A member of the nightshade family (along with potatoes, tomatoes, and peppers), eggplants received their name during the British occupation of India, where the white, egg-shaped plants were quite popular. Though we typically envision dark purple eggplant, they can be found in a variety of colors (striped white and purple, solid dark purple, white, pale green) and sizes. Refrain from peeling eggplant, as the skin is full of anthocyanins and other phytonutrients. In addition to these, eggplant provides plenty of fiber, important for digestive and heart health, as well as vitamin C, folate, potassium, and magnesium. Bigger is not necessarily better in the case of eggplant; smaller ones tend to be less bitter than larger ones. As the interior flesh of an eggplant often acts like a sponge, be sure to limit the amount of oil used during cooking by quickly sautéing or grilling it. When making our Stir-Fried Eggplant with Garlic-Basil Sauce (page 226), we used just 2 tablespoons of oil to cook the eggplant before adding our other ingredients.

AVOCADOS

Most famous as the star of guacamole, avocados are one of the only fruits that have an abundance of heart-healthy monounsaturated fat. Because they are rich in fats, avocados enable your body to better absorb fat-soluble vitamins that may be in other foods eaten with it. In addition, avocados are a great source of fiber, vitamins C, E, and K, riboflavin, copper, and potassium. Avocados also contain lutein and zeaxanthan, which may help with eye and skin health. Although avocados are higher in calories than other fruits, they are a great alternative to fatty condiments like mayonnaise, as they provide so many benefits (mix some with yogurt for a sandwich spread; see page 83). We paired buttery avocado with bright tomatoes and oranges in a vitamin-packed topping for steak (Grilled Flank Steak with Tomato, Orange, and Avocado, page 172). And our Avocado and Bean Toast (page 64) made a good thing better by incorporating beans for added fiber and heartiness.

A LITTLE FAT IS A GOOD THING

Sure, avocados and tomatoes taste great together—the creamy avocado balancing the tomato's bright acidity—but there's a nutritional benefit to the pairing. The fat in the avocado dramatically increases our ability to absorb the antioxidant lycopene in the tomato—as much as sevenfold. Fat also helps us absorb the beta-carotene in carrots and dark leafy greens. And fat is necessary for the absorption of vitamins A, D, E, and K. (The ideal ratio of fat to vitamins is not known, but they should be consumed at the same meal.) So there's no reason to settle for an austere vegetables-only salad; adding some avocado, nuts, or dressing actually makes it healthier, not to mention more delicious.

TOMATOES

Whether you consider tomatoes to be fruits or vegetables, the one thing we can all agree on is their substantial health benefits. Like most bright red produce, tomatoes are high in potassium and vitamins A and C. However, they are best known for their high levels of lycopene, an antioxidant whose free radical–fighting properties may be linked with reducing the risk of certain cancers. Lycopene also has a role in heart health and may help reduce LDL ("bad") cholesterol and lower blood pressure. Applying heat (through cooking, canning, or other processing) increases the bioavailability of lycopene, making cooked tomatoes richer sources than their raw counterparts (and eating lycopene-rich food with some healthy fat further increases its bioavailability). Look for low-sodium or no-salt-added canned tomato products if you are concerned about sodium. Taking advantage of their versatility, we incorporated tomatoes into a variety of our dishes, cooked and raw, from Turkish Tomato, Bulgur, and Red Pepper Soup (page 94) to our MLT (mushroom, lettuce, and tomato sandwich, page 83).

BEETS

Famous for their deep purple color that stains virtually everything it touches, beets are full of B vitamins, minerals, and fiber. The root's rich purple hue comes from betalains, a pigment compound that may have protective properties against carcinogens and suppress certain types of cancer. (Golden yellow beets contain lutein and zeaxanthin instead.) Beets are also rich in nitrates, which, in addition to lowering blood pressure, have been shown to boost endurance performance (elite athletes often eat beets or drink beet juice prior to competing). Though beets are most often consumed cooked, their natural sugar content makes them delicious in raw preparations, such as our Raw Beet and Carrot Noodle Salad with Almond-Sesame Dressing (page 122). Though we typically utilize the root, beet greens can also be consumed and are high in calcium, iron, and vitamins. We stirred the leaves into a vibrant Beet Barley Risotto (page 189).

RED BELL PEPPERS

SUBSTITUTE
Orange or yellow bell peppers

Peppers originated in South America and date back to 5000 B.C. Bell peppers first turn green and, as they mature, can become red, yellow, orange, and even purplish brown. They provide vitamin C, as well as folate, vitamin K, and potassium. Red skin indicates even more beneficial properties from lycopene, the same antioxidant found in tomatoes. As they ripen and turn from green to red, they become sweeter and milder, and increase their levels of vitamins A and C. (Red peppers contain nine times more beta-carotene and twice as much vitamin C as green peppers; just a cup of red peppers has three times the vitamin C of a navel orange.) Yellow and orange peppers, though not quite as rich in vitamin A or lycopene, still contain plenty of nutrients. Crisp and juicy, peppers make a great raw snack but also stand up well to sautéing, broiling, and grilling. They added color and crispness to our Baked Stuffed Trout with Red Pepper and Preserved Lemon (page 149).

DOES COOKING DESTROY NUTRIENTS?

As a fruit or vegetable cooks, it softens and loses color, eventually turning limp and dull. But does that mean raw is best? That depends. Vitamin C and the B vitamins are heat-sensitive, so foods retain more of them when cooked minimally. On the flip side, cooking breaks down a plant's cells, which can make nutrients like beta-carotene and lycopene more bioavailable. Cooking makes proteins more digestible and increases our ability to absorb some minerals. Of course, we aren't consuming nutrients in isolation: Spinach offers more vitamin C when raw, but more beta-carotene and iron when cooked. A consistent culprit in nutrient loss is boiling, which leaches water-soluble vitamins. But rather than fret about heat or no heat, we aim to eat a mix of raw and cooked vegetables—and plenty of them.

ARTICHOKES

It might be a surprise to see artichokes listed among the most nutrient-dense vegetables, but they are a great source of fiber (one of the highest-fiber vegetables), as well as vitamins C and K, magnesium, and more. They also contain a number of different phytonutrients that act as antioxidants. If trimming fresh whole artichokes is overwhelming, you can buy frozen or canned—just beware of added sodium. Fresh artichokes may have slightly more fiber, and water-packed artichokes may lose some of their vitamin C, but the differences are minimal. We let fresh artichokes shine in a simple side dish of Roasted Artichokes with Lemon Vinaigrette (page 202). And artichokes' many layers of leaves helped trap the flavorful basil pesto in our Pesto Farro Salad with Cherry Tomatoes and Artichokes (page 117).

ASPARAGUS

Often symbolic of spring's arrival, asparagus boasts plenty of fiber and can be helpful for digestive health. The vegetable contains asparagine, a natural diuretic that can reduce bloating and may help prevent urinary tract infections. Eating asparagus will ensure you get plenty of folate, vitamins C, E, and K, and chromium, a mineral important for blood sugar control. While you'll most often find green asparagus, you can also find purple and white varieties. The purple spears are typically more tender and sweeter and contain anthocyanins. Be sure to avoid overcooking asparagus; boiling or sautéing too long will cause vitamins to leach out. We sauté the spears until just crisp-tender for our Asparagus, Arugula, and Cannellini Bean Salad with Walnuts (page 114).

ORGANIC OR CONVENTIONAL?

In this book, we call for organic eggs, poultry, and milk products because of the superior nutritional profile they provide. When it comes to produce, nutrition doesn't vary much between conventional and organic (local and seasonal are better markers of optimal nutrients). But there are pesticides to consider. The Environmental Working Group's "clean fifteen" and "dirty dozen" describe which conventional produce is safest to eat and which contains more pesticide residue, making organic a smart choice.

CLEAN FIFTEEN Corn, avocados, pineapples, cabbage, onions, frozen sweet peas, papayas, asparagus, mangoes, eggplant, honeydew melon, kiwi, cantaloupe, cauliflower, grapefruit

DIRTY DOZEN Strawberries, spinach, nectarines, apples, peaches, pears, cherries, grapes, celery, tomatoes, sweet bell peppers and hot peppers, potatoes

MUSHROOMS

Mushrooms are often referred to as the "meat" of the vegetable world, and for good reason. The composition of these fungi bridges the gap between plants and animals, with a structure that gives them a chewy, meat-like texture. Like animals, mushrooms can use the ultraviolet rays in sunlight to synthesize vitamin D. Mushrooms also provide B vitamins—especially helpful for those who don't eat meat. They are also rich sources of minerals such as iron, selenium, and copper, and the antioxidant ergothioneine, which may help strengthen the immune system and improve cognitive function, skin, and eye health. Dried mushrooms are also a great option; in fact, the drying process concentrates the nutrients. Contrary to popular belief, mushrooms don't absorb a lot of water when washed, and can be rinsed under gently running water to remove debris. Mushrooms are noted for their characteristic savory umami flavor when cooked, making them a good stand-in for meat. We used a mix of portobello mushrooms and dried porcinis to make a savory, meatless Mushroom Bourguignon (page 186). And we sautéed wild mushrooms to bring earthy depth and a boost of minerals to our Mushroom and Artichoke Hash with Parmesan Croutons (page 78).

ONIONS

Though they may make us cry, there is nothing sad nutritionally about onions. Onions and other members of the allium family (which includes shallots, leeks, scallions, garlic, and ramps) contain sulfur compounds that, when chopped, crushed, or chewed, release strong chemicals that provide their distinct pungent flavor and aroma. Developed to help defend the plant from microbes and insects (they are also the cause of onion tears), these potent chemicals can also act as antioxidants and may help to lower cholesterol and triglycerides in our bodies. Onions are also a great source of vitamin C, fiber, and flavonoids, including quercetin, another powerful antioxidant. When preparing onions, make sure to remove as few of the outer layers as possible, as they are thought to contain the highest concentration of flavonoids. Onions permeate our cooking, but their flavor starred in a pickled red onion topping for our Avocado and Bean Toast (page 64).

GREEN BEANS

SUBSTITUTE
Peas

Green beans are legumes, a family of plants that contain seeds within a pod. There are more than 130 different varieties, the most common including snap beans, string beans, and the long, thin haricots verts. Green beans contain about 90 percent water and are a surprisingly versatile vegetable, performing equally well in quick stir-fries (such as our Beef Stir-Fry with Bok Choy and Green Beans, page 175) as in long, slow braises. They contain vitamins A, C, K, and B vitamins, plus iron, calcium, magnesium, potassium, phosphorus, and plenty of phytonutrients. Green beans get their color from chlorophyll, and yellow wax beans are simply green beans that have been bred to have none of this pigment.

EDAMAME

A familiar starter in Japanese restaurants, edamame are protein-rich and have a savory, nutty flavor and firm, dense texture. Though the terms "edamame" and "soybeans" are often used interchangeably, there is a slight difference: Soybeans are mature, whereas edamame are larger and harvested while the beans are still green and young. Edamame offer a variety of nutrients, including vitamin C, folate, fiber, calcium, potassium, iron, magnesium, manganese, copper, phosphorus, and zinc. Among legumes, edamame and all soybeans are noteworthy due to their high concentration of phytonutrients called isoflavones, plant hormones that may help prevent certain types of cancer and help ease symptoms of menopause. There is a lot of conflicting research when it comes to soy, but there's a possibility that soy may help prevent memory loss, lower cholesterol, and ward off osteoporosis. You can buy preshelled edamame frozen or dry-roasted soybeans, or frozen edamame still in the shell. We liked the convenience of pre-shelled edamame and used the beans to add a protein boost to our Edamame Salad with Arugula and Radishes (page 225), where their mild flavor balances pungent greens. We also liked their pop of texture and vibrant green color in our Quinoa Pilaf with Shiitakes, Edamame, and Ginger (page 249).

DRIED BEANS

Dried beans are a healthy plant-based protein source that contains no saturated fat. While the variety is quite broad—including kidney, black, pinto, and navy beans and chickpeas—most dried beans share a fairly similar nutritional profile, notably a rich vitamin and mineral content—including B vitamins (with the exception of B12), magnesium, zinc, potassium, phosphorus, and copper to name a few—as well as a high fiber content, which can help with satiety and blood sugar control and may even lower the risk of certain cancers. Dried beans are rich in protein; however, they are not considered a complete protein due to their lack of the amino acid tryptophan. (This amino acid can be found in grains, making dishes such as rice and beans a complete protein source.) Canned beans offer very similar nutritional benefits to dried beans you cook yourself, so we happily rely on their convenience in most instances. Just be sure to drain and rinse them to remove excess sodium. To make a plant-based alternative to chicken salad sandwiches, we turned to canned chickpeas for our Chickpea Salad Sandwiches (page 89). You can also find bean flours available in stores; we took advantage of nutrient-dense chickpea flour when making our Cauliflower-Chickpea Flatbread with Romesco (page 198).

LENTILS

Among the first crops domesticated for human consumption, lentils come in many different types, varying in color from yellow to red-orange, green, brown, and black (though red and yellow lentils are nothing more than the common brown and green lentils hulled). Because of their small size, relatively high surface-area-to-volume ratio, and thin seed coat, lentils absorb water rapidly and cook in much less time than other dried legumes, making dried lentils convenient pantry items. In addition to protein, lentils provide a plethora of vitamins and minerals. They're a particularly excellent source of potassium, phosphorus, and folate, important for preventing birth defects, as well as iron, which can help curb fatigue. And, as an added bonus, lentils are super economical, allowing you to get a serious nutritional bang for your buck. We loved how quickly red lentils turned soft and contributed body and creaminess to our Red Lentil Soup with North African Spices (page 101).

SALMON (WILD)

We love salmon because it's rich without being aggressively fishy, and needs no dressing up to taste good. Salmon's rich flavor is due to how its fat is stored: Unlike the fat in white fish, which is mostly stored in the liver, the fat in salmon is spread throughout the flesh. And much of it takes the form of omega-3 fatty acids, an essential polyunsaturated fat that is linked with a reduced risk of heart disease in adults and promotes brain development and healthy vision in infants. In this book, we cooked with wild salmon due to its optimal fat content; it is rich in omega-3 fats but lower in total fat than farm-raised. If wild-caught salmon is unavailable, you'll still get omega-3 fats from the farm-raised variety, but the saturated fat content may be higher. Because wild salmon is leaner than farmed, it can be prone to overcooking, so we cook it to a slightly lower temperature. We turned to salmon often in these recipes to help bring more fish into our diet, from Salmon Tacos with Super Slaw (page 139), where it provided richness without the need for frying, to Japanese-style Black Rice Bowls with Salmon (page 143).

ANCHOVIES & SARDINES

These tiny silver-skinned fish boast large amounts of heart-healthy omega-3 fatty acids, and are also high in vitamin A, protein, and calcium. Because manufacturers typically preserve the fish in salt, rinse and pat them dry before using to remove excess sodium. You can also look for fresh sardines and anchovies or those packed in water. In recipes like our Anchovy Dip (page 267), the anchovies are the star of the recipe and provide potent, savory flavor. But when used more judiciously, the umami-producing glutamates present in either fish can help to boost a dish's savory notes and add a dose of healthy fats without adding fishy flavor, as the anchovies do in our Kale Caesar Salad (page 108).

TROUT

SUBSTITUTE
Mackerel

Oily fish such as trout don't aways win the popularity contest where fish is concerned, but they are well worth seeking out as a protein-rich alternative to red meat. Similar to salmon, trout are full of omega-3 fatty acids and rich in B vitamins (which facilitate digestion and enable the body to use energy from food), particularly B12 and niacin (great news for pescetarians). They also offer abundant minerals, including calcium, iron, copper, magnesium, zinc, manganese, and selenium. There are many different trout species in the U.S., but you're most likely to find rainbow trout due to the lower risk of pollutants and mercury. In addition to fresh trout, you can find smoked trout in grocery stores, a convenient way to add more fish to your diet. We flaked bite-size chunks of the smoky fish for our Fennel and Apple Salad with Smoked Trout (page 130), where its richness balanced the fresh, crisp flavors of the fennel and apple. We also utilized the entire fresh fish in Baked Stuffed Trout with Red Pepper and Preserved Lemon (page 149).

WHITE FISH

SUBSTITUTE
Cod, halibut

"White fish" is a term that encompasses many species of deepwater saltwater fish, all of which are mild flavored and white fleshed. At the market, you will most often see flounder and sole (delicate and flaky); cod, haddock, and sea bass (medium-flaky); and grouper, halibut, and monkfish (firm and meaty). Most white fish store fat primarily in their livers, leaving very little fat within the muscle tissue itself, making it a very lean protein choice. Though each fish has its own nutritional profile, the group as a whole is a rich source of phosphorus, vitamin D, potassium, and a moderate amount of omega-3 fatty acids. These fish are particularly high in vitamin B12, key for proper nerve function and energy production, as well as niacin and selenium. To complement the mildness of cod without turning to butter or cream, we cooked it gently in coconut milk for our Cod in Coconut Broth with Lemon Grass and Ginger (page 146). And to keep its lean flesh tender and moist without deep frying, we used an elevated rack to bake our Nut-Crusted Cod Fillets (page 144).

a better way to eat

TOFU & TEMPEH

Tofu is one of the most important sources of protein in Asia. But while soybeans have been grown in America since the early 19th century, they were first used mainly for animal feed. It took the health food movement of the 1970s to give soy—and tofu—any heft as a food for human consumption. As a nutrient-dense food, tofu doesn't offer just protein; it's an excellent source of calcium and iron, as well as manganese, magnesium, and phosphorus. Soy consumption has been shown to decrease cholesterol and reduce the risk of obesity-related diseases. Tofu comes in varying degrees of firmness, making it extremely versatile, and it absorbs flavors well, making it ideal for simmering in an aromatic broth, as we did for our Thai Red Curry with Lentils and Tofu (page 178). Tempeh, by contrast, is always firm; it's made from fermenting soybeans and pressing them into blocks, and has a different nutritional profile: In addition to protein, it offers copper, manganese, riboflavin, and niacin. Keep in mind that tempeh is relatively calorie-dense, as one cup provides 18 grams of fat (though most of this fat is unsaturated). When cooking tempeh, we focused on crisping cubes before treating them as a mild canvas for our flavorful Stir-Fried Tempeh with Orange Sauce (page 181).

EGGS

The healthfulness of eggs has been controversial over the last few decades, but it's safe to say they deserve a place on any superfood list. Both the yolk and the white have unique nutritional properties. More than half of an egg's protein resides in the white, which also contains many B vitamins, plus magnesium and potassium. The yolk contains the majority of the egg's fat, cholesterol, and calories, but also fat-soluble vitamins A, D, E, and K, plus calcium, copper, iron, zinc, and more. It contains the majority of an egg's choline as well, which may help prevent breast cancer, reduce inflammation, and improve brain function. And the antioxidants lutein and zeaxanthin, associated with preventing vision loss, reside there, too. In these recipes, we opted for organic eggs and poultry. Certified organic producers must follow stricter guidelines than others, including providing a cleaner environment, access to the outdoors, 100 percent certified organic feed, and no hormones or other drugs to promote growth. This not only translates to healthier chickens but eggs that may have a superior nutritional profile, with potentially higher concentrations of omega-3 fats, vitamin E, and antioxidants. Such an exceptional ingredient needed worthy partners in the kitchen. Stirring soft-scrambled eggs into sautéed kale and black beans made for a nutrient-packed breakfast burrito (page 69). And we cracked eggs directly into a skillet of smoked trout hash (page 76) for a hearty way to start our morning sunny-side up.

LEAN WHITE POULTRY

Americans eat a lot of chicken. In fact, in 1992, the amount of chicken consumed in the United States surpassed that of beef, according to the USDA. The average American now eats about 82 pounds of chicken per year versus about 50 pounds of beef. We eat some whole birds and some wings, but chicken breasts account for 60 percent of the chicken sold in stores. And no wonder: When it comes to an easy, all-purpose protein, chicken breasts are hard to beat, making them a useful option when trying to eat moderate amounts of red meat. And lean turkey is almost as versatile, especially ground turkey, which can stand in for beef in burgers, meatballs, and more. In addition to protein, chicken and turkey are rich in selenium, choline, and B vitamins. We opted for organic in these recipes to ensure an optimal nutritional profile and better conditions for the animals (see Eggs, page 26). Relying on lean poultry did pose some challenges in the kitchen when it came to cooking options. But rather than limit ourselves to quick sautés, we devised new ways of ensuring moist, juicy results, by roasting bone-in chicken breasts for even cooking in our One-Pan Chicken with Kale and Butternut Squash (page 154), and brining turkey breasts before simmering them right in the sauce for our Pulled BBQ Turkey with Red Cabbage Slaw (page 170).

GRASS-FED LEAN RED MEAT

Red meat doesn't get much credit as a "healthy food," but for the carnivores out there, rest assured there are plenty of benefits to be had by eating the right type (lean) and quantity of red meat. Beef contains high levels of B vitamins, particularly B12, as well as iron (a type more easily absorbed than plant-based iron), phosphorus, selenium, and zinc. In these recipes, we cooked with grass-fed beef. Most beef sold today is grain-fed, meaning that after the animals are 6 months old, they are fed a diet of corn and other grains. But since cows' bodies are not designed to digest corn, this diet can make them sick, often requiring antibiotics. Grass-fed cows, on the other hand, eat grass and hay, are not fed antibiotics or growth hormones, and are not confined. As a result, grass-fed beef tends to have more antioxidants and less total fat. Depending on the breed of cow, grass-fed beef may contain between two and five times more omega-3 fatty acids than grain-fed. (The amount is still significantly less than that in oily fish.) Note that because it is leaner, grass-fed beef is less forgiving when it comes to cooking, so check the meat for doneness at the beginning of the time range. The best way to source grass-fed meat is to seek out a high-end grocery store or a local butcher shop. A lean cut, such as flank steak, is a great go-to; we used it in our Grilled Flank Steak with Tomato, Orange, and Avocado (page 172) and our Beef Stir-Fry with Bok Choy and Green Beans (page 175).

WALNUTS

Among tree nuts, walnuts stand out nutritionally for their high levels of various antioxidants and rich amounts of omega-3 and omega-6 fatty acids, polyunsaturated fats that may help reduce the risk of certain cancers and heart disease and lower cholesterol. (The fats do result in high calorie counts, so it's important to be mindful of portion size.) Like other tree nuts, walnuts are a great source of thiamine, vitamin E, copper, and manganese. The high level of fat makes walnuts highly perishable, so store them in an airtight container in the freezer. When shopping, avoid nuts that are packaged or roasted in oil; instead, eat them raw or dry-roasted and look for varieties without any added salt. We use walnuts as a healthy and easy way to add richness and crunch to our cooking, from a Mediterranean Chopped Salad (page 111) to Skillet-Roasted Apples with Dried Figs, Walnuts, and Maple Yogurt (page 294).

ALMONDS

While walnuts may offer the highest levels of omega-3s, all tree nuts are nutrient dense, and consumption of tree nuts in general is linked with a variety of consistent and positive health outcomes. We've spotlighted almonds because they are among the lowest-calorie, highest-protein nuts and provide a favorable fat profile. They also offer fiber, magnesium, vitamin E, and phosphorus, and contain more calcium than other nuts, making them an especially healthful option for anyone avoiding dairy. Furthermore, almonds are one of the most useful nuts in the kitchen: They come in many forms, whole, sliced, and slivered; look for raw or dry-roasted almonds to avoid added salt. Throughout the book we found ways to take almonds beyond just an add-in, from grinding them into meal to add richness to Whole-Wheat Blueberry-Almond Muffins (page 58) to making them a healthy base for granola (page 43) and muesli (page 40).

SUNFLOWER SEEDS & PEPITAS

Like nuts, seeds can be a healthful way to enhance dishes by lending additional nutrients. Sunflower seeds (technically kernels) and pepitas, or pumpkin seeds, are full of vitamin E, as well as selenium, which works with vitamin E to protect against cell damage in the body. They're also a good source of monounsaturated and polyunsaturated fats, which can help lower cholesterol. And the benefits don't stop there: they're rich in protein, folate, fiber, magnesium, copper, and zinc. Their convenience makes them a supersimple way to add nutrients to virtually any meal. As with nuts, we suggest buying raw or dry-roasted varieties without added salt. You can also find sunflower seed butter available. We sprinkled these nutrient-packed seeds throughout recipes, incorporating sunflower seeds into a pesto (instead of traditional pine nuts) for our Whole-Wheat Pizza with Kale and Sunflower Seed Pesto (page 196) and mixing pepitas into a nutrient-packed chocolate bark (page 301).

OATS

The USDA recommends making half your grains whole grains, and oats are an easy, tasty way to get there. With a greater proportion of soluble fiber than any other grain, plus protein and plenty of iron, oats are versatile and satiating. Oats can be found in many different forms. Rolled oats are steamed and rolled into flakes, which makes them thin and quick-cooking but doesn't diminish their nutrients. Steel-cut oats, made by slicing whole oat groats with steel blades into nubby grains, produces stellar oatmeal, but requires more time to cook; so to turn our Steel-Cut Oatmeal with Carrots and Cherries (page 46) into a quick breakfast, we presoaked the grains overnight. Oats are also available as flour; we incorporated it into our Cranberry-Orange Oat Muffins (page 60), where the fairly neutral-tasting flour boosted nutrients without overpowering the flavor of the orange zest.

QUINOA

SUBSTITUTE
Amaranth

Referred to as "the mother of all grains" by the Incas, quinoa is a powerhouse grain (though technically it's a grain-like seed). Not only is it full of protein, but it's one of only a few plant foods that's considered a "complete" protein, containing all the essential amino acids we need but can't make on our own and have to obtain through our diets. Of all the whole grains, quinoa contains the most potassium, which helps control blood pressure, and it's especially high in fiber. It also has a high ratio of protein to carbohydrate compared to other grains. Though most often beige-colored, quinoa can also be found in red and black varieties. Thoroughly washing quinoa before cooking removes traces of its bitter, mildly toxic saponin coating, nature's way of making the high-protein seeds unattractive to birds and other seed eaters. Many brands of quinoa available in stores today are prewashed; for only a few cents more per ounce, we think the convenience is worth it. To take advantage of the seed's versatility, we used quinoa for breakfast in our Quinoa Granola with Sunflower Seeds and Almonds (page 43). Its mild savoriness paired well with Southwestern flavors and served as a tasty, creative substitute for ground beef in our Quinoa Taco Salad (page 120).

WHOLE GRAINS

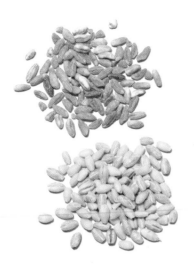

Whole grains, such as farro, wheat berries, and buckwheat, are considered whole because the bran, germ, and endosperm are present in the same proportions as when the grain was growing. Once processed, a whole grain must still offer the same nutrients as found in the original form. The bran contains most of the fiber, while the germ contains some B vitamins, protein, minerals, and healthy fats. The endosperm contains starchy carbohydrates, proteins, and traces of vitamins and minerals. The many phytonutrients found in whole grains have been shown to reduce risk of heart disease, stroke, diabetes, and certain types of cancer. But refining grains diminishes their nutritional quality: Processing can strip away 90 percent of the vitamin E, virtually all of the fiber, and over half of the B vitamins. Many refined grains are then enriched with B vitamins and iron to compensate, but fiber and phytonutrients are not added back. Because different types of whole grains boast different ratios of nutrients, it's best to consume a variety. When it came to cooking with grains, we took them beyond only side-dish treatments, using barley instead of Arborio rice in hearty Beet Barley Risotto (page 189) and trading white pasta for chewy farro in our Pesto Farro Salad with Cherry Tomatoes and Artichokes (page 117).

WILD, BLACK, RED, OR BROWN RICE

Rice feeds more than half of the global population, and there are approximately 40,000 different varieties of the grain. Many factors influence a rice's nutritional value, such as how processed it is, the type of soil it was grown in, and how it may be enriched—and some choices are better than others. A 1-cup serving of brown rice has 3.5 grams of fiber compared to just 0.6 gram of fiber in the same serving of white rice. Besides fiber, brown rice also contains B vitamins, magnesium, phosphorus, and calcium. Wild rice (actually a grass seed) has a chewy texture, long, slender grain, and can be found in a range of colors. Like brown rice, it's high in B vitamins, as well as potassium and phosphorus. Black rice, sometimes labeled "forbidden rice," gets its dark purple-black color from the antioxidant anthocyanin. Similarly, red rice, which contains ten times the antioxidants of brown rice, can thank anthocyanins for its red hue. Instead of a typical white rice pilaf, we used brown rice in our Brown Rice Pilaf with Dates and Pistachios (page 250). Nutty black rice made the perfect base for our Black Rice Bowls with Salmon (page 143).

PLAIN YOGURT

As evidenced by the expansive selection available in grocery stores, yogurt has blossomed in popularity recently, and for good reason. This cultured milk product is soured and thickened by adding lactic acid–producing cultures (aka probiotics) to milk. The lactic acid coagulates the milk protein, thickening it and adding sour flavor. The probiotics help to balance gut microflora, which can improve digestive health. In addition to the probiotic benefits, yogurt is a great source of potassium, phosphorous, calcium, zinc, some B vitamins, and vitamin D. Greek yogurt is simply yogurt that has been strained more to remove the whey, leading to higher protein and half the sodium and carbohydrates as regular yogurt. When shopping, check labels carefully, as many fruit yogurts contain excessive added sugar; plain is best. Probiotics can diminish when exposed to higher temperatures, such as during baking. In the U.S., manufacturers can pay for the right to display a "Live & Active Culture" seal on containers; this requires that the yogurt contains 100 million cultures per gram at the time of manufacture. In this book, we opted for organic yogurt and other dairy products to ensure optimal nutrition. Yogurt made the perfect base for a tangy frosting to top our Beet-Chocolate Cupcakes (page 288) and Carrot Snack Cake (page 290). We also used yogurt to replace some of the mayonnaise in recipes such as Chickpea Salad Sandwiches (page 88).

DARK CHOCOLATE

Though chocolate is certainly a treat, limited amounts of dark chocolate have been shown to provide numerous possible health benefits. Just an ounce is full of phytonutrients, including flavanols, which can improve heart health (including improved blood pressure and decreased stroke risk), brain function, and blood flow to the brain and heart. Chocolate's phytonutrients may also reduce heart disease risk by helping to lower cholesterol levels. In addition, dark chocolate boasts a plethora of minerals such as potassium, zinc, selenium, and iron. As chocolate is relatively high in sugar and calories, keep portion size in mind (a 1-ounce serving should be enough to reap the benefits). Note that most chocolate candy bars are highly processed, so stick to plain bars and/or chips instead of chocolate concoctions involving caramel, marshmallows, or candies that add extra fat and sugar. In our recipes, we opted for dark chocolate, preferably 70 percent cacao or higher, which brings the most antioxidant benefits, as well as unsweetened cocoa powder. We used both dark chocolate and cocoa powder to add rich chocolate flavor to our Chocolate-Avocado Pudding (page 298). And dark chocolate made the perfect base for our Chocolate Bark with Pepitas and Dried Goji Berries (page 301).

FLAVOR, FLOUR, AND FAT: BUILDING A NUTRIENT-DENSE PANTRY

After lining up 50 foods that would constitute the base of our meals, we looked to build our pantry. But we were surprised to find there wasn't much left to tackle. Our plate was already quite full—of vegetables and fruits, fish and meat, also of dried beans and whole grains, eggs and yogurt, nuts and seeds. Ingredients traditionally found on the sidelines had been brought closer to the center of the plate, edging out the traditional large piece of meat. All we needed to round things out was a handful of seasonings, some (healthy) fat for the skillet and salad bowl, a couple of good cooking liquids, and some whole-grain flours for baking wholesome morning breads and desserts.

HIGH-PERFORMING SPICES AND HERBS

Roots, seeds, berries, bark, and leaves (aka spices and herbs) offer aromatic flavors that make food more exciting and help us rely less on salt and saturated fats. All offer a host of phytonutrients with anti-oxidant properties, which, like their flavors, are fleeting (if you can't recall when you last bought a particular spice, it's time to restock). Whether adding a flourish of parsley or a warm undertone of turmeric, we explored ways to dial up these seasonings in our recipes for bold but balanced results.

CUMIN Often used as a natural health remedy, cumin's essential oils may help aid digestion. New research shows that the spice may also help lower blood sugar. Just 1 tablespoon contains an impressive 20 percent daily value of iron and is also a rich source of magnesium. Cumin added warmth to our Pumpkin Turkey Chili (page 169).

GINGER An ancient medicinal plant, this rhizome (a relative of turmeric and galangal) boasts numerous antioxidants. Studies have found it may provide relief from muscle and joint pain and have anti-inflammatory properties. Ginger stimulates digestion and is sometimes recommended to help reduce nausea. We used generous amounts to infuse our Shiitake, Tofu, and Mustard Greens Soup (page 104).

TURMERIC A popular spice in India, golden turmeric is having its moment in the sun, appearing in everything from lattes to tooth-paste. The reason is curcumin, the source of its color and a strong anti-inflammatory agent that may be associated with inhibiting tumor growth and delaying loss of brain function. Black pepper improves curcumin's absorption: We used both to kick up the flavor in Turmeric Chicken Salad Sandwiches (page 85).

CAYENNE The capsaicin that gives cayenne and all fresh and dried chiles their heat is a phytonutrient that may also boost metabolism, reduce inflammation, and regulate insulin levels. Ironically, the way capsaicin triggers the sensation of pain in the mouth ultimately has a desensitizing effect, which has led to the compound's being used in topical pain-relieving treatments.

BLACK PEPPER It's a rare occasion where we don't turn to the dried berries of the pepper plant to add their heat and sharp bite to our cooking. Good thing, then, that black pepper not only stimulates salivary glands but triggers the release of stomach acid, which aids in digestion. We recommend grinding whole peppercorns just before using for maximum flavor and nutritional benefits.

FRESH HERBS

GINGER

CUMIN

TURMERIC

GARLIC

BLACK PEPPER

CAYENNE

CINNAMON

CINNAMON Cinnamon sticks are rolled strips of inner bark from the Cinnamomum genus of evergreen trees. The quintessential warm spice has some of the highest anti-oxidant activity of any spices, including anti-inflammatory activity, cholesterol-lowering abilities, and possible connections to preventing Alzheimer's and Parkinson's diseases. Cinnamon provided warmth and depth of flavor to our Pumpkin Spice Waffles (page 57).

FRESH HERBS Fresh herbs (and dried herbs when stored properly) can be much more than a pretty garnish. Different types of herbs offer varying levels of essential nutrients including vitamins A, C, and K, as well as protective phyto-nutrients. Rather than limit ourselves to a sprinkle, we used a handful each of mint and basil in our Eda-mame Salad with Arugula and Radishes (page 225) and showered our Tofu Rancheros (page 74) with a full cup of cilantro leaves.

GARLIC Everyday garlic is highly touted for the ability to boost the immune system. Research shows it may help to lower high blood pres-sure and cholesterol and improve circulation. We used a whopping 25 cloves to give toasty sweet flavor to our Garlic-Chicken and Wild Rice Soup (page 97).

a better way to eat

FLAX, CHIA, HEMP,
AND SESAME SEEDS

VINEGAR

LEMONS
AND LIMES

GOJI BERRIES

OTHER FLAVOR BOOSTERS

FLAX, CHIA, HEMP, AND SESAME SEEDS Small but mighty, these seeds are great sources of healthy fats, protein, and plenty of vitamins and minerals. They provide great texture and are easy to have on hand as pantry staples to add to baked goods, smoothies, dips, and more. Note that flaxseeds (we prefer the golden variety) have to be chopped or ground in order to reap their nutritional benefits. Neutral-flavored hemp seeds make a convenient, healthy protein addition to smoothies.

GOJI BERRIES Native to China, once-exotic goji berries are now more widely available. Though fresh and frozen berries do exist in the U.S., they're difficult to find; the berries are most often available dried. Studies have explored their possible connection to preventing vision degeneration, defeating cancer cells, and even combating the flu. Whether or not they are more powerful than other nutrient-dense foods, the sweet-tart berries are rich sources of vitamins, minerals, fiber, and phytonutrients.

LEMONS AND LIMES While we rarely consume the flesh of these tart citrus, as we do with oranges and grapefruits, we still reap many benefits from the juice and zest. We've even grilled the halved citrus to extract even more flavor from the juice, as in our Grilled Broccoli with Lemon and Parmesan (page 208). We used plenty of orange zest to add citrus notes to our Cherry, Chocolate, and Orange Trail Mix (page 281).

VINEGAR Trying to cut back on sodium? Vinegar makes for a healthier flavor enhancer. Salt works its magic mainly by suppressing our perception of bitterness, allowing underlying flavors to come to the fore. Like salt, acids such as vinegar and citrus juice compete with bitter flavor compounds, lessening our perception of these tastes as they "brighten" remaining ones. We used rice vinegar to add bright punch to our Shiitake, Tofu, and Mustard Greens Soup (page 104), which helped us to use a more moderate hand with the soy sauce.

FLOUR POWER

Offering all the same nutritional benefits as the unmilled grains, whole-grain flours make a desirable starting point in baking, but you can't just swap them in, as doing so poses challenges to structure, texture, flavor, and moistness. We set a bar of at least 50 percent whole grains in our baked goods—and sought to see how far up we could go. To our surprise, the answer turned out to be 100 percent in some cases, such as our Carrot Snack Cake (page 290) where whole-wheat flour's earthy flavors tasted right at home. Even where a little all-purpose flour was needed for structure, we were often able to go as high as 75 percent whole-grain by adjusting the moisture level with ingredients like yogurt.

WHAT WE USED Readily available whole-wheat flour and neutral-flavored and high-fiber oat flour. (Note that you can grind your own oat flour in a food processor or spice grinder, but the results will be denser.) In addition to grain flours, we employed ground almond flour in our Whole-Wheat Blueberry-Almond Muffins (page 58) and nutrient-dense chickpea flour in our Cauliflower-Chickpea Flatbread with Romesco (page 198).

THE HEALTHY KIND OF FAT

It may sound like an oxymoron, but fat is essential to our bodies: Fat stores energy, builds cell membranes, coats nerves, and enables the absorption of some vitamins and minerals. Notions of eating "low fat" have changed over the years, and now many nutritionists believe that limiting fat intake matters less than the kind of fat you eat. (Simply eating less fat, they say, often translates into eating more sugar and refined carbs.) The USDA recommends replacing saturated fats with unsaturated fats, and limiting saturated fats to 10 percent of calories per day. To maximize the nutrition of these recipes, we've avoided cooking with solid fats such as butter and focused on primarily unsaturated oils.

Choosing a healthy oil can be bewildering, however. An oil's healthfulness is affected by its ratio of monounsaturated, polyunsaturated, and saturated fats, as well as whether it was refined. We chose

A NOTE ON SUGAR

Whole fruits offer sweetness in a nutrient-dense form, since their sugars are accompanied by the plant's fiber, vitamins, and minerals. The FDA now draws a distinction in labeling between "total sugar," which includes the sugars present in whole foods, and "added sugars," which include table sugar, brown sugar, honey, maple syrup, and molasses—a distinction we've carried into our nutrition information. The USDA advises we eat more fruits (giving no cap on total sugar), but limit added sugars to less than 10 percent of daily calories, or 50 grams on a 2,000-calorie diet. (Americans' biggest source of added sugars? Sweetened beverages.) A dessert will always be a treat, but to ensure ours fit into these guidelines, we often got sweetness from whole fruits (as in Skillet Roasted Apples with Dried Figs, Walnuts, and Maple Yogurt, page 294), and kept added sugar levels as low as reasonably possible, often under 20 or even 10 grams per serving. But it's not all about restriction: All of our desserts offer nutrient density in the form of fruits (and vegetables!), nuts, yogurt, chocolate, and whole-grain flours.

two all-purpose cooking oils, expeller-pressed canola oil and cold-pressed extra-virgin olive oil, both high in monounsaturated fats. But many other oils fit into a healthy diet and will work in our recipes. Here are some rules of thumb:

- Use oils high in unsaturated fats (monounsaturated and polyunsaturated), such as canola, olive, sunflower, grapeseed, sesame, and walnut.

- Expeller- or cold-pressed oils are healthier but involve trade-offs: Both refer to minimally refined oils, processed without chemicals. Cold pressing involves lower temperatures and is used for heat-sensitive oils such as olive oil. These oils retain more of their antioxidants but spoil more quickly and may need to be refrigerated. They may also have lower smoking points.

- Avoid oils labeled "vegetable oil," which gives no indication of what's in it.

TOOLS OF THE TRADE

Eating well shouldn't mean having to spend hours and hours preparing your meals. We continuously found ourselves turning to these useful pieces of equipment to save us time.

SPIRALIZER Using a spiralizer allowed us to get perfectly thin vegetable noodles.
Winner Paderno World Cuisine Tri-Blade Plastic Spiral Vegetable Slicer $33.24

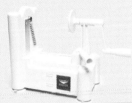

SPICE GRINDER (ELECTRIC) Grinding spices ourselves ensured they had the best fresh flavor, and it encouraged us to use more of them.
Winner Krups Fast-Touch Coffee Mill, Model 203 $19.99

MANDOLINE Making homemade vegetable chips was supereasy when we used a mandoline, which created perfectly thin, consistent chips every time.
Winner Swissmar Börner Original V-Slicer Plus Mandoline $29.99

FOOD PROCESSOR A kitchen must-have; we used our food processor to make our dips and sauces super-smooth.
Winner Cuisinart Custom 14 Food Processor $199.99
Winner (small) Cuisinart Elite Collection 4-Cup Chopper/Grinder $59.95

BLENDER Blenders can do much more than make smoothies; we used ours to achieve a velvety smooth Super Greens Soup (page 92).
Winner (midpriced) Breville the Hemisphere Control $199.95
Winner (upscale) Vitamix 5200 $449.00

HOMEMADE BROTHS

Useful for far more than soup, broth is a nutritious way to infuse food with flavor. Homemade broth not only offers far better flavor than storebought, but also puts you in control of the sodium.

CHICKEN BROTH
makes about 8 cups

This rich and well-rounded chicken broth is perfect as a base for soups, stews, and sauces; as a cooking medium; and even on its own. Many recipes for chicken broth call for simmering a whole chicken, but we found that cutting the chicken into pieces yielded more flavor by providing more surface area for browning. If using a slow cooker, you will need one that holds 5 ½ to 7 quarts.

- 1 **tablespoon cold-pressed extra-virgin olive oil (see page 35)**
- 3 **pounds whole organic chicken legs, backs, and/or wings, hacked into 2-inch pieces**
- 1 **onion, chopped**
- 8 **cups water**
- 3 **bay leaves**
  Kosher salt

1 Heat oil in Dutch oven over medium-high heat until just smoking. Pat chicken dry with paper towels. Brown half of chicken, about 5 minutes; transfer to large bowl. Repeat with remaining chicken; transfer to bowl.

2 Add onion to fat left in pot and cook over medium heat until softened, about 5 minutes. Stir in 2 cups water, bay leaves, and 1 teaspoon salt, scraping up any browned bits.

3A **FOR THE STOVETOP** Stir remaining 6 cups water into pot, then return browned chicken and any accumulated juices to pot and bring to simmer. Reduce heat to low, cover, and simmer gently until broth is rich and flavorful, about 4 hours.

3B **FOR THE SLOW COOKER** Transfer browned chicken and any accumulated juices and onion mixture to slow cooker. Stir in remaining 6 cups water. Cover and cook until broth is rich and flavorful, about 4 hours on low.

4 Remove large bones from pot, then strain broth through fine-mesh strainer into large container; discard solids. Let broth settle for 5 to 10 minutes, then defat using wide, shallow spoon or fat separator. (Cooled broth can be refrigerated for up to 4 days or frozen for up to 1 month.)

VEGETABLE BROTH BASE
makes about 1¾ cups base; enough for 7 quarts broth

Long-simmered vegetable broth tends to be murky and off-tasting. After testing, we realized we prefer the clean, fresh flavor—not to mention the ease—of vegetable broth made by stirring boiling water into a paste of vegetables and herbs, which can be conveniently stored in the freezer. Dried minced onions minimized wateriness; unlike dehydrated onions they are freeze-dried and maintain more flavor compounds. For the best balance, measure the prepped vegetables by weight. Kosher salt aids in grinding the vegetables. The base contains enough salt to keep it from freezing solid, making it easy to scoop out a little at a time. To make 1 cup of broth, combine 1 tablespoon of fresh or frozen broth base with 1 cup of boiling water. If particle-free broth is desired, let the broth steep for 5 minutes and then strain it through a fine-mesh strainer.

- 2 leeks, white and light green parts only, chopped and washed thoroughly (2½ cups or 5 ounces)
- 2 carrots, peeled and cut into ½-inch pieces (⅔ cup or 3 ounces)
- ½ small celery root, peeled and cut into ½-inch pieces (¾ cup or 3 ounces)
- ½ cup (½ ounce) fresh parsley leaves and thin stems
- 3 tablespoons dried minced onions
- 2 tablespoons kosher salt
- 1½ tablespoons tomato paste
- 3 tablespoons low-sodium soy sauce

Homemade broth puts you in control of the sodium.

1 Process leeks, carrots, celery root, parsley, minced onions, and salt in food processor, scraping down sides of bowl frequently, until paste is as fine as possible, 3 to 4 minutes. Add tomato paste and process for 1 minute, scraping down sides of bowl every 20 seconds. Add soy sauce and continue to process 1 minute longer.

2 Transfer mixture to airtight container and tap firmly on counter to remove air bubbles. Press small piece of parchment paper flush against surface of mixture and cover. Freeze for up to 6 months.

CHICKEN BROTH (PER 1 CUP)
Cal 20; Total Fat 0g, Sat Fat 0g; Chol 0mg; Sodium 280mg; Total Carbs 0g, Fiber 0g, Total Sugar 0g, Added Sugar 0; Protein 4g

VEGETABLE BROTH BASE (PER 1 CUP PREPARED)
Cal 10; Total Fat 0g, Sat Fat 0g; Chol 0mg; Sodium 380mg; Total Carbs 2g, Fiber 0g, Total Sugar 1g, Added Sugar 0g; Protein 0g

BREAKFAST

40 Pepita, Almond, and Goji Berry Muesli

Sunflower Seed, Hazelnut, and Cherry Muesli

43 Quinoa Granola with Sunflower Seeds and Almonds

45 Flourless Nut and Seed Loaf

46 Steel-Cut Oatmeal with Carrots and Cherries

49 Three-Grain Breakfast Bowl

51 Chia Pudding with Fresh Fruit and Coconut

52 Blueberry-Oat Pancakes

55 100 Percent Whole-Wheat Pancakes

57 Pumpkin Spice Waffles

58 Whole-Wheat Blueberry-Almond Muffins

60 Cranberry-Orange Oat Muffins

63 Whole-Wheat Date-Nut Bread

64 Avocado and Bean Toast

Quick Sweet-and-Spicy Pickled Red Onions

67 Fried Eggs over Garlicky Chard and Bell Pepper

69 Kale and Black Bean Breakfast Burritos

70 Fluffy Omelet with Smoked Salmon and Asparagus

72 Frittata with Broccoli and Turmeric

74 Tofu Rancheros

76 Smoked Trout Hash with Eggs

78 Mushroom and Artichoke Hash with Parmesan Croutons

PEPITA, ALMOND, AND GOJI BERRY MUESLI

1½ cups (4½ ounces) old-fashioned rolled oats

¼ cup raisins

¼ cup goji berries

¼ cup sliced almonds, toasted and chopped

¼ cup pepitas, toasted

1⅔ cups organic 1 percent low-fat milk

5 ounces (1 cup) blueberries, raspberries, and/or blackberries

why this recipe works • *Muesli, a nutrient-packed breakfast dish created by a Swiss physician for his patients, started as a combination of rolled oats, nuts, seeds, and dried fruit soaked overnight in milk or water for improved texture and digestibility. Today's mueslis include all manner of ingredients (we counted as many as 20 in some recipes) but we saw no reason to get fussy. An oat-forward mixture of 3 parts oats to 2 parts add-ins—a nut, a seed, and two dried fruits—offered an ideal balance of flavor and texture. While traditional methods leave everything raw, we found that toasting the nuts and seeds brought greater depth and complexity to this simple dish. For our nut, sliced almonds required almost no prep work. Picking a seed proved trickier. Soaked flaxseed and chia seeds had overpowering flavor. Pepitas were ideal; we loved the big flavor they took on from toasting. To round out our muesli, we added raisins and antioxidant-packed goji berries, which benefit from the soaking, as it softens their chewy texture. Muesli can also be served like cereal (no soaking overnight). This recipe can easily be doubled. To make a single serving, combine ½ cup muesli with ⅓ cup milk in bowl, cover, and refrigerate overnight. Serve with maple syrup if desired.*

1 Combine oats, raisins, goji berries, almonds, and pepitas in bowl. (Muesli can be stored at room temperature for up to 2 weeks.)

2 Stir milk into muesli until combined. Cover bowl with plastic wrap and refrigerate overnight.

3 Sprinkle with berries and serve.

VARIATION

SUNFLOWER SEED, HAZELNUT, AND CHERRY MUESLI

Substitute unsweetened dried tart cherries for goji berries; toasted, skinned, and chopped hazelnuts for almonds; and sunflower seeds for pepitas.

PER SERVING
Cal 310; Total Fat 10g, Sat Fat 2g; Chol 5mg; Sodium 65mg; Total Carbs 45g, Fiber 6g, Total Sugar 20g, Added Sugar 0g; Protein 12g

EXCELLENT SOURCE OF
Protein, Fiber, Vitamin A, Magnesium, Manganese, Phosphorus

QUINOA GRANOLA WITH SUNFLOWER SEEDS AND ALMONDS

- ½ cup maple syrup
- 4 teaspoons vanilla extract
- ½ teaspoon salt
- ¼ cup cold-pressed extra-virgin olive oil (see page 35)
- 2 cups whole almonds, chopped coarse
- 2 cups unsweetened flaked coconut
- 1 cup quinoa flakes
- 1 cup prewashed white quinoa
- 1 cup raw sunflower seeds
- 2 cups unsweetened dried tart cherries, chopped

why this recipe works • *Granola can be a healthy, nutrient-dense breakfast or snack, but it often comes laden with sugar, saturated fats, and overly processed ingredients. We wanted to bring granola back to where it began: a collection of toasted nuts, grains, and seeds held together in clumps by a kiss of sweetness. We opted to omit oats from our recipe to try something new. We loved the crunch toasted quinoa added, and balanced it with quinoa flakes, which mimicked the texture of rolled oats and added a more delicate crunch, which we found appealing. Almonds and sunflower seeds were mild enough to pair well with the quinoa, while unsweetened flaked coconut contributed flavor without making our granola too sweet. Maple syrup and a hefty amount of vanilla rounded things out with rich, warm sweetness and, once baked, held everything together in granola's signature clumps. Stirring in unsweetened dried tart cherries gave the finished quinoa granola pleasant fruitiness. If you buy unwashed quinoa (or if you are unsure whether it has been washed), be sure to rinse it before cooking to remove its bitter protective coating (called saponin).*

1 Adjust oven rack to upper-middle position and heat oven to 325 degrees. Line rimmed baking sheet with parchment paper.

2 Whisk maple syrup, vanilla, and salt together in large bowl. Whisk in oil. Fold in almonds, coconut, quinoa flakes, quinoa, and sunflower seeds until thoroughly coated.

3 Transfer mixture to prepared baking sheet and spread into thin, even layer. Using stiff metal spatula, press on quinoa mixture until very compact. Bake until deep golden, 45 to 55 minutes.

4 Remove granola from oven and let cool on wire rack for 1 hour. Break cooled granola into pieces of desired size and stir in dried cherries. Serve. (Granola can be stored at room temperature for up to 2 weeks.)

PER ½ CUP
Cal 330; Total Fat 20g, Sat Fat 5g; Chol 0mg; Sodium 70mg; Total Carbs 33g, Fiber 6g, Total Sugar 13g, Added Sugar 5g; Protein 7g

EXCELLENT SOURCE OF
Fiber, Vitamin E, Manganese

breakfast

FLOURLESS NUT AND SEED LOAF

makes 1 loaf, serves 12

1 cup sunflower seeds

1 cup sliced almonds

½ cup pepitas

1¾ cups (5¼ ounces)
old-fashioned rolled oats

¼ cup whole flaxseeds

3 tablespoons powdered
psyllium husk

1½ cups water

3 tablespoons expeller-pressed
canola oil (see page 35)

2 tablespoons maple syrup

¾ teaspoon salt

why this recipe works • *Composed almost entirely of wholesome nuts, seeds, and oats, this loaf is something of a miracle bread. The secret to its structure is powdered psyllium husk, a plant fiber with strong binding properties when hydrated. We toasted our nuts and seeds to enhance their flavor, mixed in oats, flaxseeds, and psyllium, plus canola oil and maple syrup for a hint of sweetness, and let everything hydrate for two hours in a loaf pan. We baked the loaf briefly to set the outside, then turned it out onto a wire rack to finish baking, which promoted evaporation, avoiding a wet center. The outcome? A loaf full of protein, fiber, and healthy fats, perfect for snacking or breakfast. Do not use quick, instant, or thick-cut oats in this recipe. Both brown and golden flaxseeds will work well here. Note that this recipe calls for an 8½ by 4½-inch loaf pan; if you use a 9 by 5-inch loaf pan, the loaf will not be quite as tall.*

1 Adjust oven rack to middle position and heat oven to 350 degrees. Combine sunflower seeds, almonds, and pepitas on rimmed baking sheet and bake, stirring occasionally, until lightly browned, 10 to 12 minutes.

2 Transfer toasted nut-seed mixture to bowl and let cool slightly. Stir in oats, flaxseeds, and psyllium. In separate bowl, whisk water, oil, maple syrup, and salt together until well combined. Using rubber spatula, stir water mixture into nut-seed mixture until completely incorporated.

3 Line bottom of 8½ by 4½-inch loaf pan with parchment paper and spray with canola oil spray. Scrape mixture into pan. Using wet hands, press dough into corners and smooth top. Cover loosely with plastic wrap and let sit at room temperature until mixture is fully hydrated and cohesive, about 2 hours.

4 Heat oven to 350 degrees. Remove plastic and bake loaf for 20 minutes.

5 Invert loaf onto wire rack set inside rimmed baking sheet. Remove loaf pan and discard parchment. Bake loaf (still inverted) until deep golden brown and loaf sounds hollow when tapped, 35 to 45 minutes.

6 Let loaf cool completely on rack, about 2 hours. Serve. (Loaf can be stored at room temperature, uncovered, for up to 3 days; do not wrap. It can also be wrapped in double layer of plastic and frozen for up to 1 month.)

PER ⅔-INCH SLICE
Cal 240; Total Fat 17g, Sat Fat 2g;
Chol 0mg; Sodium 150mg; Total
Carbs 19g, Fiber 5g, Total Sugar 5g,
Added Sugar 2g; Protein 7g

EXCELLENT SOURCE OF
Fiber, Magnesium, Manganese

STEEL-CUT OATMEAL WITH CARROTS AND CHERRIES

serves 4

- 3 cups water
- 1 cup steel-cut oats
- ½ teaspoon salt
- ½ cup carrot juice
- ½ cup organic 1 percent low-fat milk
- ½ cup finely grated carrot
- 3 tablespoons packed dark brown sugar
- ⅓ cup unsweetened dried tart cherries
- ½ teaspoon ground cinnamon
- ½ cup pecans, toasted and chopped coarse

why this recipe works • *While we love a simple bowl of oatmeal topped with dried fruits and nuts, we wanted to bring some variety to this morning mainstay while amping up the nutrition of the already fiber-packed oats. Carrots fit the bill perfectly. We infused the oats' cooking liquid with vitamin A–rich carrot juice and milk and stirred in shredded carrot for texture, which lent a vibrant orange hue along with a subtle sweetness that was complemented by cinnamon and brown sugar. Using steel-cut oats offered the best flavor and texture, but we weren't thrilled with their 40-minute cook time. We wanted a 10-minute breakfast, so we soaked the oats in water overnight, allowing them to gently hydrate and soften. In the morning, we added milk and carrot juice along with some dried cherries, then simmered the oats for just 4 to 6 minutes, until they were thick and creamy. A brief rest off the heat let them thicken to the perfect consistency: creamy with a subtle chew and nutty flavor. For added flavor and texture, we topped the oatmeal with chopped toasted pecans. The oatmeal will continue to thicken as it cools. If you prefer a looser consistency, thin with boiling water.*

1 Bring water to boil in large saucepan over high heat. Remove pan from heat; stir in oats and salt. Cover saucepan and let sit overnight.

2 Stir carrot juice, milk, carrot, sugar, cherries, and cinnamon into oats and bring to boil over medium-high heat. Reduce heat to medium and cook, stirring occasionally, until oats are softened but still retain some chew and mixture thickens and resembles warm pudding, 4 to 6 minutes. Remove pan from heat and let stand for 5 minutes. Stir and serve, sprinkling individual portions with 2 tablespoons pecans.

PER SERVING
Cal 360; Total Fat 13g, Sat Fat 1.5g; Chol 0mg; Sodium 340mg; Total Carbs 55g, Fiber 8g, Total Sugar 18g, Added Sugar 10g; Protein 10g

EXCELLENT SOURCE OF
Protein, Fiber, Vitamin A, Manganese

THREE-GRAIN BREAKFAST BOWL

serves 4

 4 cups water
 ½ cup millet, rinsed
 ½ cup prewashed white quinoa
 ¼ cup amaranth, rinsed
 ½ teaspoon salt
 1 cup organic 1 percent low-fat
    milk, plus extra as needed
 ½ teaspoon ground cinnamon
 ⅛ teaspoon ground nutmeg
7½ ounces (1½ cups) blueberries,
    raspberries, and/or blackberries
 2 tablespoons maple syrup

why this recipe works • *Eating a variety of whole grains is the best way to take advantage of their many nutritional benefits. A hearty porridge was the perfect opportunity to enjoy several kinds in one bowl. We chose a combination of millet, quinoa, and amaranth. The millet's mellow corn flavor and fine, starchy texture balanced the quinoa's nutty, earthy flavor, while a smaller amount of amaranth added bold anise flavor and an intriguing caviar-like texture. Cooking the grains in plenty of liquid encouraged them to swell and some to burst and release their starches, creating a porridge with a creamy texture. However, we felt the 30-minute simmering time was too long for a quick breakfast. So, following our Steel-Cut Oatmeal with Carrots and Cherries (page 46), we hydrated the grains in water the night before. Stirring in blueberries and warm spices and finishing with a bit of maple syrup accentuated the millet's sweetness, balanced the often-bitter quinoa, and tamed the flavor of the amaranth. If you buy unwashed quinoa (or if you are unsure whether it has been washed), be sure to rinse it before cooking to remove its bitter protective coating (called saponin).*

1 Bring water to boil in large saucepan over high heat. Remove pan from heat; stir in millet, quinoa, amaranth, and salt. Cover pan and let sit overnight.

2 Stir milk, cinnamon, and nutmeg into grains and bring to simmer over medium-high heat. Reduce heat to medium-low and cook, stirring occasionally, until grains are fully tender and mixture is thickened, 8 to 10 minutes.

3 Stir in berries and syrup, and adjust consistency with hot milk as needed; porridge will thicken as it sits. Serve.

PER SERVING
Cal 310; Total Fat 4g, Sat Fat 1g;
Chol 3mg; Sodium 330mg; Total
Carbs 60g, Fiber 9g, Total Sugar 16g,
Added Sugar 6g; Protein 11g

EXCELLENT SOURCE OF
Protein, Fiber, Manganese

breakfast

CHIA PUDDING WITH FRESH FRUIT AND COCONUT

- 2 cups organic 1 percent low-fat milk, plus extra for serving
- ½ cup chia seeds
- 2 tablespoons maple syrup, plus extra for serving
- 1½ teaspoons vanilla extract
- ¼ teaspoon salt
- 2 cups (10 ounces) blueberries, raspberries, blackberries, or sliced strawberries, and/or sliced bananas
- ¼ cup unsweetened flaked coconut, toasted

why this recipe works • *Chia pudding comes together by what seems like Jack and the Beanstalk–level magic. When chia seeds are combined with liquid and left to soak overnight they create a gel, which thickens and produces a no-cook tapioca-like pudding—a spectacular base for a simple, healthy breakfast. Pudding alchemy aside, chia is great because it's a nutritional powerhouse, packed with fiber, protein, and omega-3 fatty acids; plus, it has a neutral flavor that's the perfect canvas for fruity toppings. This recipe takes little effort, just time. We tried to cut back on that by scalding the milk to speed up the thickening process. And indeed we could: After just 15 minutes the pudding had thickened as much as it had after a cold overnight soak. But that speed came with downsides: a decidedly grassier, "seedier" flavor and the loss of the fresh, milky notes we enjoyed in the soaked pudding. So we stuck with the hands-off overnight method. Before we put it to bed for the night, we gave the pudding a quick second whisk 15 minutes after its initial mixing to make sure all the chia hydrated and to prevent clumping. To flavor the pudding, we kept things simple with vanilla extract and maple syrup, which pair nicely with almost any toppings you have at your breakfast table.*

1 Whisk milk, chia seeds, maple syrup, vanilla, and salt together in bowl. Let mixture sit for 15 minutes, then whisk again to break up any clumps. Cover bowl with plastic wrap and refrigerate for at least 8 hours or up to 1 week.

2 Adjust consistency of pudding with additional milk as needed. Top individual portions of pudding with ½ cup fruit and 1 tablespoon coconut, and drizzle with maple syrup to taste before serving.

PER SERVING
Cal 250; Total Fat 11g, Sat Fat 4.5g; Chol 5mg; Sodium 210mg; Total Carbs 32g, Fiber 13g, Total Sugar 16g, Added Sugar 6g; Protein 9g

EXCELLENT SOURCE OF
Fiber, Riboflavin, Niacin, Vitamin C, Calcium, Magnesium, Manganese, Phosphorus, Selenium

breakfast

BLUEBERRY-OAT PANCAKES

2 cups organic low-fat buttermilk, plus extra as needed
1 cup (3 ounces) old-fashioned rolled oats
1½ cups (4½ ounces) oat flour
½ cup (2½ ounces) all-purpose flour
2½ teaspoons baking powder
1 teaspoon ground cinnamon
¼ teaspoon salt
⅛ teaspoon ground nutmeg
2 large organic eggs
3 tablespoons plus 2 teaspoons expeller-pressed canola oil (see page 35)
3 tablespoons sugar
2 teaspoons vanilla extract
7½ ounces (1½ cups) blueberries

why this recipe works • *A stack of classic pancakes makes for a delicious breakfast but doesn't offer much in the way of nutrition. To give this breakfast a boost, we turned to whole grains and zeroed in on oats for their nutty flavor, hearty texture, and high fiber content. We were able to create a smooth base for our batter using three-quarters oat flour, with ½ cup all-purpose flour providing structure and lift. We stirred whole rolled oats into our batter as well. Pre-soaked until just softened, they gave our pancakes a satisfying, nubby texture. Fresh blueberries, cinnamon, and nutmeg paired nicely with the toasty oats. Lastly, switching from whole milk to low-fat buttermilk kept our pancakes light and fluffy. An electric griddle set at 350 degrees can be used in place of a skillet. We prefer using store-bought oat flour, as it has a very fine grind and creates the most fluffy pancakes, but you can make your own in a pinch: Grind 1½ cups (4½ ounces) old-fashioned rolled oats in a food processor to a fine meal, about 2 minutes; note pancakes will be denser if using ground oats. Do not use toasted oat flour, or quick, instant, or thick-cut oats in this recipe. Serve with maple syrup and additional blueberries if desired.*

1 Adjust oven rack to middle position and heat oven to 200 degrees. Set wire rack in rimmed baking sheet and place in oven. Combine 1 cup buttermilk and oats in bowl and let sit at room temperature until softened, about 15 minutes.

2 Whisk oat flour, all-purpose flour, baking powder, cinnamon, salt, and nutmeg together in large bowl. In separate bowl, whisk remaining 1 cup buttermilk, eggs, 3 tablespoons oil, sugar, and vanilla together until frothy, about 1 minute. Whisk buttermilk mixture into flour mixture until smooth. Using rubber spatula, fold in oat-buttermilk mixture.

3 Heat 1 teaspoon oil in 12-inch nonstick skillet over medium heat until shimmering, 3 to 5 minutes. Using paper towels, wipe out oil, leaving thin film in pan. Using ¼-cup measure, portion batter into pan, spreading each into 4-inch round using back of spoon. Sprinkle each pancake with 1 tablespoon blueberries. Cook until edges are set and first side is golden, 2 to 3 minutes.

4 Flip pancakes and cook until second side is golden, 2 to 3 minutes. Serve or transfer to wire rack in oven. Repeat with remaining batter, whisking additional buttermilk into batter as needed to loosen, and adding remaining oil to pan as necessary.

PER SERVING
Cal 350; Total Fat 12g, Sat Fat 2g; Chol 65mg; Sodium 390mg; Total Carbs 48g, Fiber 5g, Total Sugar 14g, Added Sugar 6g; Protein 12g

EXCELLENT SOURCE OF
Protein, Fiber

100 PERCENT WHOLE-WHEAT PANCAKES

makes 15 pancakes; serves 6

- 2 cups (11 ounces) whole-wheat flour
- 2 tablespoons sugar
- 1½ teaspoons baking powder
- ½ teaspoon baking soda
- ¾ teaspoon salt
- 2¼ cups organic low-fat buttermilk
- 5 tablespoons plus 2 teaspoons expeller-pressed canola oil (see page 35)
- 2 large organic eggs

why this recipe works • *Pancakes seemed like the perfect opportunity to showcase whole-wheat flour; its earthy, robust flavor would pair well with maple syrup and fresh fruit. But would the results be dense and heavy? Most whole-wheat pancake recipes we saw shied away from using only whole-wheat flour, cutting the mix with white. But when we prepared a batch of 100 percent whole-wheat pancakes, rather than being leaden, they turned out as light, fluffy, and tender as any pancakes we'd ever made. The reason? The bran present in the whole-wheat flour—the same stuff that contributes healthful fiber—cuts through any gluten strands that form, preventing the batter from becoming tough. In fact, while recipes for pancakes made with white flour advise undermixing to avoid tough pancakes, with whole-wheat flour we were guaranteed light and tender cakes even as we whisked our batter to a smooth, thick consistency. An electric griddle set at 350 degrees can be used in place of a skillet. Serve with maple syrup and fresh fruit.*

1 Adjust oven rack to middle position and heat oven to 200 degrees. Set wire rack in rimmed baking sheet and place in oven.

2 Whisk flour, sugar, baking powder, baking soda, and salt together in large bowl. In separate bowl, whisk buttermilk, 5 tablespoons oil, and eggs together until combined. Whisk buttermilk mixture into flour mixture until smooth. (Mixture will be thick; do not add more buttermilk.)

3 Heat 1 teaspoon oil in 12-inch nonstick skillet over medium heat until shimmering, 3 to 5 minutes. Using paper towels, wipe out oil, leaving thin film in pan. Using ¼-cup measure, portion batter into pan, spreading each into 4-inch round using back of spoon. Cook until edges are set, first side is golden, and bubbles on surface are just beginning to break, 2 to 3 minutes.

4 Flip pancakes and cook until second side is golden, 1 to 2 minutes longer. Serve or transfer to wire rack in oven. Repeat with remaining batter, adding remaining oil to pan as necessary.

PER SERVING
Cal 360; Total Fat 15g, Sat Fat 2g; Chol 70mg; Sodium 630mg; Total Carbs 47g, Fiber 6g, Total Sugar 9g, Added Sugar 4g; Protein 12g

EXCELLENT SOURCE OF
Protein, Fiber, Niacin, Manganese, Phosphorus, Selenium

breakfast

PUMPKIN SPICE WAFFLES

makes five 7-inch
Belgian waffles

2½ cups (7½ ounces) oat flour
½ cup (2½ ounces) all-purpose
  flour
1 teaspoon ground cinnamon
1 teaspoon baking powder
½ teaspoon baking soda
¾ teaspoon salt
¼ teaspoon ground nutmeg
¼ teaspoon ground cardamom
1 (15-ounce) can unsweetened
  pumpkin puree
1¼ cups organic plain
  low-fat yogurt
2 large organic eggs
¼ cup expeller-pressed canola
  oil (see page 35), plus extra
  for brushing
¼ cup (1¾ ounces) sugar
1 teaspoon grated fresh ginger

why this recipe works • *While we love a plain waffle, with its crisp exterior and custardy interior, it didn't take much arm twisting to convince tasters to try a pumpkin version, with its sunset-orange color and aroma of autumn spices. Canned pumpkin puree proved a delicious way to bring nutrients such as vitamin A, fiber, and iron into our morning baking, along with a sweet, earthy flavor. However, pumpkin also brings moisture, which initially thwarted our efforts to get a crispy edge. Blotting the puree with paper towels helped eliminate excess moisture, producing a thick, not overly wet batter that crisped up while retaining the waffles' custardy center. Low-fat yogurt helped make our batter extra thick and provided richness and tang. Taking a cue from our Blueberry Oat Pancakes (page 52), we traded out most of the all-purpose flour for mild-tasting whole-grain oat flour. A touch of cinnamon, nutmeg, cardamom, and fresh ginger rounded out the flavor. We prefer using store-bought oat flour, as it has a very fine grind and creates the best waffles, but you can make your own in a pinch. Grind 2½ cups (7½ ounces) old-fashioned rolled oats in a food processor to a fine meal, about 2 minutes; note waffles will be denser if using ground oats. Do not use toasted oat flour in this recipe. Serve with maple syrup and fresh fruit.*

1 Adjust oven rack to middle position and heat oven to 200 degrees.

2 Whisk oat flour, all-purpose flour, cinnamon, baking powder, baking soda, salt, nutmeg, and cardamom together in large bowl.

3 Line rimmed baking sheet with triple layer of paper towels. Spread pumpkin on paper towels in even layer. Cover pumpkin with second triple layer of paper towels and press firmly until paper towels are saturated. Peel back top layer of towels and discard. Grasp bottom towels and fold pumpkin in half; peel back towels. Transfer pumpkin to separate bowl and discard towels. Whisk in yogurt, eggs, oil, sugar, and ginger until combined. Whisk pumpkin mixture into flour mixture until well combined and smooth. Set wire rack in now-empty baking sheet and place in oven.

4 Heat waffle iron according to manufacturer's instructions and brush well with additional oil. Add scant 1 cup batter to waffle iron and cook according to manufacturer's instructions until each waffle is deep golden and has crisp, firm exterior. Serve immediately or transfer to wire rack in oven. Repeat with remaining batter, brushing waffle iron with additional oil.

PER WAFFLE
Cal 450; Total Fat 17g, Sat Fat 2.5g;
Chol 80mg; Sodium 630mg; Total
Carbs 59g, Fiber 7g, Total Sugar 17g,
Added Sugar 10g; Protein 16g

EXCELLENT SOURCE OF
Protein, Fiber, Vitamin A, Iron

breakfast

WHOLE-WHEAT BLUEBERRY-ALMOND MUFFINS

makes 12 muffins

- 1 cup sliced almonds, lightly toasted
- 1 cup (5½ ounces) whole-wheat flour
- ¾ cup (3¾ ounces) all-purpose flour
- 2 teaspoons baking powder
- ½ teaspoon baking soda
- ¾ teaspoon salt
- 1 cup organic low-fat buttermilk
- ⅔ cup packed (4⅔ ounces) dark brown sugar
- 2 large organic eggs
- ¼ cup expeller-pressed canola oil (see page 35)
- 2 teaspoons vanilla extract
- 7½ ounces (1½ cups) blueberries

PER MUFFIN
Cal 240; Total Fat 10g, Sat Fat 1g; Chol 30mg; Sodium 310mg; Total Carbs 32g, Fiber 3g, Total Sugar 14g, Added Sugar 11g; Protein 6g

EXCELLENT SOURCE OF
Manganese

why this recipe works • *We wanted to build a healthier blueberry muffin using whole-wheat flour. Problem is, most whole-wheat muffins are dense, bland sinkers that nobody wants to eat. Could we create a version that was tender and delicious? First, we needed to address the cardboard-like flavor that plagues so many whole-wheat muffins. We replaced part of the whole-wheat flour with ground toasted almonds and loved how their richness and nuttiness complemented the whole wheat's own earthy, nutty flavor. But the muffins were still squat and dense. Switching gears, we combined two leaveners— baking soda and baking powder. We were surprised to find how tender our muffins became—too tender. Because whole-wheat flour forms a relatively weak gluten network (which was further weakened by the fat in the almonds), these muffins lacked the structure to even come out of the pan. Incorporating ¾ cup all-purpose flour into the mix brought structural integrity back to our muffins while keeping them tender. Do not overmix the batter. You can substitute frozen (unthawed) blueberries for fresh in this recipe.*

1 Adjust oven rack to middle position and heat oven to 400 degrees. Spray 12-cup muffin tin, including top, generously with canola oil spray. Pulse ¼ cup almonds in food processor until coarsely chopped, 4 to 6 pulses; transfer to small bowl and set aside for topping.

2 Add whole-wheat flour, all-purpose flour, baking powder, baking soda, salt, and remaining ¾ cup almonds to now-empty food processor and process until well combined and almonds are finely ground, about 30 seconds; transfer to large bowl.

3 In separate bowl, whisk buttermilk, sugar, eggs, oil, and vanilla together until combined. Using rubber spatula, stir buttermilk mixture into almond-flour mixture until just combined (do not overmix). Gently fold in blueberries until incorporated.

4 Divide batter evenly among prepared muffin cups (cups will be filled to rim) and sprinkle with reserved chopped almonds. Bake until golden brown and toothpick inserted in center comes out with few crumbs attached, 16 to 18 minutes, rotating muffin tin halfway through baking.

5 Let muffins cool in tin on wire rack for 10 minutes. Remove muffins from tin and let cool for at least 10 minutes before serving.

nutritious DELICIOUS

CRANBERRY-ORANGE OAT MUFFINS

makes 12 muffins

2¼ cups (6¾ ounces) oat flour
1⅓ cups (6⅔ ounces) all-purpose flour
2 teaspoons baking powder
½ teaspoon baking soda
½ teaspoon salt
1¼ cups organic plain low-fat yogurt
¾ cup (5¼ ounces) sugar
½ cup expeller-pressed canola oil (see page 35)
2 large organic eggs
1 teaspoon grated orange zest
6 ounces (1½ cups) fresh cranberries, chopped coarse
1 cup pepitas, toasted and chopped

why this recipe works • *Cranberry-orange muffins sound healthy but can veer into cupcake territory when you add a streusel topping or sugary glaze. To enliven our muffin in a healthier fashion, we started with plenty of fresh, antioxidant-rich cranberries, then folded in protein- and mineral-rich pumpkin seeds, or pepitas. Their richness tamed the bright, acidic fruit. To further temper the sour punch of the berries, we chopped them coarsely. This distributed them more evenly throughout the batter, and enabled us to reduce the amount of sugar. We then replaced over half of our all-purpose flour with oat flour—as much as we could without compromising the muffin's structure—and replaced butter with canola oil. At this point, our muffin tasted lean and "too healthy." Low-fat yogurt provided the dairy richness we were lacking. For a final touch, we sprinkled the muffins with extra pumpkin seeds, which developed a rich, nutty flavor as the muffins baked—nobody missed the streusel. We prefer using store-bought oat flour, as it has a very fine grind and creates the best muffins, but you can make your own in a pinch. Grind 2¼ cups (6¾ ounces) old-fashioned rolled oats in a food processor to a fine meal, about 2 minutes; note muffins will be more squat and somewhat dense if using ground oats. Do not use toasted oat flour in this recipe. You can use thawed, frozen cranberries in place of the fresh.*

1 Adjust oven rack to middle position and heat oven to 375 degrees. Spray 12-cup muffin tin, including top, generously with canola oil spray.

2 Whisk oat flour, all-purpose flour, baking powder, baking soda, and salt together in large bowl.

3 In separate bowl, whisk yogurt, sugar, oil, eggs, and zest together until combined. Using rubber spatula, stir yogurt mixture into flour mixture until just combined (do not overmix). Gently fold in cranberries and ¾ cup pepitas until incorporated.

4 Divide batter evenly among prepared muffin cups (cups will be filled and mounded above rim) and sprinkle with remaining ¼ cup pepitas. Bake until golden and toothpick inserted in center comes out clean, 22 to 26 minutes, rotating pan halfway through baking.

5 Let muffins cool in tin on wire rack for 10 minutes. Remove muffins from tin and let cool for at least 10 minutes before serving.

PER MUFFIN
Cal 340; Total Fat 17g, Sat Fat 2.5g; Chol 35mg; Sodium 250mg; Total Carbs 39g, Fiber 3g, Total Sugar 15g, Added Sugar 12g; Protein 10g

EXCELLENT SOURCE OF
Protein, Manganese

nutritious DELICIOUS

WHOLE-WHEAT DATE-NUT BREAD

makes 1 loaf, serves 12

- 10 ounces pitted dates, chopped coarse (1⅔ cups)
- 1 cup boiling water
- 1 teaspoon baking soda
- 1½ cups (8¼ ounces) whole-wheat flour
- ½ cup (2½ ounces) all-purpose flour
- 1 teaspoon baking powder
- ½ teaspoon salt
- ⅔ cup organic low-fat buttermilk
- ⅓ cup packed (2⅓ ounces) dark brown sugar
- ¼ cup expeller-pressed canola oil (see page 35)
- 1 large organic egg
- 1 cup walnuts, toasted and chopped coarse

why this recipe works • *Dates and walnuts are nutritional power-houses, full of fiber and omega-3 fats, respectively. Their sweet and fragrant flavors pair naturally together, especially in a classic date-nut quick bread. Unfortunately, date-nut bread often suffers from unmitigated sweetness and hard, chewy dates. We wanted a more wholesome loaf that was full of soft, sweet dates and toasty nuts and featured a tender, not-too-sweet crumb. Our first step was to soften the fibrous dates in an alkaline mix of hot water and baking soda; we included both the softened dates and their flavorful soaking liquid in the batter. Given the dates' sweetness, we found that just ⅓ cup of dark brown sugar was enough to complement their flavor and give our loaf an appealing, rich color. Swapping out butter for canola oil was easy; we tasted no difference. Incorporating whole-wheat flour also seemed like a natural choice and, indeed, tasters loved the nutty, hearty flavor of this whole grain in combination with the dates and walnuts. We found we could use 75 percent whole-wheat flour, with just a bit of all-purpose flour providing structure and lift. For an accurate measurement of boiling water, bring a full kettle of water to a boil and then measure out the desired amount. Note that this recipe calls for an 8½ by 4½-inch loaf pan; if you use a 9 by 5-inch loaf pan, the loaf will not be quite as tall.*

1 Adjust oven rack to middle position and heat oven to 350 degrees. Grease 8½ by 4½-inch loaf pan. Combine dates, boiling water, and baking soda in medium bowl, cover, and let stand until dates have softened, about 30 minutes.

2 Whisk whole-wheat flour, all-purpose flour, baking powder, and salt together in large bowl. In separate bowl, whisk buttermilk, sugar, oil, and egg together until smooth, then stir in dates and their soaking liquid until combined. Using rubber spatula, gently fold buttermilk mixture into flour mixture until just combined; do not overmix. Gently fold in walnuts.

3 Scrape batter into prepared pan and smooth top. Bake until golden and skewer inserted in center comes out clean, 55 minutes to 1 hour, rotating pan halfway through baking.

4 Let bread cool in pan on wire rack for 10 minutes. Remove bread from pan and let cool completely on wire rack, about 2 hours. Serve.

PER ⅔-INCH SLICE
Cal 290; Total Fat 12g, Sat Fat 1g; Chol 15mg; Sodium 260mg; Total Carbs 44g, Fiber 4g, Total Sugar 22g, Added Sugar 5g; Protein 6g

EXCELLENT SOURCE OF
Manganese, Selenium

breakfast

AVOCADO AND BEAN TOAST

serves 4

- **4** ounces cherry tomatoes, quartered
- **4** teaspoons cold-pressed extra-virgin olive oil (see page 35)
  Salt and pepper
- **1** (15-ounce) can black beans, rinsed
- **¼** cup boiling water
- **½** teaspoon grated lime zest plus 1 tablespoon juice
- **4** (½-inch-thick) slices rustic 100 percent whole-grain bread
- **1** ripe avocado, halved, pitted, and sliced thin
- **¼** cup Quick Sweet-and-Spicy Pickled Red Onions (optional)
- **¼** cup fresh cilantro leaves

why this recipe works • *Avocado toast is one of our favorite healthy snacks, but we wanted a topped toast that was a bit more substantial and could stand alone as breakfast. We chose a bold Southwestern flavor profile to liven up our morning: Mashed black beans on toast elevated with a bit of spice, fresh tomato, and squeeze of lime is hard to argue with. By simply mashing our beans with hot water, oil, and lime zest and juice, we were able to get a flavorsome, well-textured base. We really liked the addition of spicy quick-pickled onions, which can be made up to a week ahead. (If you don't have them on hand, a pinch of red pepper flakes will provide heat.) For an accurate measure of boiling water, bring a full kettle of water to boil and then measure out the desired amount.*

1 Combine tomatoes, 1 teaspoon oil, pinch salt, and pinch pepper in bowl; set aside. Mash beans, boiling water, lime zest and juice, ½ teaspoon salt, pinch pepper, and remaining 1 tablespoon oil with potato masher to coarse puree in second bowl, leaving some whole beans intact.

2 Adjust oven rack 4 inches from broiler element and heat broiler. Place bread on aluminum foil–lined baking sheet and broil until golden, 1 to 2 minutes per side.

3 Spread mashed bean mixture evenly on toasts, then top with avocado and season with salt to taste. Top with pickled onions, if using, tomatoes, and cilantro. Serve.

QUICK SWEET-AND-SPICY PICKLED RED ONIONS
makes about 2 cups

- **1** red onion, halved and sliced thin through root end
- **1** cup red wine vinegar
- **⅓** cup sugar
- **2** jalapeño chiles, stemmed, seeded, and sliced into thin rings
- **¼** teaspoon salt

Place onion in bowl. Bring vinegar, sugar, jalapeños, and salt to simmer over medium-high heat in small saucepan, stirring occasionally, until sugar dissolves. Pour vinegar mixture over onion, cover, and let cool completely, about 1 hour. Drain cooled vegetables in colander. (Pickled onions can be refrigerated for up to 1 week; onions will turn harsh after 1 week.)

PER SERVING
Cal 250; Total Fat 13g, Sat Fat 2g; Chol 0mg; Sodium 690mg; Total Carbs 26g, Fiber 8g, Total Sugar 3g, Added Sugar 0g; Protein 8g

EXCELLENT SOURCE OF
Fiber, Vitamin K, Manganese

FRIED EGGS OVER GARLICKY CHARD AND BELL PEPPER

serves 4

2 tablespoons cold-pressed extra-virgin olive oil (see page 35), plus extra for serving

5 garlic cloves, minced

2 pounds Swiss chard, stemmed, 1 cup stems chopped fine, leaves sliced into ½-inch-wide strips

1 small red bell pepper, stemmed, seeded, and cut into ¼-inch pieces
 Salt and pepper

⅛ teaspoon red pepper flakes

4 large organic eggs
 Lemon wedges

why this recipe works • *Greens for breakfast? When considering options for weekday mornings, Swiss chard doesn't immediately come to mind. However, the hearty leaves made an ideal partner for a fried egg (a welcome change from toast), especially when the rich, drippy yolk broke and mingled with the earthy greens. (Chard leaves contain abundant antioxidants and are also rich in vitamins K, A, E, and C.) To keep our breakfast quick, we simply bloomed minced garlic in olive oil, then wilted handfuls of chard before adding red bell pepper for sweetness and a pinch of red pepper flakes to perk everything up. The greens became tender and vibrant in 5 minutes. We then drained our vegetables to banish excess liquid before portioning them out, and used the same skillet to quickly fry 4 eggs before sliding them atop our greens. A complementary spritz from a lemon wedge added pleasant brightness. You will need a 12-inch nonstick skillet with a tight-fitting lid for this recipe.*

1 Heat 1 tablespoon oil and garlic in 12-inch nonstick skillet over medium-low heat, stirring occasionally, until garlic is light golden, 3 to 5 minutes. Increase heat to high, add chopped chard stems then chard leaves, 1 handful at a time, and cook until wilted, about 2 minutes. Stir in bell pepper, ¼ teaspoon salt, and pepper flakes and cook, stirring often, until chard is tender and peppers are softened, about 3 minutes. Off heat, season with salt and pepper to taste. Transfer to colander set in bowl.

2 Crack 2 eggs into small bowl and season with salt and pepper. Repeat with remaining 2 eggs in second bowl. Heat remaining 1 tablespoon oil in now-empty skillet over medium-high heat until shimmering; quickly swirl to coat pan. Working quickly, pour one bowl of eggs in one side of pan and second bowl of eggs in other side. Cover and cook for 1 minute.

3 Remove skillet from heat and let sit, covered, 15 to 45 seconds for runny yolks (white around edge of yolk will be barely opaque), 45 to 60 seconds for soft but set yolks, or about 2 minutes for medium-set yolks.

4 Divide chard mixture evenly among serving plates, top each with one egg, and drizzle with oil to taste. Serve immediately with lemon wedges.

PER SERVING
Cal 170; Total Fat 12g, Sat Fat 2.5g; Chol 185mg; Sodium 540mg; Total Carbs 8g, Fiber 3g, Total Sugar 3g, Added Sugar 0g; Protein 9g

EXCELLENT SOURCE OF
Vitamin A, Riboflavin, Vitamin C, Vitamin E, Vitamin K, Iron, Magnesium, Manganese, Potassium, Selenium

KALE AND BLACK BEAN BREAKFAST BURRITOS

serves 6

2 tablespoons cold-pressed extra-virgin olive oil (see page 35), plus extra for serving

1 small onion, chopped fine

1 poblano chile, stemmed, seeded, and chopped fine
 Salt and pepper

2 garlic cloves, minced

½ teaspoon ground cumin

1 (15-ounce) can black beans, rinsed

¾ cup water

12 ounces kale, stemmed and chopped

8 large organic eggs

2 tablespoons organic 1 percent low-fat milk or water

6 (10-inch) whole-grain tortilla wraps

1 tomato, cored and chopped fine

PER SERVING
Cal 390; Total Fat 13g, Sat Fat 3g; Chol 250 mg; Sodium 770mg; Total Carbs 50g, Fiber 9g, Total Sugar 3g, Added Sugar 0g; Protein 19g

EXCELLENT SOURCE OF
Protein, Fiber, Vitamin A, Riboflavin, Folate, Vitamin C, Vitamin K, Copper, Iron, Selenium

why this recipe works • *Breakfast burritos often rely on greasy meat for bulk and flavor. To fill our burrito with more nutritious options, we swapped in black beans and kale along with fluffy scrambled eggs. To build a flavorful base, we sautéed aromatic onion, garlic, a poblano, and cumin. We added our beans, mashing half to create a cohesive mixture. Next, we quickly braised our kale until tender, then used the same skillet to scramble eggs before folding in the kale. We spread the bean mixture onto whole-grain tortillas, added the kale-egg scramble, and finished with tomato and a drizzle of olive oil. Softening the tortillas in the microwave makes them easy to roll. Serve with hot sauce if desired.*

1 Heat 1 tablespoon oil in 12-inch nonstick skillet over medium-high heat until shimmering. Add onion, poblano, and ¼ teaspoon salt and cook until softened, about 5 minutes. Stir in garlic and cumin and cook until fragrant, about 30 seconds. Stir in beans and ½ cup water and cook until beans are heated through, about 4 minutes. Off heat, mash half of beans to chunky paste; transfer all the mixture to bowl and cover to keep warm. Wipe out skillet.

2 In now-empty skillet, heat 2 teaspoons oil over medium-high heat until shimmering. Add kale and ¼ teaspoon salt, cover, and cook until kale begins to wilt, about 2 minutes. Stir in remaining ¼ cup water, cover, and cook until kale is tender, 2 to 4 minutes; transfer to second bowl. Wipe out skillet.

3 Beat eggs, milk, ¼ teaspoon salt, and ¼ teaspoon pepper with fork until eggs are thoroughly combined and color is pure yellow.

4 Heat remaining 1 teaspoon oil in now-empty skillet over medium-high heat until shimmering. Add egg mixture and, using rubber spatula, constantly and firmly scrape along bottom and sides of skillet until eggs begin to clump and spatula leaves trail on bottom of pan, 1½ to 2½ minutes. Off heat, gently stir in kale and constantly fold eggs and kale until eggs have finished cooking, 30 to 60 seconds. Cover to keep warm.

5 Wrap tortillas in damp dish towel and microwave until warm and pliable, about 1 minute. Lay warm tortillas on counter and spread bean mixture evenly across center of each tortilla, close to bottom edge. Top with kale-egg mixture then sprinkle with tomato and drizzle with oil to taste. Working with 1 tortilla at a time, fold sides then bottom of tortilla over filling, then continue to roll tightly into wrap. Serve immediately.

FLUFFY OMELET WITH SMOKED SALMON AND ASPARAGUS

serves 2

2 tablespoons plus 1 teaspoon cold-pressed extra-virgin olive oil (see page 35)
1 shallot, sliced thin
5 ounces asparagus, trimmed and cut on bias into ¼-inch lengths
  Salt and pepper
1 ounce smoked salmon, chopped
½ teaspoon lemon juice
4 large organic eggs, separated
¼ teaspoon cream of tartar
1 ounce Parmesan cheese, grated (½ cup)

why this recipe works • *The beauty of this omelet (other than impressive height)? It's forgiving. Unlike traditional omelets that involve dexterous flipping, our fluffy omelet is relatively hands-off. To give it a soufflé-like consistency, we whipped egg whites with cream of tartar to get stiff peaks, then folded in our yolks. We spread the mixture out in a skillet, then let the oven do the work for us; its steady heat prevented overcooking. Such a delicate omelet would be weighted down by a heavy filling like ham and cheese. A small amount of flavorful ingredients—smoked salmon, asparagus, and a bit of Parmesan—worked perfectly, yielding a dish that was sophisticated yet surprisingly packed with nutrients. After sliding the finished omelet onto a cutting board, we effortlessly folded it in half before serving. A teaspoon of white vinegar or lemon juice can be used in place of the cream of tartar. A hand-held mixer or a whisk can be used in place of the stand mixer.*

1 Adjust oven rack to middle position and heat oven to 375 degrees. Heat 1 teaspoon oil in 12-inch ovensafe nonstick skillet over medium-high heat until shimmering. Add shallot and cook until softened and beginning to brown, about 2 minutes. Add asparagus and pepper to taste and cook, stirring frequently, until crisp-tender, 5 to 7 minutes. Transfer asparagus mixture to bowl and stir in salmon and lemon juice; set aside and wipe out skillet.

2 Whisk egg yolks, 1 tablespoon oil, and ⅛ teaspoon salt together in bowl. Place egg whites in bowl of stand mixer and sprinkle cream of tartar over surface. Fit stand mixer with whisk and whip egg whites on medium-low speed until foamy, about 2 minutes. Increase speed to medium-high and whip until stiff peaks just start to form, 2 to 3 minutes. Fold egg yolk mixture into egg whites until no white streaks remain.

3 Heat remaining 1 tablespoon oil in now-empty skillet over medium-high heat until shimmering, swirling to coat bottom of pan. Quickly add egg mixture, spreading into even layer with spatula. Remove pan from heat and gently sprinkle asparagus mixture and Parmesan evenly over top of omelet. Transfer to oven and cook until center of omelet springs back when lightly pressed, 4½ minutes for slightly wet omelet or 5 minutes for dry omelet.

4 Run spatula around edges of omelet to loosen, shaking gently to release. Slide omelet onto cutting board and let stand for 30 seconds. Using spatula, fold omelet in half. Cut omelet in half crosswise and serve immediately.

PER SERVING
Cal 390; Total Fat 31g, Sat Fat 8g; Chol 385mg; Sodium 640mg; Total Carbs 6g, Fiber 2g, Total Sugar 3g, Added Sugar 0g; Protein 23g

EXCELLENT SOURCE OF
Protein, Riboflavin, Niacin, Folate, Vitamin B12, Vitamin D, Vitamin K, Calcium, Phosphorus, Selenium

FRITTATA WITH BROCCOLI AND TURMERIC

serves 6

12 large organic eggs

⅓ cup organic 1 percent low-fat milk or water

¼ cup grated Parmesan cheese

2 tablespoons cold-pressed extra-virgin olive oil (see page 35)

1 tablespoon minced fresh tarragon
   Salt and pepper

12 ounces broccoli florets, cut into ½-inch pieces (4 cups)

1 shallot, minced

1 teaspoon ground turmeric

3 tablespoons water

½ teaspoon grated lemon zest plus ½ teaspoon juice

why this recipe works • *A frittata is a hearty brunch option but is often loaded with potatoes, cheese, and sausage or bacon. For a more nutritious version, we nixed the meat and swapped out potatoes for broccoli. To make a substantial, veggie-packed frittata, we used a dozen eggs and a full 4 cups of broccoli, chopping the florets small so they would be surrounded by the eggs, ensuring a cohesive whole. Adding healthful turmeric and black pepper gave the filling a bold, slightly spicy flavor. But we weren't ready to omit cheese entirely. We opted for Parmesan, since a little bit goes a long way in terms of cheesy flavor; just ¼ cup was all we needed. To ensure our frittata cooked fully and evenly, we started it on the stovetop, stirring until a spatula left a trail in the curds, and then transferred it to the oven to gently finish. Adding milk and salt to the eggs ensured they stayed tender and fluffy, as the liquid makes it harder for the proteins to coagulate and turn rubbery, while the salt weakens their interactions and produces a softer curd. This frittata can be served warm or at room temperature. When paired with a salad, it can serve as a meal.*

1 Adjust oven rack to middle position and heat oven to 350 degrees. Whisk eggs, milk, Parmesan, 1 tablespoon oil, tarragon, and ¼ teaspoon salt in bowl until well combined.

2 Heat remaining 1 tablespoon oil in 12-inch ovensafe nonstick skillet over medium-high heat until shimmering. Add broccoli, shallot, turmeric, ¼ teaspoon salt, and ¼ teaspoon pepper and cook, stirring frequently, until broccoli is crisp-tender and spotty brown, 7 to 9 minutes. Stir in water and lemon zest and juice and continue to cook, stirring constantly, until broccoli is just tender and no water remains in skillet, about 1 minute longer.

3 Add egg mixture and cook, using rubber spatula to stir and scrape bottom of skillet until large curds form and spatula leaves trail through eggs but eggs are still very wet, about 30 seconds. Smooth curds into even layer and cook, without stirring, for 30 seconds. Transfer skillet to oven and bake until frittata is slightly puffy and surface bounces back when lightly pressed, 5 to 8 minutes. Using rubber spatula, loosen frittata from skillet and transfer to cutting board. Let sit for 5 minutes before slicing and serving.

PER SERVING
Cal 220; Total Fat 15g, Sat Fat 4g; Chol 375mg; Sodium 400mg; Total Carbs 6g, Fiber 2g, Total Sugar 2g, Added Sugar 0g; Protein 16g

EXCELLENT SOURCE OF
Protein, Vitamin A, Riboflavin, Folate, Vitamin C, Vitamin D, Phosphorus, Selenium

nutritious DELICIOUS

TOFU RANCHEROS

serves 6

2 (28-ounce) cans diced tomatoes
1 tablespoon plus 1 teaspoon lime juice, plus lime wedges for serving
1 tablespoon packed brown sugar
1 onion, chopped
½ cup chopped canned green chiles
¼ cup cold-pressed extra-virgin olive oil (see page 35)
2 tablespoons plus ½ teaspoon chili powder
4 garlic cloves, sliced thin
14 ounces firm tofu, halved lengthwise, then cut crosswise into twelve ½-inch-thick slabs Salt and pepper
1 cup cilantro leaves
4 scallions, white parts sliced thin, green parts cut into 1-inch pieces
1 avocado, halved, pitted, and diced
8 (6-inch) corn tortillas, warmed

why this recipe works • *Huevos rancheros, with its fine-tuned combination of eggs, spicy sauce, and rich toppings, makes for an eye-opening breakfast. To introduce some variety to our breakfast, we found that we could easily replace the eggs (the "huevos") with supple squares of firm tofu as the source of protein. Like a poached egg, the tofu achieved a creamy, silky interior texture while still holding its shape during cooking. The backbone of our tofu rancheros is the sauce, so nailing it was key: For maximum flavor with little effort, we roasted canned diced tomatoes with brown sugar, lime juice, onion, green chiles, garlic, and chili powder. Roasting on a sheet pan allowed moisture to quickly evaporate and a nice char to form on the vegetables. We seared seasoned tofu while the sauce cooked to give it a beautiful golden-brown color. Finishing the sauce and tofu together on the stovetop allowed the flavors to meld and gave the tofu a perfect texture. Instead of sprinkling the dish with a few herbs, we supercharged the toppings by adding a vibrant salad of avocado, cilantro, and scallions. Served with warm corn tortillas, tofu rancheros is a spicy, hearty way to start the day. Use a heavyweight rimmed baking sheet for this recipe, as flimsy sheets will warp in the 500-degree oven.*

1 Adjust oven rack to middle position and heat oven to 500 degrees. Line rimmed baking sheet with parchment paper. Drain tomatoes in fine-mesh strainer set over bowl, pressing to extract as much juice as possible. Reserve 1¼ cups tomato juice and discard remainder. Whisk 1 tablespoon lime juice and sugar into tomato juice.

2 Combine onion, chiles, 2 tablespoons oil, 2 tablespoons chili powder, garlic, and drained tomatoes in second bowl. Transfer tomato mixture to prepared baking sheet and spread in even layer to edges of sheet. Roast until charred in spots, 35 to 40 minutes, stirring and redistributing into even layer halfway through baking.

3 Meanwhile, spread tofu on paper towel–lined baking sheet and let drain for 20 minutes. Gently press dry with paper towels, season with salt and pepper, and sprinkle both sides with remaining ½ teaspoon chili powder.

4 Heat 1 tablespoon oil in 12-inch nonstick skillet over medium-high heat until just smoking. Add tofu and cook until golden and crisp on both sides, 5 to 7 minutes; transfer to paper towel–lined plate.

5 Transfer roasted tomato mixture to now-empty skillet and stir in reserved tomato juice mixture. Season with salt and pepper to taste, then nestle tofu into sauce. Bring to simmer over medium heat, cover, and cook until tofu is warmed through and sauce thickens slightly, about 2 minutes.

6 Whisk remaining 1 tablespoon oil and 1 teaspoon lime juice together in large bowl. Add cilantro, scallions, and avocado and toss to coat. Season to taste with salt and pepper. Serve rancheros with warm tortillas and lime wedges, topped with herb and avocado salad.

SMOKED TROUT HASH WITH EGGS

serves 4

1 pound russet potatoes, peeled and cut into ¼-inch pieces

2 tablespoons cold-pressed extra-virgin olive oil (see page 35)
Salt and pepper

1½ pounds mustard greens, stemmed and cut into 1-inch pieces

1 onion, chopped fine

1 garlic clove, minced

6 ounces smoked trout, flaked

4 large organic eggs

1 tablespoon minced fresh dill
Lemon wedges

why this recipe works • *Smoked trout is a great breakfast protein that is full of omega-3 fatty acids. Instead of the classic pairing with a hefty bagel and schmear of cream cheese, we looked to fit the rich fish into a vegetable hash. Because smoked trout is often paired with mustard or horseradish, we chose mustard greens, a nutritional powerhouse that carries a horseradish-like bite. Their spicy flavor stood up perfectly to the fish and provided leafy chew, crisp lacy edges, and nutrients: flavonoids, vitamins, iron, and more. But our hash needed a saucy element in order to complete and further tame the smokiness of the fish, so we cooked 4 eggs right in the hash once it finished browning. The runny yolks gave us the rich, saucy component we wanted, while the whites brought extra protein into the mix. A squeeze of lemon brightened everything up for a balanced hash. You will need a 12-inch nonstick skillet with a tight-fitting lid for this recipe.*

1 Microwave potatoes, 1 tablespoon oil, ½ teaspoon salt, and ¼ teaspoon pepper in covered bowl until potatoes are translucent around edges, 5 to 8 minutes, stirring halfway through microwaving.

2 Microwave mustard greens in second large covered bowl until wilted, 8 to 10 minutes, stirring halfway through microwaving. Transfer to colander, drain well, then add to bowl with potatoes; set aside.

3 Heat remaining 1 tablespoon oil in 12-inch nonstick skillet over medium-high heat until shimmering. Add onion and cook until softened and lightly browned, 5 to 7 minutes.

4 Stir in garlic and cook until fragrant, about 30 seconds. Stir in potatoes and mustard greens, breaking up any clumps. Using back of spatula, firmly pack potato mixture into skillet and cook undisturbed for 2 minutes. Flip hash, one portion at a time, and repack into skillet. Repeat flipping process every few minutes until potatoes are well browned and mustard greens are tender, 6 to 8 minutes.

5 Off heat, sprinkle trout evenly over hash. Make 4 shallow indentations (about 2 inches wide) in surface of hash using back of spoon. Crack 1 egg into each indentation and season eggs with salt and pepper. Cover and cook over medium-low heat until egg whites are just set and yolks are still runny, 4 to 6 minutes. Sprinkle with dill and serve with lemon wedges.

PER SERVING
Cal 320; Total Fat 15g, Sat Fat 3.5g; Chol 220mg; Sodium 380mg; Total Carbs 25g, Fiber 5g, Total Sugar 3g, Added Sugar 0g; Protein 23g

EXCELLENT SOURCE OF
Protein, Fiber, Vitamin A, Thiamine, Riboflavin, Niacin, Pantothenic Acid, Vitamin B6, Vitamin B12, Vitamin C, Vitamin K, Manganese, Phosphorus, Potassium, Selenium

MUSHROOM AND ARTICHOKE HASH WITH PARMESAN CROUTONS

serves 4

6 tablespoons cold-pressed extra-virgin olive oil (see page 35)

2 slices rustic 100 percent whole-grain bread, cut into ½-inch pieces

¼ cup grated Parmesan cheese

1½ pounds chanterelle, cremini, oyster, and/or shiitake mushrooms, stemmed and cut into ½-inch pieces
Salt and pepper

2½ cups jarred whole baby artichoke hearts packed in water, drained, quartered, and patted dry

2 garlic cloves, minced

2 teaspoons minced fresh sage

⅛ teaspoon red pepper flakes

½ cup Lemon-Yogurt Sauce (page 152)

PER SERVING
Cal 370; Total Fat 24g, Sat Fat 4g; Chol 4mg; Sodium 730mg; Total Carbs 27g, Fiber 9g, Total Sugar 5g, Added Sugar 0g; Protein 11g

EXCELLENT SOURCE OF
Protein, Fiber, Riboflavin, Niacin, Vitamin C, Vitamin D, Copper, Iron, Manganese, Potassium

why this recipe works • *Meaty breakfast hashes, such as classic corned beef hash, may be delicious, but they are typically loaded with fat and salt and provide you with little nutrition. For a healthier but equally satisfying hash, we turned to fiber-filled artichokes and deeply flavored, "meaty" mushrooms. To get these superstar vegetables crisp, we tried oven roasting, which provided rich browning but took close to an hour and a half. And the results didn't quite feel hash-like, more like a savory medley of roasted vegetables. Our hash needed cohesiveness and a starchy element. White potatoes are typically found in hash, but we wanted to incorporate a wholesome grain instead, so we made Parmesan croutons from rustic whole-grain bread. Returning to our skillet, we pressed our mixture into the pan with the back of a spatula, flipping and packing it a few times to achieve good browning while also creating a cohesive, hash-like texture. A dollop of bright Lemon-Yogurt Sauce on top livened up all the flavors and turned the hash into a satiating breakfast or brunch dish. We recommend using a high-quality, rustic whole-grain bread for the best-textured croutons. Any mix of wild mushrooms can be used here.*

1 Heat 2 tablespoons oil in 12-inch nonstick skillet over medium heat until shimmering. Add bread and cook, stirring constantly, until beginning to brown, 3 to 5 minutes. Add Parmesan and continue to cook, stirring constantly and breaking up clumps, until croutons are golden brown, about 2 minutes. Transfer croutons to bowl.

2 Heat 2 tablespoons oil in now-empty skillet over medium-high heat until shimmering. Add mushrooms and ½ teaspoon salt, cover, and cook, stirring occasionally, until mushrooms have released their liquid, 8 to 10 minutes.

3 Uncover and stir in remaining 2 tablespoons oil, the artichokes, garlic, sage, pepper flakes, and reserved croutons. Using back of spatula, firmly pack hash into skillet and cook undisturbed for 2 minutes. Flip hash, one portion at a time, and repack into skillet. Repeat flipping process every few minutes until hash is well browned, about 6 minutes. Season with salt and pepper to taste. Top individual portions with Lemon-Yogurt Sauce and serve.

LUNCH

83 MLTs

85 Turmeric Chicken Salad Sandwiches

86 Egg Salad Sandwiches with Radishes and Watercress

89 Chickpea Salad Sandwiches

Curried Chickpea Salad Sandwiches

90 Pinto Bean–Beet Burgers

92 Super Greens Soup

94 Turkish Tomato, Bulgur, and Red Pepper Soup

97 Garlic-Chicken and Wild Rice Soup

98 Mushroom and Wheat Berry Soup

101 Red Lentil Soup with North African Spices

103 Hearty 15-Bean and Vegetable Soup

104 Shiitake, Tofu, and Mustard Greens Soup

107 Italian Wedding Soup with Kale and Farro

108 Kale Caesar Salad

111 Mediterranean Chopped Salad

112 Super Cobb Salad

114 Asparagus, Arugula, and Cannellini Bean Salad with Walnuts

117 Pesto Farro Salad with Cherry Tomatoes and Artichokes

119 Three-Bean Salad with Arugula

120 Quinoa Taco Salad

122 Raw Beet and Carrot Noodle Salad with Almond-Sesame Dressing

124 Chinese Chicken Salad

127 Chicken and Arugula Salad with Figs and Warm Spices

129 Salmon, Avocado, Grapefruit, and Watercress Salad

130 Fennel and Apple Salad with Smoked Trout

133 Summer Rolls with Spicy Almond Butter Sauce

MLTs

1 tablespoon cold-pressed
   extra-virgin olive oil
   (see page 35)
1 shallot, minced
1½ pounds portobello mushroom
   caps (4 to 5 inches in
   diameter), gills removed,
   sliced into ½-inch-thick strips
   Salt and pepper
1 garlic clove, minced
½ teaspoon smoked paprika
1 ripe avocado, halved and pitted
2 tablespoons organic plain
   low-fat yogurt
8 slices rustic 100 percent
   whole-grain bread, toasted
2 tomatoes, cored and sliced thin
2 ounces (2 cups) baby arugula

PER SANDWICH
Cal 310; Total Fat 14g, Sat Fat 2g;
Chol 0mg; Sodium 520mg; Total
Carbs 38g, Fiber 11g, Total
Sugar 11g, Added Sugar 0g;
Protein 13g

EXCELLENT SOURCE OF
Protein, Fiber, Vitamin A, Thiamine,
Riboflavin, Niacin, Pantothenic Acid,
Vitamin B6, Folate, Vitamin C,
Vitamin K, Copper, Magnesium,
Manganese, Phosphorus, Potassium,
Selenium

why this recipe works • *The simple beauty of a classic BLT lies in the balance of a few ingredients—salty-crisp bacon, sweet-juicy tomatoes, and refreshing lettuce—tied together with a slick of mayonnaise. Could we re-create this appealing balance using a nutrient-packed ingredient lineup? Strips of portobello mushrooms proved a good stand-in for bacon. When sautéed and seasoned with smoked paprika and a little salt, they brought meaty texture, umami character, and even some smokiness without all the fat and preservatives. (Being fungi rather than plants, they also offered a unique nutritional profile, including stores of minerals such as copper and selenium.) Using a full 1½ pounds of mushrooms provided plenty of meatiness without causing the sandwich to fall apart. We kept the juicy tomatoes. As for the lettuce, we traded romaine for arugula, enjoying how its peppery bite perked up the other flavors. Finally, we needed a creamy spread: Mixing avocado and yogurt captured the richness and tang of mayonnaise, and we happily slathered it on toasted whole-grain bread (instead of traditional white bread) to complete the sandwich.*

1 Heat oil in 12-inch nonstick skillet over medium heat. Add shallot and cook until softened, about 2 minutes. Add mushrooms and ½ teaspoon salt, cover, and cook, stirring occasionally, until mushrooms have released their moisture, 10 to 12 minutes.

2 Uncover, increase heat to medium-high, and cook until mushrooms are lightly browned, about 10 minutes. Stir in garlic and smoked paprika and cook until fragrant, about 30 seconds. Remove pan from heat and let mushrooms cool slightly, about 10 minutes.

3 Just before serving, combine avocado, yogurt, and ⅛ teaspoon salt in small bowl and mash until smooth. Spread avocado mixture evenly over 4 toast slices. Assemble 4 sandwiches by evenly layering mushrooms, tomatoes, then arugula. Top with remaining 4 toast slices. Serve.

lunch

TURMERIC CHICKEN SALAD SANDWICHES

serves 6

Salt and pepper

2 (4- to 6-ounce) organic boneless, skinless chicken breasts, no more than 1 inch thick, trimmed of all visible fat

1 teaspoon cold-pressed extra-virgin olive oil (see page 35)

½ teaspoon ground turmeric
Pinch ground cinnamon

¼ cup organic plain low-fat yogurt

2 tablespoons mayonnaise

2 teaspoons lemon juice

½ teaspoon Dijon mustard

1 garlic clove, minced

⅓ cup walnuts, toasted and chopped coarse

⅓ cup fresh parsley leaves

¼ cup unsweetened dried tart cherries

1 shallot, minced

12 slices hearty 100 percent whole-grain sandwich bread

2 ounces (2 cups) baby spinach

PER SANDWICH
Cal 290; Total Fat 11g, Sat Fat 1.5g; Chol 30mg; Sodium 470mg; Total Carbs 30g, Fiber 5g, Total Sugar 7g, Added Sugar 0g; Protein 17g

EXCELLENT SOURCE OF
Protein, Fiber, Vitamin A, Niacin, Vitamin B6, Vitamin K, Manganese, Phosphorus, Selenium

why this recipe works • *To apply some modern tricks to old-school chicken salad, we turned to our spice rack. Most spices boast an impressive portfolio of phytonutrients—often the very same compounds that give them such potent flavor. Mild, creamy chicken salad was an ideal canvas. First, we found we could replace two-thirds of the mayonnaise with low-fat yogurt (and use less dressing overall) and still deliver enough creamy tang to keep everyone happy. To spice up our dressing, we added turmeric and black pepper. Long used as a medicinal spice in India, turmeric is associated with many health benefits. Black pepper—commonly paired with turmeric— may boost the potency of turmeric, especially in the presence of a little heart-healthy fat. With our dressing ready, we poached chicken breasts to perfection by heating them just until the water reached 170 degrees, then removing the pot from the heat and letting the chicken cook through slowly and gently. For add-ins, we opted for dried cherries and toasted walnuts to provide crunch. Instead of a whisper of herbs, we stirred in ⅓ cup of parsley leaves (herbs, like spices, contain concentrated nutrients), which added a pop of green color and an herbal back note. Two cups of tender baby spinach provided a fresh finish to our updated chicken salad sandwiches.*

1 Dissolve 1 tablespoon salt in 6 cups cold water in Dutch oven. Submerge chicken in water. Heat pot over medium heat until water registers 170 degrees. Turn off heat, cover pot, and let stand until chicken registers 165 degrees, 15 to 17 minutes. Transfer chicken to paper towel–lined rimmed baking sheet and refrigerate until cool, about 30 minutes.

2 Combine oil, turmeric, and cinnamon together in bowl and microwave until fragrant, about 30 seconds; let cool slightly. In large bowl, whisk oil mixture, yogurt, mayonnaise, lemon juice, mustard, garlic, ½ teaspoon pepper, and ¼ teaspoon salt together until smooth.

3 Pat cooled chicken dry with paper towels and cut into ½-inch pieces. Add chicken, walnuts, parsley, cherries, and shallot to bowl with yogurt mixture, toss to combine, and season with salt and pepper to taste. Divide chicken salad evenly over 6 bread slices, then top with spinach. Top with remaining 6 bread slices. Serve.

lunch

serves 6

- 10 large organic eggs
- 2½ tablespoons mayonnaise
- 2½ tablespoons organic plain low-fat yogurt
- 1½ tablespoons lemon juice
- 1 tablespoon Dijon mustard
  Salt and pepper
- 3 scallions, sliced thin
- 12 slices hearty 100 percent whole-grain sandwich bread
- 6 radishes, trimmed and sliced thin
- 2 ounces (2 cups) watercress

why this recipe works • *Eggs are among the most nutritionally rich foods available, so an egg salad sandwich would seem like a good thing. But the hallmark of egg salad—the creaminess—typically has more to do with the amount of mayonnaise in the mix. We wanted a version that would do our eggs justice. To achieve creaminess without relying solely on mayo, we took a cue from our method for deviled eggs and mashed the yolks. Knocking a few minutes off the cooking time produced yolks that mashed up perfectly creamy, with no hint of chalkiness. From there, we added just 2½ tablespoons of mayonnaise and an equal amount of yogurt, plus lemon juice, mustard, salt, and pepper. This yielded a velvety base into which we folded the chopped egg whites and fresh scallions. For crunch, we added a layer of vibrant radishes. And we traded the token lettuce leaf for a mound of vitamin-rich watercress for freshness. Be sure to use large eggs that have no cracks and are cold from the refrigerator. If you don't have a steamer basket, use a spoon or tongs to gently place the eggs in the water. It does not matter if the eggs are above the water or partially submerged.*

1 Bring 1 inch water to rolling boil in large saucepan over high heat. Place eggs in steamer basket in single layer. Transfer basket to saucepan. Cover, reduce heat to medium-low, and cook eggs for 11 minutes.

2 When eggs are almost finished cooking, fill medium bowl halfway with ice and water. Using slotted spoon, transfer eggs to bowl of ice water and let sit for 15 minutes to cool.

3 Peel eggs and halve lengthwise. Transfer egg yolks to large bowl. Using potato masher, mash yolks with mayonnaise, yogurt, lemon juice, mustard, ½ teaspoon salt, and ⅛ teaspoon pepper. Whisk mixture until smooth.

4 Chop egg whites into ¼-inch pieces. Fold whites and scallions into yolk mixture and refrigerate for 30 minutes. Season with salt and pepper to taste. Spread egg salad evenly over 6 bread slices. Arrange radishes evenly over egg salad, then top with watercress. Top with remaining 6 bread slices. Serve.

PER SANDWICH
Cal 310; Total Fat 14g, Sat Fat 3.5g; Chol 310mg; Sodium 620mg; Total Carbs 25g, Fiber 4g, Total Sugar 4g, Added Sugar 0g; Protein 18g

EXCELLENT SOURCE OF
Protein, Riboflavin, Niacin, Folate, Vitamin K, Manganese, Phosphorus, Selenium

nutritious DELICIOUS

CHICKPEA SALAD SANDWICHES

2 (15-ounce) cans chickpeas, rinsed

¼ cup mayonnaise

¼ cup organic plain low-fat yogurt

1 tablespoon lemon juice
  Salt and pepper

1 celery rib, minced

⅓ cup dill pickle chips, patted dry and chopped fine

½ small red onion, chopped fine

2 tablespoons minced fresh parsley, dill, or tarragon

12 slices hearty 100 percent whole-grain sandwich bread

2 ounces (2 cups) baby spinach

1 tomato, cored and sliced thin

why this recipe works • *For a healthy change of pace when lunchtime rolls around, we wanted an easy bean-based sandwich that offered all the satisfaction of traditional deli-style options. Chickpeas promised plenty of fiber and served as a meat-free protein source; and the legume's tender but not overly pasty texture would combine well with a creamy dressing. As for the dressing, normally a bit of mayonnaise provides creaminess, but since we were already using chickpeas, why not make a hummus-style puree for our base? We processed a portion of the chickpeas with equal parts mayo and yogurt for just a bit of richness, plus lemon juice for brightness. Then we added the remaining chickpeas to the mixture and briefly pulsed them to give us the right textural contrast. To round things out, we turned to classic flavors: Chopped celery provided crunch, dill pickles brought some brininess, and red onion and herbs finished the salad with vibrant, fresh flavor. Served on whole-grain bread with baby spinach, this salad makes a healthful, luscious sandwich sure to satisfy any lunchtime craving.*

1 Process ¾ cup chickpeas, mayonnaise, yogurt, lemon juice, and ¼ teaspoon salt in food processor until smooth, about 30 seconds, scraping down sides of bowl as needed.

2 Add remaining chickpeas to food processor and pulse until coarsely chopped with some larger pieces remaining, about 4 pulses.

3 Combine chickpea mixture, celery, pickles, onion, and parsley in large bowl and season with salt and pepper to taste. Spread chickpea salad evenly over 6 bread slices, then top with spinach and tomato. Top with remaining 6 bread slices. Serve.

VARIATION
CURRIED CHICKPEA SALAD SANDWICHES
Add 1 tablespoon curry powder to chickpea mixture in food processor in step 1. Substitute ½ cup golden raisins for pickles.

PER SANDWICH
Cal 300; Total Fat 11g, Sat Fat 2g; Chol 5mg; Sodium 700mg; Total Carbs 39g, Fiber 9g, Total Sugar 5g, Added Sugar 0g; Protein 13g

EXCELLENT SOURCE OF
Protein, Fiber, Niacin, Vitamin B6, Folate, Vitamin K, Manganese, Phosphorus, Selenium

lunch

PINTO BEAN–BEET BURGERS

Salt and pepper
⅔ cup medium-grind bulgur, rinsed
1 large beet (9 ounces), trimmed, peeled, and shredded
¾ cup walnuts
½ cup fresh basil leaves
2 garlic cloves, minced
1 (15-ounce) can pinto beans, rinsed
1 (4-ounce) jar carrot baby food
2 tablespoons water
1 tablespoon whole-grain mustard
1½ cups 100 percent whole-wheat panko bread crumbs
6 tablespoons expeller-pressed canola oil (see page 35), plus extra as needed

why this recipe works • *A homemade veggie burger is a welcome alternative to beef—at least in theory. But too many are either mushy or dry and lack flavor. For a modern burger with superior composition, we stepped beyond run-of-the-mill bean patties and combined pinto beans with sweet, earthy beets, rich walnuts, and chewy bulgur. This not only delivered fantastic texture and flavor, but amassed an enviable nutritional profile for a burger: protein and fiber from beans, minerals and vitamins from the bulgur and beets, and omega-3 fatty acids from the walnuts. Carrot baby food (conveniently pureed) provided an unconventional but effective binder that lent the patties a subtle sweetness. Any brand of plain carrot baby food will work here. Use a coarse grater or the shredding disk of a food processor to shred the beet. When shopping, don't confuse bulgur with cracked wheat, which has a much longer cooking time. Serve these burgers with Garlic Aïoli, Lemon-Yogurt Sauce, or Tahini Yogurt Sauce (pages 152–53) as well as favorite burger fixings.*

1 Bring 1½ cups water and ½ teaspoon salt to boil in small saucepan. Off heat, stir in bulgur, cover, and let stand until tender, 15 to 20 minutes. Drain bulgur, spread onto rimmed baking sheet, and let cool slightly.

2 Meanwhile, pulse beet, walnuts, basil, and garlic in food processor until finely chopped, about 12 pulses, scraping down sides of bowl as needed. Add beans, carrot baby food, water, mustard, 1½ teaspoons salt, and ½ teaspoon pepper and pulse until well combined, about 8 pulses. Transfer mixture to large bowl and stir in panko and cooled bulgur.

3 Adjust oven rack to middle position and heat oven to 200 degrees. Divide mixture into 8 equal portions and pack into 3½-inch-wide patties.

4 Heat 3 tablespoons oil in 12-inch nonstick skillet over medium-high heat until shimmering. Gently lay 4 patties in skillet and cook until crisp and well browned on first side, about 4 minutes. Gently flip patties and cook until crisp and well browned on second side, about 4 minutes, adding extra oil if skillet looks dry.

5 Transfer burgers to wire rack set in rimmed baking sheet and place in oven to keep warm. Wipe out skillet with paper towels and repeat with remaining 3 tablespoons oil and remaining patties. Serve.

PER BURGER
Cal 310; Total Fat 18g, Sat Fat 1.5g; Chol 0mg; Sodium 610mg; Total Carbs 32g, Fiber 7g, Total Sugar 4g, Added Sugar 0g; Protein 8g

EXCELLENT SOURCE OF
Fiber, Vitamin K, Manganese

SUPER GREENS SOUP

serves 6

½ cup organic plain low-fat yogurt

2 tablespoons plus ½ teaspoon cold-pressed extra-virgin olive oil (see page 35)

½ teaspoon minced fresh tarragon

¼ teaspoon finely grated lemon zest plus ½ teaspoon juice
Salt and pepper

1 onion, halved through root end and sliced thin

¾ teaspoon light brown sugar

3 ounces white mushrooms, trimmed and sliced thin

2 garlic cloves, minced
Pinch cayenne pepper

3 cups water

3 cups homemade or low-sodium chicken or vegetable broth (see page 36)

⅓ cup Arborio rice

12 ounces Swiss chard, stemmed and chopped coarse

9 ounces kale, stemmed and chopped coarse

¼ cup fresh parsley leaves

2 ounces (2 cups) baby arugula

PER SERVING
Cal 150; Total Fat 6g, Sat Fat 1g; Chol 0mg; Sodium 550mg; Total Carbs 19g, Fiber 3g, Total Sugar 5g, Added Sugar 1g; Protein 6g

EXCELLENT SOURCE OF
Vitamin A, Folate, Vitamin C, Vitamin K, Copper, Manganese

why this recipe works • *When considering uses for sturdy greens like kale and Swiss chard, a smooth pureed soup may not immediately come to mind. But we had high hopes for a silky-smooth soup that delivered a big dose of healthy greens packed with essential nutrients. First, we built a flavorful foundation of sweet caramelized onions and earthy sautéed mushrooms. We added broth, water, and lots of leafy greens (we liked a mix of chard, kale, arugula, and parsley, each with unique nutritional qualities), and simmered the greens until tender before blending them until smooth. We were happy with the soup's depth of flavor, but it was watery and too thin. Many pureed soups call for excessive amounts of cream to create a velvety consistency. Instead, we used Arborio rice: The rice's high starch content thickened our soup perfectly and without dulling the bright flavors of the greens. And rather than adding dairy richness by the cupful, we drizzled each bowl with just a tablespoon or two of yogurt enlivened with lemon and tarragon.*

1 Combine yogurt, ½ teaspoon oil, tarragon, and lemon zest and juice in bowl. Season with salt and pepper to taste, cover, and refrigerate until ready to serve.

2 Heat remaining 2 tablespoons oil in Dutch oven over medium-high heat until shimmering. Stir in onion, sugar, and ½ teaspoon salt and cook, stirring occasionally, until onion releases some moisture, about 5 minutes. Reduce heat to low and cook, stirring often and scraping up any browned bits, until onion is deeply browned and slightly sticky, about 30 minutes. (If onion is sizzling or scorching, reduce heat. If onion is not browning after 15 to 20 minutes, increase heat.)

3 Stir in mushrooms and cook until they have released their moisture, about 5 minutes. Stir in garlic and cayenne and cook until fragrant, about 30 seconds. Stir in water, broth, and rice, scraping up any browned bits, and bring to boil. Reduce heat to low, cover, and simmer for 15 minutes.

4 Stir in chard, kale, and parsley, 1 handful at a time, until wilted and submerged in liquid. Return to simmer, cover, and cook until greens are tender, about 10 minutes.

5 Off heat, stir in arugula until wilted. Working in batches, process soup in blender until smooth, about 1 minute. Return pureed soup to clean pot and season with salt and pepper to taste. Drizzle individual portions with lemon-tarragon yogurt, and serve.

nutritious DELICIOUS

TURKISH TOMATO, BULGUR, AND RED PEPPER SOUP

serves 8

- 2 tablespoons cold-pressed extra-virgin olive oil (see page 35)
- 1 onion, chopped
- 2 red bell peppers, stemmed, seeded, and chopped
  Salt and pepper
- 3 garlic cloves, minced
- 1 teaspoon dried mint, crumbled
- ½ teaspoon smoked paprika
- ⅛ teaspoon red pepper flakes
- 1 tablespoon tomato paste
- ½ cup dry white wine
- 1 (28-ounce) can diced fire-roasted tomatoes
- 4 cups homemade or low-sodium chicken or vegetable broth (see page 36)
- 2 cups water
- ¾ cup medium-grind bulgur, rinsed
- ⅓ cup chopped fresh mint

why this recipe works • *We love a cozy bowl of tomato soup, but too often it lacks complexity and winds up tasting more of cream than tomato. Forgetting the cream, we turned to a simple tomato and red pepper soup inspired by Turkish cuisine, which is enriched not with dairy but with herbs, spices, and grains to yield an irresistible flavor. We started by softening onion and red bell peppers before creating a solid flavor backbone with garlic, tomato paste, white wine, dried mint, smoked paprika, and red pepper flakes. To impart additional smokiness, canned fire-roasted tomatoes did the trick. For a grain, we turned to bulgur. When stirred into soup, this quick-cooking whole grain absorbs the surrounding flavors and gives off starch that creates a silky texture—no cream needed. We stirred in the bulgur toward the end, giving it just enough time to become tender. A sprinkle of fresh mint gave the soup a final punch of flavor. When shopping, don't confuse bulgur with cracked wheat, which has a much longer cooking time and will not work in this recipe.*

1 Heat oil in Dutch oven over medium heat until shimmering. Add onion, bell peppers, ¾ teaspoon salt, and ¼ teaspoon pepper and cook until softened and lightly browned, 6 to 8 minutes. Stir in garlic, dried mint, smoked paprika, and pepper flakes and cook until fragrant, about 30 seconds. Stir in tomato paste and cook for 1 minute.

2 Stir in wine, scraping up any browned bits, and simmer until reduced by half, about 1 minute. Add tomatoes and their juice and cook, stirring occasionally, until tomatoes soften and begin to break apart, about 10 minutes.

3 Stir in broth, water, and bulgur and bring to simmer. Reduce heat to low, cover, and simmer gently until bulgur is tender, about 20 minutes. Season with salt and pepper to taste. Serve, sprinkling individual portions with fresh mint.

PER SERVING
Cal 140; Total Fat 4g, Sat Fat 0.5g; Chol 0mg; Sodium 660mg; Total Carbs 20g, Fiber 4g, Total Sugar 6g, Added Sugar 0g; Protein 3g

EXCELLENT SOURCE OF
Vitamin A, Vitamin C, Manganese

nutritious DELICIOUS

GARLIC-CHICKEN AND WILD RICE SOUP

serves 6

3 tablespoons cold-pressed extra-virgin olive oil (see page 35)

½ cup minced garlic (about 25 cloves)

2 carrots, peeled and sliced ¼ inch thick

1 onion, chopped fine

1 celery rib, minced
Salt and pepper

2 teaspoons minced fresh thyme or ½ teaspoon dried

1 teaspoon tomato paste

6 cups homemade or low-sodium chicken broth (see page 36)

2 bay leaves

⅔ cup wild rice, rinsed

8 ounces organic boneless, skinless chicken breasts, trimmed of all visible fat and cut into ¾-inch pieces

3 ounces (3 cups) baby spinach

¼ cup chopped fresh parsley

why this recipe works • *Both chicken soup and garlic soup have been lauded as powerful home remedies for cold and flu infections and restorative tonics. Our goal was to combine these powerhouse soups by supercharging our hearty Chicken Broth (page 36) with a megadose of garlic, before adding tender morsels of chicken. We tested our way through increasing amounts of garlic, starting with what we thought was a hefty amount—2 tablespoons. Much to our surprise and satisfaction, tasters rallied behind a whopping ½ cup of minced garlic, praising its bright yet balanced presence in our full-flavored soup. Mincing and blooming the garlic before adding liquid gave it a toasty sweetness without the trouble of roasting. To build flavor, we added aromatic vegetables, thyme, bay leaves, and tomato paste along with our chicken broth. In place of noodles or white rice we opted for toothsome wild rice, one of the most nutrient-dense whole grains (technically it is not a rice but a marsh grass), cooking it directly in the soup to infuse it with garlicky flavor. To keep our chicken tender and juicy, we simmered it during the last few minutes of cooking. Finally we added several handfuls of baby spinach and a generous amount of chopped parsley to give our soup a vegetal boost that complemented the deep garlic notes.*

1 Heat oil and garlic in Dutch oven over medium-low heat, stirring occasionally, until garlic is light golden, 3 to 5 minutes. Add carrots, onion, celery, and ¼ teaspoon salt, increase heat to medium, and cook, stirring occasionally, until vegetables are just beginning to brown, 10 to 12 minutes.

2 Stir in thyme and tomato paste and cook until fragrant, about 30 seconds. Stir in broth and bay leaves, scraping up any browned bits, and bring to simmer. Stir in rice, return to simmer, cover, and cook over medium-low heat until rice is tender, 40 to 50 minutes.

3 Discard bay leaves. Stir in chicken and spinach and cook over low heat, stirring occasionally, until chicken is cooked through and spinach is wilted, 3 to 5 minutes. Off heat, stir in parsley and season with salt and pepper to taste. Serve.

PER SERVING
Cal 240; Total Fat 9g, Sat Fat 1g; Chol 30mg; Sodium 430mg; Total Carbs 24g, Fiber 3g, Total Sugar 2g, Added Sugar 0g; Protein 17g

EXCELLENT SOURCE OF
Protein, Vitamin A, Niacin, Vitamin B6, Vitamin C, Vitamin K, Manganese

lunch

MUSHROOM AND WHEAT BERRY SOUP

serves 8

1 cup wheat berries, rinsed

3 tablespoons cold-pressed extra-virgin olive oil (see page 35)

1½ pounds cremini mushrooms, trimmed and sliced thin

Salt and pepper

1 onion, chopped fine

6 garlic cloves, minced

2 teaspoons tomato paste

1 cup dry sherry

8 cups homemade or low-sodium chicken or vegetable broth (see page 36)

1 tablespoon low-sodium soy sauce

1 sprig fresh thyme

1 bay leaf

½ ounce dried shiitake mushrooms, finely ground using spice grinder

4 ounces mustard greens, stemmed and chopped

¼ teaspoon grated lemon zest

PER SERVING
Cal 210; Total Fat 6g, Sat Fat 0.5g; Chol 0mg; Sodium 440; Total Carbs 25g, Fiber 4g, Total Sugar 3g, Added Sugar 0g; Protein 10g

EXCELLENT SOURCE OF
Riboflavin, Vitamin C, Vitamin K, Copper, Manganese

why this recipe works • *A healthy alternative to mushroom soups loaded with cream, this combination of mushrooms and wheat berries is rich and substantial but not heavy, and full of satisfying, savory flavors. Wheat berries are whole, unprocessed kernels of wheat and an excellent source of nutrients. To bring out their nutty flavor, we toasted them in a dry Dutch oven. Next we slowly cooked our cremini mushrooms in a covered pot to concentrate their flavors and extract the juices. To amplify the earthiness of the wheat berries and creminis, we built a flavorful base from ground dried shiitake mushrooms, tomato paste, soy sauce, dry sherry, and plenty of garlic. Grinding the shiitakes ensured their flavor permeated the broth. After simmering our wheat berries, we finished the soup with vitamin-packed mustard greens and some lemon zest for freshness. White mushrooms can be substituted for the cremini. We used a spice grinder to process the dried shiitake mushrooms, but a blender also works.*

1 Toast wheat berries in Dutch oven over medium heat, stirring often, until fragrant and beginning to darken, about 5 minutes; transfer to bowl.

2 Heat 2 tablespoons oil in now-empty pot over medium heat until shimmering. Add cremini mushrooms and ¼ teaspoon salt, cover, and cook until mushrooms have released their liquid, about 3 minutes. Uncover, increase heat to medium-high, and cook until mushrooms begin to brown, 5 to 7 minutes; transfer to plate.

3 Heat remaining 1 tablespoon oil in now-empty pot over medium heat until shimmering. Add onion and cook until softened, about 5 minutes. Stir in garlic and tomato paste and cook until slightly darkened, about 2 minutes.

4 Stir in sherry, scraping up any browned bits, and cook until nearly evaporated, about 2 minutes. Stir in toasted wheat berries, broth, soy sauce, thyme, bay leaf, and ground shiitakes and bring to boil over medium-high heat. Cover, reduce heat to low, and simmer until wheat berries are tender but still chewy, 45 minutes to 1 hour. Discard bay leaf and thyme sprig.

5 Off heat, stir in reserved cremini and any accumulated juices, mustard greens, and lemon zest, cover, and let sit until greens are wilted, about 5 minutes. Season with salt and pepper to taste and serve.

RED LENTIL SOUP WITH NORTH AFRICAN SPICES

serves 6

¼ cup cold-pressed extra-virgin olive oil (see page 35)

1 large onion, chopped fine
  Salt and pepper

¾ teaspoon ground coriander

½ teaspoon ground cumin

¼ teaspoon ground ginger

⅛ teaspoon ground cinnamon
  Pinch cayenne pepper

1 tablespoon tomato paste

1 garlic clove, minced

4 cups homemade or low-sodium chicken or vegetable broth, plus extra as needed (see page 36)

2 cups water

10½ ounces (1½ cups) red lentils, picked over and rinsed

2 tablespoons lemon juice

1½ teaspoons dried mint, crumbled

1 teaspoon paprika

¼ cup chopped fresh cilantro

why this recipe works • *When we're in the mood for soup, it's easy to open up a can. But while canned soups are convenient, they can be one of the worst culprits when it comes to added sodium and other processed ingredients. Some homemade soups are almost as fast, and a lot healthier—and red lentil soup fits the bill. Loaded with fiber, protein, potassium, and iron, red lentils break down rapidly into a creamy, thick puree. Their flavor does require some enhancement, and for that we looked to our spice rack to boost flavor. A North African–style mix of coriander, cumin, ginger, cinnamon, black pepper, and cayenne brought warm complexity in minutes as we bloomed them in our pot after sautéing an onion. Tomato paste and garlic completed the base before the addition of the lentils, and a mix of broth and water gave the soup a full, rounded character. After only 15 minutes of cooking, the lentils were soft enough to be pureed with a whisk. A generous dose of lemon juice brought the flavors into focus, and a drizzle of spice-infused oil and a sprinkle of fresh cilantro completed the transformation of commonplace ingredients into an exotic yet comforting, quick soup.*

1 Heat 2 tablespoons oil in large saucepan over medium heat until shimmering. Add onion and ½ teaspoon salt and cook, stirring occasionally, until softened, about 5 minutes. Stir in coriander, cumin, ginger, cinnamon, cayenne, and ¼ teaspoon pepper and cook until fragrant, about 2 minutes. Stir in tomato paste and garlic and cook for 1 minute.

2 Stir in broth, water, and lentils and bring to vigorous simmer. Cook, stirring occasionally, until lentils are soft and about half are broken down, about 15 minutes.

3 Whisk soup vigorously until broken down to coarse puree, about 30 seconds. Adjust consistency with extra hot broth as needed. Stir in lemon juice and season with salt to taste. Cover and keep warm.

4 Heat remaining 2 tablespoons oil in small skillet over medium heat until shimmering. Off heat, stir in mint and paprika. Serve soup, drizzling individual portions with 1 teaspoon spiced oil and sprinkling with cilantro.

PER SERVING
Cal 310; Total Fat 11g, Sat Fat 1.5g; Chol 0mg; Sodium 410mg; Total Carbs 40g, Fiber 7g, Total Sugar 4g, Added Sugar 0g; Protein 16g

EXCELLENT SOURCE OF
Protein, Fiber, Folate, Copper, Iron, Manganese

lunch

HEARTY 15-BEAN AND VEGETABLE SOUP

serves 10

Salt and pepper

1 pound 15-bean soup mix, flavoring pack discarded, beans picked over and rinsed

2 tablespoons cold-pressed extra-virgin olive oil (see page 35)

1 small onion, chopped

1 carrot, peeled and chopped fine

1 pound Swiss chard, stems chopped, leaves sliced into ½-inch-wide strips

½ ounce dried porcini mushrooms, rinsed and minced

12 ounces white mushrooms, trimmed and quartered

6 garlic cloves, minced

2 teaspoons minced fresh thyme or ½ teaspoon dried

8 cups homemade or low-sodium chicken or vegetable broth (see page 36)

2 bay leaves

1 large tomato, cored and chopped

PER SERVING
Cal 220; Total Fat 4g, Sat Fat 0g; Chol 0mg; Sodium 380mg; Total Carbs 35g, Fiber 8g, Total Sugar 5g, Added Sugar 0g; Protein 12g

EXCELLENT SOURCE OF
Protein, Fiber, Vitamin A, Vitamin C, Vitamin K, Iron, Manganese, Potassium

why this recipe works • *We wanted the ultimate bean soup, showcasing an array of textures, colors, and nutrients and supercharged with hearty vegetables. A 15-bean soup mix proved a convenient starting point, but we discarded the seasoning packet, knowing we could add flavor in a healthier manner. Bean soup mixes can disappoint because different beans cook at different rates, leaving some blown-out and disintegrating while others remain hard. To prevent blowouts, we brined the beans to soften their skins. Then we brought the soup to a simmer before transferring it to the oven to cook gently in the low, constant heat. To build flavor, we sautéed plenty of aromatics and added thyme, bay leaves, and savory dried porcini. Swiss chard, white mushrooms, and fresh tomato balanced the beans with hearty vegetable flavor. You can find 15-bean soup mix alongside the other bagged dried beans in the supermarket; 15-bean mix is the most common, but any 1-pound bag of multiple varieties of beans will work in this recipe. The different varieties of beans cook at different rates, so be sure to taste several beans to ensure they are all tender before serving.*

1 Dissolve 3 tablespoons salt in 4 quarts cold water in large container. Add beans and soak at room temperature for at least 8 hours or up to 24 hours. Drain and rinse well.

2 Adjust oven rack to lower-middle position and heat oven to 250 degrees. Heat oil in Dutch oven over medium heat until shimmering. Add onion, carrot, chard stems, and porcini mushrooms and cook until vegetables are softened, 7 to 10 minutes.

3 Stir in white mushrooms, cover, and cook until mushrooms have released their liquid, about 5 minutes. Uncover and continue to cook until mushrooms are browned, 5 to 10 minutes.

4 Stir in garlic and thyme and cook until fragrant, about 30 seconds. Stir in soaked beans, broth, and bay leaves and bring to a boil. Cover pot, transfer to oven, and cook until beans are almost tender, 1 to 1¼ hours.

5 Stir in chard leaves and tomato and continue to cook in oven, covered, until beans and vegetables are fully tender, 30 to 40 minutes longer. Discard bay leaves and season with salt and pepper to taste. Serve.

lunch

SHIITAKE, TOFU, AND MUSTARD GREENS SOUP

serves 6

1 tablespoon expeller-pressed canola oil (see page 35)
1 onion, chopped
  Salt
1 (4-inch) piece ginger, peeled and sliced thin
5 garlic cloves, smashed
4 cups homemade or low-sodium chicken or vegetable broth (see page 36)
4 cups water
8 ounces shiitake mushrooms, stemmed and sliced thin (stems reserved)
½ ounce dried shiitake mushrooms, rinsed
2 tablespoons low-sodium soy sauce
14 ounces firm tofu, cut into ½-inch pieces
8 ounces mustard greens, stemmed and cut into 2-inch pieces
2 tablespoons rice vinegar
3 scallions, sliced thin
  Chili oil (optional)

why this recipe works • *We wanted a clean-tasting but deeply satisfying soup full of umami, but without skyrocketing sodium levels. We started by infusing chicken broth with generous amounts of ginger and garlic as well as dried shiitake mushrooms to build an aromatic backbone. Then we added just enough low-sodium soy sauce to contribute savory character. Since we would be adding fresh shiitake mushroom caps later, we tossed in the tough stems to bring even more depth and mushroom flavor. After straining, our broth was aromatic, but needed punch and a little sweetness, which we got from a splash of rice vinegar. We then considered what to stir in. We wanted a vegetable-focused soup, but with bold flavor. So we added sliced shiitake mushroom caps, which reinforced the mushroomy broth, and a hefty amount of mustard greens, which gave a wonderful wasabi-like back note that really perked up our soup. In lieu of noodles, we added tofu cubes to ensure our soup was satiating. A sprinkle of sliced scallions lent a fresh, clean bite. Some tasters enjoyed a drizzle of chili oil to ramp up the spicy flavor, but it is completely optional.*

1 Heat oil in large saucepan over medium-high heat until shimmering. Stir in onion and ½ teaspoon salt and cook until softened and lightly browned, 5 to 7 minutes. Stir in ginger and garlic and cook until lightly browned, about 2 minutes.

2 Stir in broth, water, reserved mushroom stems, dried mushrooms, and soy sauce and bring to boil. Reduce heat to low, cover, and simmer until flavors meld, about 1 hour.

3 Strain broth through fine-mesh strainer set over large bowl, pressing on solids to extract as much broth as possible; discard solids. Wipe saucepan clean with paper towels and return strained broth to saucepan.

4 Stir in sliced mushrooms, tofu, mustard greens, and vinegar and cook until mushrooms and tofu are warmed through and greens are wilted, about 3 minutes. Sprinkle individual portions with scallions and drizzle with chili oil, if using. Serve.

PER SERVING
Cal 140; Total Fat 6g, Sat Fat 0.5g; Chol 0mg; Sodium 580mg; Total Carbs 12g, Fiber 3g, Total Sugar 3g, Added Sugar 0g; Protein 11g

EXCELLENT SOURCE OF
Protein, Vitamin A, Vitamin C, Vitamin K, Copper, Manganese

ITALIAN WEDDING SOUP WITH KALE AND FARRO

- 1 tablespoon cold-pressed extra-virgin olive oil (see page 35)
- 1 fennel bulb, fronds minced to make ¼ cup, stalks discarded, and bulb halved, cored, and sliced thin
- 1 onion, sliced thin
- 5 garlic cloves, 4 peeled and smashed, 1 minced to a paste
- ¼ ounce dried porcini mushrooms, rinsed and minced
- ½ cup dry white wine
- 1 tablespoon Worcestershire sauce
- 4 cups homemade or low-sodium chicken broth (see page 36)
- 4 cups water
- 1 slice hearty 100 percent whole-grain sandwich bread, torn into 1-inch pieces
- 5 tablespoons organic 1 percent low-fat milk
- 12 ounces organic ground turkey
- ¼ cup grated Parmesan cheese
- ¼ cup minced fresh parsley
  Salt and pepper
- 1 cup whole farro, rinsed
- 8 ounces kale, stemmed and cut into ½-inch pieces

PER SERVING
Cal 310; Total Fat 6g, Sat Fat 2g; Chol 25mg; Sodium 780mg; Total Carbs 37g, Fiber 6g, Total Sugar 6g, Added Sugar 0g; Protein 27g

EXCELLENT SOURCE OF
Protein, Fiber, Vitamin A, Vitamin C, Vitamin K, Copper, Manganese

why this recipe works • *Traditional Italian wedding soup is so named because of the harmonious marriage of meatballs, greens, and pasta in a savory, fortified broth. We loved the idea of a hearty, meal-in-a-bowl soup but wanted to fine-tune the components, eliminating greasy meat and white pasta. For a fast path to a complex broth, we simmered chicken broth with aromatic fennel, onion, garlic, and dried porcini mushrooms, adding white wine for sharpness and Worcestershire sauce for meaty depth. In place of traditional beef and pork, we prepared turkey meatballs, boosting their flavor with chopped parsley, Parmesan, and minced fronds from our fennel bulb. After gently poaching them in the broth, we were pleasantly surprised to find that they turned out delicate and tender. Chopped kale lent its assertive texture. Finally, we replaced ditalini pasta with hearty farro; the nutty whole grain rounded out the soup perfectly. A rasp-style grater makes quick work of turning the garlic into a paste. Be sure to use 93 percent lean ground turkey, not 99 percent fat-free ground turkey breast, or the meatballs will be tough.*

1 Heat oil in Dutch oven over medium-high heat until just shimmering. Stir in sliced fennel, onion, smashed garlic, and porcini and cook, stirring frequently, until just softened and lightly browned, 5 to 7 minutes. Stir in wine and Worcestershire and cook for 1 minute. Stir in broth and water and bring to simmer. Reduce heat to low, cover, and simmer for 30 minutes.

2 Meanwhile, combine bread and milk in large bowl and, using fork, mash mixture to uniform paste. Add turkey, Parmesan, parsley, ¼ cup minced fennel fronds, minced garlic, ½ teaspoon salt, and ⅛ teaspoon pepper to bowl with bread mixture and knead gently with hands until evenly combined. Using wet hands, roll heaping 1 teaspoons of meat mixture into meatballs and transfer to rimmed baking sheet. (You should have 35 to 40 meatballs.) Cover with greased plastic wrap and refrigerate for 30 minutes.

3 Strain broth through fine-mesh strainer set over large bowl, pressing on solids to extract as much broth as possible; discard solids. Wipe pot clean with paper towels and return strained broth to pot.

4 Bring broth to boil over medium-high heat. Add farro and ½ teaspoon salt, reduce heat to medium-low, cover, and simmer until farro is just tender, about 15 minutes. Uncover, stir in meatballs and kale and cook, stirring occasionally, until meatballs are cooked through and farro is tender, 5 to 7 minutes. Season with salt and pepper to taste, and serve.

lunch

KALE CAESAR SALAD

serves 4

12 ounces curly kale, stemmed
   and cut into 1-inch pieces
   (16 cups)

3 ounces rustic 100 percent
   whole-grain bread, cut into
   ½-inch cubes (1½ cups)

2 tablespoons cold-pressed
   extra-virgin olive oil
   (see page 35)
   Salt and pepper

3 tablespoons mayonnaise

3 tablespoons organic plain
   low-fat yogurt

1 ounce Parmesan cheese,
   grated (½ cup)

1 tablespoon lemon juice

2 teaspoons white wine vinegar

2 teaspoons Worcestershire
   sauce

2 teaspoons Dijon mustard

3 anchovy fillets, rinsed and
   minced

1 garlic clove, minced

why this recipe works • *Kale is closing in on romaine as the Caesar salad green of choice; the hearty, nutrient-dense leaves, with their pungent earthiness, pair surprisingly well with the tangy Caesar dressing—perhaps even better than romaine. While raw kale may sound healthiest, we learned that soaking the kale slightly helps to break down the fibrous cell walls, making nutrients such as vitamins A and C and iron more available for absorption. A 10-minute soak in warm water did the trick and also tenderized the kale. How else could we improve on the salad? We traded white-bread croutons for whole-grain; their rustic chew tasted right at home in our bowl. At first, an egg-based dressing sounded like the way to go, but we found a thicker mayonnaise-based dressing stood up better to the greens. What to do? We cut half of the mayonnaise with yogurt, then decreased the oil to just 2 tablespoons. We added three anchovy fillets, which brought savoriness and healthy omega-3 fats. Decreasing the Parmesan lowered saturated fat without sacrificing the cheese's nutty flavor. With our dressing reworked, the salad was ready to toss; we did, and gave it a 20-minute rest to blend flavors before serving.*

1 Adjust oven rack to middle position and heat oven to 350 degrees. Place kale in large bowl and cover with warm tap water (110 to 115 degrees). Swish kale around to remove grit. Let kale sit in warm water bath for 10 minutes. Remove kale from water and spin dry in salad spinner in multiple batches. Pat leaves dry with paper towels if still wet.

2 Toss bread, 1 tablespoon oil, ⅛ teaspoon salt, and ⅛ teaspoon pepper together in bowl. Spread on rimmed baking sheet and bake until golden and crisp, about 15 minutes. Let croutons cool completely on sheet. (Cooled croutons can be stored at room temperature for up to 24 hours.)

3 In large bowl, whisk mayonnaise, yogurt, ¼ cup Parmesan, lemon juice, vinegar, Worcestershire sauce, mustard, anchovies, garlic, ½ teaspoon salt, and ½ teaspoon pepper together until well combined. Whisking constantly, drizzle in remaining 1 tablespoon oil until combined.

4 Toss kale with dressing and refrigerate for at least 20 minutes or up to 6 hours. Toss dressed kale with croutons and remaining ¼ cup Parmesan. Serve.

PER SERVING
Cal 280; Total Fat 19g, Sat Fat 3.5g;
Chol 10mg; Sodium 880mg; Total
Carbs 19g, Fiber 5g, Total Sugar 5g,
Added Sugar 0g; Protein 11g

EXCELLENT SOURCE OF
Protein, Fiber, Vitamin A, Folate,
Vitamin C, Vitamin K, Calcium,
Copper, Manganese

MEDITERRANEAN CHOPPED SALAD

serves 6

- 1 cucumber, halved lengthwise, seeded, and cut into ½-inch pieces
- 10 ounces grape tomatoes, quartered
  Salt and pepper
- 3 tablespoons red wine vinegar
- 1 garlic clove, minced
- 3 tablespoons cold-pressed extra-virgin olive oil (see page 35)
- 1 (15-ounce) can chickpeas, rinsed
- ½ cup pitted kalamata olives, chopped
- ½ small red onion, chopped fine
- ½ cup chopped fresh parsley
- 1 head escarole (1 pound), trimmed and cut into ½-inch pieces
- 2 ounces feta cheese, crumbled (½ cup)
- ½ cup walnuts, toasted and chopped

why this recipe works • *The appeal of a chopped salad is that all the ingredients are cut to a uniform size and tossed together, permitting a taste of everything in each bite. Virtually any ingredients may be used, yet most chopped salads are uninspired, laden with deli meats and cheeses and drowned in dressing. With a world of options at our disposal, we steered our salad in a Mediterranean direction, starting with escarole. A member of the chicory family, this under-utilized leafy green is loaded with vitamins and has a mild bitterness that pairs well with bold flavors. Next we added chopped cucumbers and grape tomatoes, salting them to remove excess moisture, and red onion. To make our salad hearty, instead of deli meat we incorporated nutty chickpeas. Kalamata olives added richness, and walnuts brought crunch and healthy fats. We tossed everything with a simple red wine vinaigrette to let the salad's flavors shine through. Finally, not wanting to completely eliminate cheese from our salad, we sprinkled on ½ cup of briny feta to round out the flavors. Cherry tomatoes can be substituted for the grape tomatoes.*

1 Toss cucumber and tomatoes with 1 teaspoon salt and let drain in colander for 15 minutes.

2 Whisk vinegar and garlic together in large bowl. Whisking constantly, drizzle in oil. Add drained cucumber-tomato mixture, chickpeas, olives, onion, and parsley and toss to coat. Let sit for at least 5 minutes or up to 20 minutes.

3 Add escarole, feta, and walnuts and toss gently to combine. Season with salt and pepper to taste. Serve.

PER SERVING
Cal 220; Total Fat 16g, Sat Fat 3g; Chol 10mg; Sodium 650mg; Total Carbs 18g, Fiber 6g, Total Sugar 3g, Added Sugar 0g; Protein 7g

EXCELLENT SOURCE OF
Fiber, Vitamin A, Folate, Vitamin C, Vitamin K, Manganese

SUPER COBB SALAD

serves 6

- **8** ounces organic boneless, skinless chicken breasts, trimmed of all visible fat and cut into ½-inch pieces
  Salt and pepper
- **2** teaspoons expeller-pressed canola oil (see page 35)
- **10** ounces shiitake mushrooms, stemmed and sliced thin
- **⅛** teaspoon smoked paprika
- **⅛** teaspoon chili powder
- **8** ounces kale, stemmed and cut into 1-inch pieces (8 cups)
- **⅓** cup finely chopped red onion
- **1** tablespoon lemon juice
- **¾** cup organic plain low-fat yogurt
- **3** tablespoons crumbled blue cheese
- **1** garlic clove, minced
- **½** small head radicchio (3 ounces), cored and cut into ½-inch pieces
- **3** hard-cooked large organic eggs, quartered
- **1** avocado, halved, pitted, and cut into ½-inch pieces
- **6** ounces cherry tomatoes, halved

PER SERVING
Cal 230; Total Fat 12g, Sat Fat 3g; Chol 125mg; Sodium 340mg; Total Carbs 13g, Fiber 4g, Total Sugar 6g, Added Sugar 0g; Protein 18g

EXCELLENT SOURCE OF
Protein, Vitamin A, Riboflavin, Niacin, Pantothenic Acid, Vitamin B6, Folate, Vitamin C, Vitamin K, Copper, Manganese, Phosphorus, Potassium, Selenium

why this recipe works • *Stunning presentation aside, Cobb salad has all the markers of a powerhouse meal, including eggs, avocados, tomato, and lean chicken—we just had to do something about all that bacon and cheese. We were sad to sacrifice bacon's smoky flavor until we tried sautéing shiitake mushrooms with smoked paprika and chili powder. Now we had smokiness and even some umami meatiness without the saturated fat and preservatives. Using kale in place of romaine upped the nutritional ante, and radicchio contributed beautiful color. For the dressing, just a bit of blue cheese whisked with yogurt, garlic, and lemon juice provided the tangy blue cheese flavor we expected. We tossed some with our greens and drizzled the rest over our still-classic, yet mindfully updated, Cobb salad.*

1 Pat chicken dry with paper towels and season with salt and pepper. Heat 1 teaspoon oil in 12-inch nonstick skillet over medium-high heat until shimmering. Add chicken and cook, stirring occasionally, until cooked through, 4 to 6 minutes. Transfer to plate and let cool.

2 Heat remaining 1 teaspoon oil in now-empty skillet over medium heat until shimmering. Add mushrooms and ¼ teaspoon salt, cover, and cook until mushrooms have released their liquid, 4 to 6 minutes. Uncover and increase heat to medium-high. Stir in paprika, chili powder, and ⅛ teaspoon pepper and cook until mushrooms are golden, 4 to 6 minutes. Transfer to second plate and let cool.

3 Place kale in large bowl and cover with warm tap water (110 to 115 degrees). Swish kale around to remove grit. Let kale sit in warm water bath for 10 minutes. Remove kale from water and spin dry in salad spinner in multiple batches. Pat leaves dry with paper towels if still wet. Toss onion with 2 teaspoons lemon juice and set aside.

4 Whisk yogurt, blue cheese, garlic, remaining 1 teaspoon lemon juice, and ¼ teaspoon salt together in bowl until well combined. Season with salt and pepper to taste.

5 Toss kale and radicchio with ½ cup dressing to coat. Transfer to serving platter and mound in even layer. Arrange cooled mushrooms, onion, eggs, avocado, and tomatoes in single, even rows over greens, leaving space at either end. Arrange half of chicken in each open space at ends of platter. Drizzle remaining dressing over salad. Serve.

ASPARAGUS, ARUGULA, AND CANNELLINI BEAN SALAD WITH WALNUTS

serves 6

5 tablespoons cold-pressed extra-virgin olive oil (see page 35)

½ red onion, sliced ⅛ inch thick

1 pound asparagus, trimmed and cut on bias into 1-inch lengths
   Salt and pepper

1 (15-ounce) can cannellini beans, rinsed

2 tablespoons plus 2 teaspoons balsamic vinegar

1 garlic clove, minced

6 ounces (6 cups) baby arugula

½ cup walnuts, toasted and chopped coarse

why this recipe works • *To elevate a basic mixed greens salad to complete-meal status and supercharge it with nutrients, we started with a vibrant base of green asparagus and arugula. Sautéing the asparagus briefly delivered the deep flavor and crisp-tender texture we were after without leaching away or degrading valuable nutrients. We added protein- and fiber-packed cannellini beans for their creamy yet firm texture, and a generous sprinkling of toasted walnuts rounded out the dish with nutty flavor and crunch. A zesty balsamic dressing gave our salad a decidedly Italian character. Rinsing the canned cannellini beans eliminates any slimy texture. Look for asparagus spears no thicker than ½ inch.*

1 Heat 2 tablespoons oil in 12-inch nonstick skillet over high heat until just smoking; stir in onion and cook until beginning to brown, about 1 minute. Stir in asparagus, ¼ teaspoon salt, and ⅛ teaspoon pepper and cook, stirring occasionally, until asparagus is browned and crisp-tender, about 3 minutes. Off heat, stir in beans; transfer to large plate and let cool for 5 minutes.

2 Whisk vinegar, garlic, ¼ teaspoon salt, and ⅛ teaspoon pepper together in small bowl until combined. Whisking constantly, slowly drizzle in remaining 3 tablespoons oil. In large bowl, toss arugula and walnuts with 2 tablespoons dressing until coated. Season with salt and pepper to taste and divide among serving plates. Toss asparagus mixture with remaining dressing, and arrange over arugula. Serve.

PER SERVING
Cal 230; Total Fat 17g, Sat Fat 2g; Chol 0mg; Sodium 135mg; Total Carbs 15g, Fiber 5g, Total Sugar 4g, Added Sugar 0g; Protein 7g

EXCELLENT SOURCE OF
Fiber, Vitamin A, Vitamin K, Manganese

PESTO FARRO SALAD WITH CHERRY TOMATOES AND ARTICHOKES

serves 6

1½ cups whole farro, rinsed
    Salt and pepper
1½ ounces (1½ cups) baby
    spinach
 2 cups fresh basil leaves
 ½ cup raw sunflower seeds,
    toasted
 1 ounce Parmesan cheese,
    grated (½ cup)
 2 garlic cloves, minced
 ½ cup cold-pressed extra-virgin
    olive oil (see page 35)
 ⅓ cup organic plain low-fat
    yogurt
12 ounces cherry tomatoes, halved
 2 cups jarred whole baby
    artichoke hearts packed in
    water, rinsed, patted dry,
    and quartered

why this recipe works • *The first thing we noticed when replacing pasta with whole-grain farro in this nourishing update on pasta salad with pesto was the grain's fantastic al dente texture. Tender with just the right amount of chew (thanks to boiling pasta-style), each grain stayed distinct, the better to become coated in luscious sauce. For a supercharged, not-too-oily pesto, we combined basil with spinach, which added nutrients and helped retain the sauce's vibrant color. We used sunflower seeds, a rich source of vitamin E and copper that may also have anti-inflammatory benefits, and about two-thirds of the typical amount of oil, combining it with ⅓ cup of yogurt, which further lightened the pesto's color and flavor and gave it a creamy but not greasy texture. Halved cherry tomatoes paired well with the basil and brightened the salad. Jarred artichoke hearts, packed with fiber and vitamins, were an easy addition. We prefer the flavor and texture of whole farro; pearled farro can be used, but the texture may be softer. Do not use quick-cooking or presteamed farro. The cooking time for farro can vary greatly among brands, so we recommend beginning to check for doneness after 10 minutes.*

1 Bring 4 quarts water to boil in Dutch oven. Add farro and 1 tablespoon salt, return to boil, and cook until grains are tender with slight chew, 15 to 30 minutes. Drain farro, spread onto rimmed baking sheet, and let cool for 20 minutes.

2 Meanwhile, pulse baby spinach, basil, sunflower seeds, Parmesan cheese, garlic, ½ teaspoon salt, and ¼ teaspoon pepper in food processor until finely ground, 20 to 30 pulses, scraping down sides of bowl as needed. With processor running, slowly add oil until incorporated. Add yogurt and pulse to incorporate, about 5 pulses; transfer pesto to large bowl.

3 Toss cooled farro with pesto until combined. Gently stir in tomatoes and artichoke hearts and season with salt and pepper to taste. Stir in warm water as needed, 1 tablespoon at a time, to adjust consistency. Serve.

PER SERVING
Cal 460; Total Fat 27g, Sat Fat 4g; Chol 5mg; Sodium 460mg; Total Carbs 46g, Fiber 7g, Total Sugar 5g, Added Sugar 0g; Protein 13g

EXCELLENT SOURCE OF
Protein, Fiber, Vitamin A, Vitamin C, Vitamin K

lunch

THREE-BEAN SALAD WITH ARUGULA

serves 6

- 3 tablespoons cider vinegar
- 2 teaspoons honey
- 1 garlic clove, minced
  Salt and pepper
- 2 tablespoons cold-pressed extra-virgin olive oil (see page 35)
- ½ small red onion, sliced thin
- 8 ounces green beans, trimmed and cut into 1-inch lengths
- 1 (15-ounce) can chickpeas, rinsed
- 1 (15-ounce) can red kidney beans, rinsed
- ¼ cup minced fresh parsley
- 3 ounces (3 cups) baby arugula

why this recipe works • *For a fresher take on three-bean salad that would feel at home on any picnic spread, we kept things simple but ditched the mushy canned string beans and sugary vinaigrette. Instead, we steamed fresh green beans to crisp-tender perfection. We tested various combinations of beans and settled on chickpeas and kidney beans to round out the trio for an appealing mix of color, texture, and flavor. Most recipes rely on a syrupy dressing made from sugar and vinegar; we opted for a bright vinaigrette, with just a hint of honey sweetness to recall the classic formula. To keep the sharpness of the red onion in check, we marinated it briefly in the vinaigrette. One last change: Just before serving, we folded in a generous bundle of baby arugula, transforming this picnic-table standby into a complete and satisfying lunch. Be sure to set up the ice water bath before cooking the green beans, as plunging them in the cold water immediately after steaming retains their bright green color and ensures that they don't overcook.*

1 Whisk vinegar, honey, garlic, ½ teaspoon salt, and ⅛ teaspoon pepper together in large bowl until well combined. Whisking constantly, slowly drizzle in oil. Stir in onion and set aside. Fill separate large bowl halfway with ice and water.

2 Bring ½ inch water to rolling boil in medium saucepan over high heat. Place green beans in steamer basket then transfer basket to saucepan. Cover, reduce heat to medium-low, and cook beans until crisp-tender, about 4 minutes. Transfer beans to bowl of ice water and let sit until chilled, about 5 minutes. Drain well and pat dry with paper towels.

3 Add green beans, chickpeas, kidney beans, and parsley to vinaigrette mixture and toss well to coat. Gently fold in arugula, and season with salt and pepper to taste. Serve.

lunch

PER SERVING
Cal 150; Total Fat 5g, Sat Fat 0.5g; Chol 0mg; Sodium 430mg; Total Carbs 20g, Fiber 5g, Total Sugar 5g, Added Sugar 2g; Protein 6g

EXCELLENT SOURCE OF
Fiber, Vitamin K

QUINOA TACO SALAD

- ¾ cup prewashed white quinoa
- 3 tablespoons cold-pressed extra-virgin olive oil (see page 35)
- 1 small onion, chopped fine
  Salt and pepper
- 2 teaspoons minced canned chipotle chile in adobo sauce
- 2 teaspoons tomato paste
- 1 teaspoon anchovy paste (optional)
- ½ teaspoon ground cumin
- 1 cup homemade or low-sodium chicken or vegetable broth (see page 36)
- 2 tablespoons lime juice
- 1 head escarole (1 pound), trimmed and sliced thin
- 2 scallions, sliced thin
- ½ cup chopped fresh cilantro
- 1 (15-ounce) can black beans, rinsed
- 8 ounces cherry or grape tomatoes, quartered
- 1 ripe avocado, halved, pitted, and chopped
- 2 ounces queso fresco, crumbled (½ cup)

PER SERVING
Cal 420; Total Fat 22g, Sat Fat 3.5g; Chol 5mg; Sodium 740mg; Total Carbs 45g, Fiber 13g, Total Sugar 5g, Added Sugar 0g; Protein 14g

EXCELLENT SOURCE OF
Protein, Fiber, Vitamin A, Pantothenic Acid, Vitamin B6, Folate, Vitamin C, Vitamin E, Vitamin K, Copper, Iron, Magnesium, Manganese, Phosphorus, Potassium

why this recipe works • *Taco salad hits a home run with any crowd. What's not to love about seasoned beef and the works on a bed of lettuce? Well, while it may be fun, we wouldn't call a salad based on greasy meat and shredded cheese healthy, even without the fried tortilla bowl. To rework taco salad to be more nutritious but still hearty, we replaced the beef with quinoa. Some tasters had doubts, but this low-saturated-fat, high-fiber source of protein—with its chewy texture and ability to absorb flavors—made a good stand-in for ground beef. Toasted and simmered in chicken broth with chipotles in adobo, tomato paste, anchovy paste, and cumin, it acquired a rich, spiced meaty flavor. We substituted escarole for lettuce, cut back on cheese, opting for queso fresco, and added an extra-hefty amount of cilantro. Black beans, avocado, cherry tomatoes, and scallions completed the picture. Tasters found the salad so hearty it didn't need tortilla chips, but if you prefer, serve with your favorite multigrain chip. We like the convenience of prewashed quinoa; rinsing removes the quinoa's bitter protective coating (called saponin). If you buy unwashed quinoa (or if you are unsure whether it's been washed), rinse it and then spread it out on a clean dish towel to dry for 15 minutes before cooking.*

1 Toast quinoa in medium saucepan over medium-high heat, stirring frequently, until quinoa is very fragrant and makes continuous popping sound, 5 to 7 minutes; transfer to bowl.

2 Heat 1 tablespoon oil in now-empty saucepan over medium heat until shimmering. Add onion and ¼ teaspoon salt and cook until onion is softened and lightly browned, 5 to 7 minutes.

3 Stir in chipotle, tomato paste, anchovy paste, and cumin and cook until fragrant, about 30 seconds. Stir in broth and toasted quinoa, increase heat to medium-high, and bring to simmer. Cover, reduce heat to low, and simmer until quinoa is tender and liquid has been absorbed, 18 to 22 minutes, stirring once halfway through cooking. Remove pan from heat and let sit, covered, for 10 minutes. Spread quinoa onto rimmed baking sheet and let cool for 20 minutes.

4 Whisk remaining 2 tablespoons oil, lime juice, ¼ teaspoon salt, and ¼ teaspoon pepper together in large bowl. Add escarole, scallions, and ¼ cup cilantro and toss to combine. Gently fold in beans, tomatoes, and avocado. Transfer to serving platter and top with quinoa, queso fresco, and remaining ¼ cup cilantro. Serve.

RAW BEET AND CARROT NOODLE SALAD WITH ALMOND-SESAME DRESSING

DRESSING
- ¼ cup almond or peanut butter
- 3 tablespoons tahini
- 3 tablespoons lime juice (2 limes), plus lime wedges for serving
- 1 tablespoon low-sodium soy sauce
- 1 tablespoon honey
- 1 tablespoon grated fresh ginger
- 2 garlic cloves, minced
- ½ teaspoon expeller-pressed toasted sesame oil (see page 35)
- ½ cup hot water

NOODLES
- 1 pound beets, trimmed and peeled
- 1 pound carrots, trimmed and peeled
- 5 scallions, sliced thin on bias
- ¼ cup fresh cilantro leaves
- 1 tablespoon sesame seeds, toasted

why this recipe works • *We're always seeking creative ways to add more vegetables to our diet, and spiralizing offers an easy way to fill our plate. We thought spiralized vegetables would prove an ideal canvas for creamy sesame dressing in place of wheat noodles, so we tested various vegetables. Zucchini noodles offered smooth texture, but for a nutritionally supercharged version, a mix of beets and carrots was the clear winner; and it looked stunning. (Those bright colors come from pigments—betalains in beets and carotenoids in carrots—associated with antioxidant and anti-inflammatory properties.) Cutting the raw vegetable into noodles gave them an appealing crisp-tender texture, a perfect foil for the dressing, which we made by whisking together almond butter, tahini, lime juice, soy sauce, honey, hefty doses of ginger and garlic, and toasted sesame oil. We tossed our veggie noodles with the dressing, scallions, and cilantro, and sprinkled them with toasted sesame seeds. Tasters loved the contrast of bright and aromatic ginger and herbs with the nutty dressing and crunchy yet tender vegetables. For the best noodles, use beets that are at least 1½ inches in diameter and carrots that are at least ¾ inch across at the thinnest end and 1½ inches across at the thickest end. We prefer to spiralize our own vegetables, but you can substitute store-bought spiralized raw beets and carrots, though they tend to be drier and less flavorful. For more on spiralizers, see page 36. You can use smooth or chunky almond or peanut butter in this recipe.*

1 FOR THE DRESSING Whisk all ingredients, except water, together in large bowl until well combined. Whisking constantly, add hot water, 1 tablespoon at a time, until dressing has consistency of heavy cream (you may not need all of water).

2 FOR THE NOODLES Using spiralizer, cut beets and carrots into ⅛-inch-thick noodles; then cut beet and carrot noodles into 6-inch lengths.

3 Add beet and carrot noodles and scallions to dressing and toss well to combine. Sprinkle with cilantro and sesame seeds. Serve with lime wedges.

PER SERVING
Cal 200; Total Fat 11g, Sat Fat 1.5g; Chol 0mg; Sodium 240mg; Total Carbs 24g, Fiber 6g, Total Sugar 13g, Added Sugar 3g; Protein 6g

EXCELLENT SOURCE OF
Fiber, Vitamin A, Folate, Vitamin C, Vitamin K, Manganese

CHINESE CHICKEN SALAD

serves 6

3 oranges

⅓ cup rice vinegar

3 tablespoons low-sodium soy sauce

3 tablespoons grated fresh ginger

1 tablespoon Asian chili-garlic sauce

1 tablespoon honey

3 tablespoons expeller-pressed canola oil (see page 35)

2 teaspoons expeller-pressed toasted sesame oil (see page 35)

1 pound organic boneless, skinless chicken breasts, trimmed of all visible fat

1 small head napa cabbage, cored and sliced thin

2 red bell peppers, stemmed, seeded, and cut into 2-inch-long matchsticks

1 cup fresh cilantro leaves

6 scallions, sliced thin

½ cup unsalted, dry-roasted peanuts, chopped

PER SERVING

Cal 330; Total Fat 17g, Sat Fat 2g; Chol 55mg; Sodium 400mg; Total Carbs 21g, Fiber 5g, Total Sugar 13g, Added Sugar 3g; Protein 23g

EXCELLENT SOURCE OF

Protein, Fiber, Vitamin A, Niacin, Vitamin B6, Vitamin C, Vitamin K, Phosphorus, Selenium

why this recipe works • *With its juicy oranges, tender chicken, and a crunchy topping, Chinese chicken salad offers an enticing variety of tastes and textures. But many versions seem to have lost their way, weighted down with gloppy sauces, lackluster chicken, sugary canned orange segments, and watery greens. We saw the potential to recast this salad in a healthier role by incorporating wholesome ingredients. To start, we traded canned oranges for fresh oranges rich in vitamin C and fiber. We cut out segments to top our salad and used the remaining juice as the basis for a bright vinaigrette, which we enlivened with 3 tablespoons of fresh ginger, a pop of Asian chili-garlic sauce, and just a touch of honey for sweetness. We used some of this flavorful liquid to simmer our chicken breasts, then we shredded the meat and returned it to the pan to soak up the rich, bright flavors. For the salad's base, we replaced the usual lettuce with nutrient-packed napa cabbage, red bell peppers, cilantro, and scallions. For crunch, we passed on sodium-laden fried chow mein noodles and added a much healthier handful of unsalted, dry-roasted peanuts. You can substitute one clove of minced garlic and ¼ teaspoon of cayenne pepper for the Asian chili-garlic sauce.*

1 Cut away peel and pith from oranges. Holding fruit over large bowl, use paring knife to slice between membranes to release segments; transfer segments to second bowl and set aside. Squeeze juice from membrane into first bowl (juice should measure 6 tablespoons).

2 Whisk vinegar, soy sauce, ginger, chili-garlic sauce, and honey into orange juice in large bowl; transfer ½ cup orange juice mixture to 12-inch skillet. Whisking constantly, slowly drizzle canola oil and sesame oil into remaining orange mixture in bowl; set aside.

3 Bring orange juice mixture in skillet to boil over medium-high heat. Add chicken, reduce heat to medium-low, cover, and simmer until meat registers 160 degrees, 10 to 15 minutes, flipping halfway through cooking.

4 Transfer chicken to plate and let cool slightly. Using 2 forks, shred chicken into bite-size pieces. Off heat, return shredded chicken and any accumulated juices into skillet and let sit for 10 minutes.

5 Add cabbage, bell peppers, cilantro, and scallions to vinaigrette in bowl and toss to combine. Transfer to serving platter and top with shredded chicken, orange segments, and peanuts. Serve.

nutritious DELICIOUS

CHICKEN AND ARUGULA SALAD WITH FIGS AND WARM SPICES

serves 6

Salt and pepper

4 (4- to 6-ounce) organic boneless, skinless chicken breasts, no more than 1 inch thick, trimmed of all visible fat

6 tablespoons cold-pressed extra-virgin olive oil (see page 35)

1 teaspoon ground coriander

½ teaspoon smoked paprika

¼ teaspoon ground cinnamon

3 tablespoons lemon juice

1 teaspoon honey

1 (15-ounce) can chickpeas, rinsed

5 ounces (5 cups) baby arugula

½ cup fresh parsley leaves

1 shallot, sliced thin

8 fresh figs, stemmed and quartered

½ cup whole almonds, toasted and chopped

PER SERVING
Cal 390; Total Fat 23g, Sat Fat 3g; Chol 55mg; Sodium 440mg; Total Carbs 26g, Fiber 6g, Total Sugar 14g, Added Sugar 1g; Protein 23g

EXCELLENT SOURCE OF
Protein, Fiber, Vitamin A, Riboflavin, Niacin, Vitamin B6, Vitamin C, Vitamin E, Vitamin K, Magnesium, Manganese, Phosphorus, Selenium

why this recipe works • *Drawing inspiration from the healthful foods of the Mediterranean, we added beautiful, deep purple figs to transform a simple salad of chicken and greens into something special. High in fiber, fresh figs have a subtle floral sweetness, which we wanted to enhance with a dressing seasoned with warm spices. We tried a variety of spice blends, and homed in on coriander for its light citrus note, along with smoked paprika and cinnamon for depth. We microwaved the spices to bloom their flavor for a bolder dressing, then whisked in lemon juice and a teaspoon of honey to balance the spice. We poached the chicken following the method in our Turmeric Chicken Salad Sandwiches (page 85), then added hearty chickpeas, which brought protein, fiber, and vitamins. A bed of peppery baby arugula complemented our dressing well. Our salad was now full of warm, bright flavors, but needed a bit of crunch to play against the soft figs. Toasted and chopped almonds, rich in vitamin E and unsaturated fats, made the perfect topping. You can substitute dried figs for fresh in this recipe.*

1 Dissolve 1 tablespoon salt in 6 cups cold water in Dutch oven. Submerge chicken in water. Heat pot over medium heat until water registers 170 degrees. Turn off heat, cover pot, and let stand until chicken registers 165 degrees, 15 to 17 minutes. Transfer chicken to cutting board and let cool slightly. Using 2 forks, shred chicken into bite-size pieces.

2 Meanwhile, microwave 1 tablespoon oil, coriander, paprika, and cinnamon in large bowl until fragrant, about 30 seconds. Whisk lemon juice, honey, ½ teaspoon salt, and ¼ teaspoon pepper into spice mixture. Whisking constantly, slowly drizzle in remaining 5 tablespoons oil.

3 Add shredded chicken, chickpeas, arugula, parsley, and shallot to dressing in bowl and gently toss to combine. Transfer salad to serving platter, arrange figs over top, and sprinkle with nuts. Serve.

lunch

SALMON, AVOCADO, GRAPEFRUIT, AND WATERCRESS SALAD

serves 4

2 (4- to 6-ounce) skin-on wild-caught salmon fillets, 1 inch thick

3 tablespoons plus 1 teaspoon cold-pressed extra-virgin olive oil (see page 35)
Salt and pepper

2 red grapefruits

1 tablespoon minced shallot

1 teaspoon white wine vinegar

1 teaspoon Dijon mustard

4 ounces (4 cups) watercress, torn into bite-size pieces

1 ripe avocado, halved, pitted, and sliced ¼ inch thick

¼ cup fresh mint leaves, torn

¼ cup blanched hazelnuts, toasted and chopped

PER SERVING
Cal 340; Total Fat 22g, Sat Fat 3g; Chol 30mg; Sodium 510mg; Total Carbs 23g, Fiber 11g, Total Sugar 11g, Added Sugar 0g; Protein 15g

EXCELLENT SOURCE OF
Protein, Fiber, Vitamin A, Niacin, Vitamin B6, Vitamin B12, Vitamin C, Vitamin K, Copper, Manganese, Potassium, Selenium

why this recipe works • *A composed salad presents an appealing mix of contrasting flavors, textures, and colors. The best can also be the simplest, as is the case with this salad showcasing four of our favorite superfoods: salmon, avocado, red grapefruit, and watercress. We chose wild-caught salmon, which typically has a higher proportion of omega-3 fatty acids than its farmed counterparts. Wild salmon is also a bit leaner, so we roasted it only until just translucent before flaking it into large chunks. Thick slices of buttery avocado added creaminess and more richness. For a bright contrast, we cut up two sweet-tart red grapefruits; the segments mimicked the shape of the avocado while delivering loads of vitamin C. We reserved some of the grapefruit juice to whisk up a simple vinaigrette. Our salad was tasting almost balanced but it needed something more. Vitamin-packed watercress was the answer, balancing the sweetness and richness with its slight bitterness and peppery punch. Finally, we added a sprinkle of crunchy, toasted hazelnuts and torn mint leaves to take our composed salad over the top. If using farmed salmon, cook until center of fillet registers 125 degrees.*

1 Adjust oven rack to lowest position, place foil-lined rimmed baking sheet on rack, and heat oven to 500 degrees.

2 Pat salmon dry with paper towels, rub with 1 teaspoon oil, and season with salt and pepper. Reduce oven to 275 degrees. Carefully place salmon skin side down on prepared sheet. Roast until center is still translucent when checked with tip of paring knife and registers 120 degrees (for medium-rare), 6 to 8 minutes. Let salmon cool to room temperature, about 20 minutes. Flake salmon into large 2-inch pieces.

3 Meanwhile, cut away peel and pith from grapefruits. Holding fruit over bowl, use paring knife to slice between membranes to release segments. Measure out 2 tablespoons grapefruit juice and transfer to separate bowl.

4 Whisk shallot, vinegar, mustard, and ½ teaspoon salt into grapefruit juice. Whisking constantly, slowly drizzle in remaining 3 tablespoons oil. Arrange watercress in even layer on platter. Arrange salmon pieces, grapefruit segments, and avocado on top of watercress. Drizzle dressing over top, then sprinkle with mint and hazelnuts. Serve.

lunch

FENNEL AND APPLE SALAD WITH SMOKED TROUT

serves 4

3 tablespoons lemon juice

1 tablespoon whole-grain mustard

1 small shallot, minced

2 teaspoons minced fresh tarragon
  Salt and pepper

¼ cup cold-pressed extra-virgin olive oil (see page 35)

5 ounces (5 cups) baby arugula

2 Granny Smith apples, cored and cut into 3-inch-long matchsticks

1 fennel bulb, stalks discarded, bulb halved, cored, and sliced thin

8 ounces smoked trout, skin and pin bones removed, flaked

why this recipe works • *We enjoy a creamy seafood salad as much as the next person, but most versions are gooped up with mayonnaise and filler ingredients. For a healthier seafood salad, we started with smoked trout, a great source of unsaturated fats, vitamin D, and protein. We then deconstructed the salad, flaking the fish atop a mix of piquant arugula and crunchy, aromatic fennel—a wonderful but underutilized salad candidate. Granny Smith apples contributed a little sweetness and more crunch, and we made sure to leave the skin on to obtain all the fruit's fiber and vitamin C. Instead of a mayo-based dressing, we made a simple lemon and oil vinaigrette with fresh tarragon, shallot, and tangy whole-grain mustard that really brought everything together in a much lighter way, letting the individual ingredients shine through. Smoked mackerel can be substituted for the smoked trout.*

1 Whisk lemon juice, mustard, shallot, 1 teaspoon tarragon, ½ teaspoon salt, and ¼ teaspoon pepper together in large bowl. Whisking constantly, slowly drizzle in oil. Add arugula, apples, and fennel and gently toss to coat. Season with salt and pepper to taste.

2 Divide salad among plates and top with flaked trout. Sprinkle with remaining tarragon. Serve immediately.

PER SERVING
Cal 320; Total Fat 19g, Sat Fat 3g; Chol 45mg; Sodium 420mg; Total Carbs 20g, Fiber 5g, Total Sugar 14g, Added Sugar 0g; Protein 18g

EXCELLENT SOURCE OF
Protein, Fiber, Vitamin A, Niacin, Vitamin B6, Vitamin B12, Vitamin C, Vitamin K, Phosphorus, Potassium

nutritious DELICIOUS

SUMMER ROLLS WITH SPICY ALMOND BUTTER SAUCE

makes 12 rolls; serves 4

SAUCE

- 3 tablespoons almond or peanut butter
- 3 tablespoons water
- 1 tablespoon rice vinegar
- 1 tablespoon low-sodium soy sauce
- 2 teaspoons grated fresh ginger
- 1 teaspoon Sriracha
- 1 garlic clove, minced

ROLLS

- 6 tablespoons rice wine vinegar
- 1 tablespoon low-sodium soy sauce
- 2 teaspoons Sriracha
- 2 scallions, sliced thin on bias
- ½ (14-ounce) package extra-firm tofu, cut into 3-inch-long by ½-inch-thick strips
- ½ small head red cabbage, halved, cored, and sliced thin (3½ cups)
- 12 (8-inch) round rice paper wrappers
- 1 cup fresh basil leaves
- 1 red bell pepper, stemmed, seeded, and cut into 2-inch-long matchsticks
- ½ seedless English cucumber, cut into 3-inch matchsticks
- 2 carrots, peeled and shredded

PER SERVING
Cal 290; Total Fat 10g, Sat Fat 1g; Chol 0mg; Sodium 470mg; Total Carbs 39g, Fiber 6g, Total Sugar 9g, Added Sugar 0g; Protein 14g

EXCELLENT SOURCE OF
Protein, Fiber, Vitamin A, Vitamin C, Vitamin E, Vitamin K, Manganese

why this recipe works • *Despite their evocative name, many summer rolls contain mostly bland rice noodles, leaving vegetables as an afterthought. For our version we gathered up a rainbow of healthful veggies to fill our rice paper packages. A mix of red cabbage, red bell pepper, cucumber, and carrots delivered color and crunch. Fresh basil added herbal notes, and strips of marinated tofu made the rolls hearty enough for lunch. Instead of a thin soy dipping sauce, we whisked up a nutrient-packed, Sriracha-spiked almond butter sauce. Thick and rich, it clung easily to our rolls, taking the dish to a new level. Be sure to make one roll at a time to keep the wrappers moist and pliable. Brands of rice paper wrappers vary in the time it takes to soak and become pliable. You can use smooth or chunky almond or peanut butter.*

1 **FOR THE SAUCE** Whisk all ingredients together until well combined; set aside.

2 **FOR THE ROLLS** Whisk 2 tablespoons vinegar, soy sauce, Sriracha, and scallions together in small bowl until well combined. Place tofu in shallow dish, then pour soy sauce mixture over top and let sit for 1 hour. Toss cabbage with remaining ¼ cup vinegar and let sit for 1 hour. Drain cabbage in fine mesh strainer, pressing gently with back of spatula to remove as much liquid as possible. Transfer to large plate and pat dry with paper towels.

3 Spread clean, damp dish towel on work surface. Fill 9-inch pie plate with 1 inch room-temperature water. Working with one wrapper at a time, submerge each in water until just pliable, 10 seconds to 2 minutes; lay softened wrapper on towel. Scatter 3 basil leaves over wrapper. Arrange 5 matchsticks each of bell pepper and cucumber horizontally on wrapper, leaving 2-inch border at bottom. Top with 1 tablespoon carrots, then arrange 2 tablespoons cabbage on top of carrots. Place 1 strip tofu horizontally on top of vegetables, being sure to shake off excess marinade.

4 Fold bottom of wrapper over filling, pulling back on it firmly to tighten it around filling, then fold sides of wrapper in and continue to roll tightly into spring roll. Transfer to platter and cover with second damp dish towel.

5 Repeat with remaining wrappers and filling. Serve with almond butter sauce. (Spring rolls are best eaten immediately but can be covered with a clean, damp dish towel and refrigerated for up to 4 hours.)

lunch

MAIN DISHES

137 Oven-Roasted Salmon with Tangerine and Ginger Relish

Oven-Roasted Salmon with Miso-Sesame Sauce

139 Salmon Tacos with Super Slaw

140 Pomegranate Roasted Salmon with Lentils and Chard

143 Black Rice Bowls with Salmon

144 Nut-Crusted Cod Fillets

146 Cod in Coconut Broth with Lemon Grass and Ginger

149 Baked Stuffed Trout with Red Pepper and Preserved Lemon

150 Poached Chicken with Warm Tomato-Ginger Vinaigrette

154 One-Pan Chicken with Kale and Butternut Squash

157 Parmesan Chicken with Warm Arugula, Radicchio, and Fennel Salad

159 Crispy Skillet Turkey Burgers

161 Spice-Rubbed Turkey Breast with Sour Orange Sauce

162 Turkey Cutlets with Barley and Swiss Chard

164 Turkey Shepherd's Pie

167 Turkey Meatballs with Lemony Brown Rice and Sun-Dried Tomatoes

169 Pumpkin Turkey Chili

170 Pulled BBQ Turkey with Red Cabbage Slaw

EASY SAUCES (PAGE 152)

Garlic Aïoli

Sriracha Aïoli

Avocado Crema

Lemon-Yogurt Sauce

Tahini Yogurt Sauce

Chimichurri Sauce

Chermoula Sauce

Kale and Sunflower Seed Pesto

172 Grilled Flank Steak with Tomato, Orange, and Avocado

175 Beef Stir-Fry with Bok Choy and Green Beans

176 Thai Grilled-Steak Salad

178 Thai Red Curry with Lentils and Tofu

181 Stir-Fried Tempeh with Orange Sauce

182 Vegetable Lasagna

185 Swiss Chard Macaroni and Cheese

186 Mushroom Bourguignon

189 Beet Barley Risotto

191 Sweet Potato, Poblano, and Black Bean Tacos

193 Swiss Chard Enchiladas

194 Cauliflower Steaks

196 Whole-Wheat Pizza with Kale and Sunflower Seed Pesto

198 Cauliflower-Chickpea Flatbread with Romesco

OVEN-ROASTED SALMON WITH TANGERINE AND GINGER RELISH

serves 4

RELISH

4 tangerines, rind and pith removed and segments cut into ½-inch pieces (1 cup)

1 scallion, sliced thin

2 teaspoons lemon juice

2 teaspoons cold-pressed extra-virgin olive oil (see page 35)

1½ teaspoons grated fresh ginger
Salt and pepper

SALMON

4 (4- to 6-ounce) skin-on wild-caught salmon fillets, 1 inch thick

1 teaspoon cold-pressed extra-virgin olive oil (see page 35)
Salt and pepper

PER SERVING
Cal 240; Total Fat 11g, Sat Fat 1.5g; Chol 60mg; Sodium 340mg; Total Carbs 12g, Fiber 2g, Total Sugar 9g, Added Sugar 0g; Protein 23g

EXCELLENT SOURCE OF
Protein, Thiamine, Riboflavin, Niacin, Pantothenic Acid, Vitamin B6, Vitamin B12, Vitamin C, Phosphorus, Potassium, Selenium

why this recipe works • *It's no wonder salmon is one of the most popular fish. Its flesh is rich-tasting, thanks to high levels of heart-healthy oils, and it takes well to many treatments. The key is to avoid overcooking it, especially wild salmon, which is leaner than farmed. Our hybrid roasting method solved this by heating the oven to 500 degrees before dropping the temperature to 275. The initial blast of heat firmed the exterior and rendered some fat while the fish gently cooked. Salmon is often roasted in butter, but we wanted a healthier approach that would contrast with the fish's richness. So we made a bright tangerine relish perked up with spicy ginger. Skin-on salmon fillets hold together better during cooking. If you can't find tangerines, you can use oranges. If your salmon is less than 1 inch thick, start checking for doneness early. If using farmed salmon, cook until thickest part of fillet registers 125 degrees.*

1 **FOR THE RELISH** Place tangerines in fine-mesh strainer set over medium bowl and drain for 15 minutes.

2 Pour off all but 1 tablespoon tangerine juice from bowl. Whisk in scallion, lemon juice, oil, and ginger. Stir in tangerines and season with salt and pepper to taste.

3 **FOR THE SALMON** Adjust oven rack to lowest position, place aluminum foil–lined rimmed baking sheet on rack, and heat oven to 500 degrees. Pat salmon dry with paper towels, rub with oil, and season with salt and pepper.

4 Once oven reaches 500 degrees, reduce oven temperature to 275 degrees. Remove sheet from oven and carefully place salmon, skin-side down, on hot sheet. Roast until center is still translucent when checked with tip of paring knife and registers 120 degrees (for medium-rare), 4 to 6 minutes.

5 Slide fish spatula along underside of fillets and transfer to individual plates or serving platter, leaving skin behind; discard skin. Top with relish and serve.

VARIATION

OVEN-ROASTED SALMON WITH MISO-SESAME SAUCE

Omit Relish. Whisk ¼ cup toasted sesame seeds, 2 tablespoons organic plain low-fat yogurt, 1 tablespoon red miso, 2 teaspoons lemon juice, 2 teaspoons sugar, 1 minced garlic clove, and ½ teaspoon water together in bowl until well combined. Serve sauce with salmon.

main dishes

SALMON TACOS WITH SUPER SLAW

serves 6

¼ teaspoon grated lime zest
   plus 2 tablespoons juice
   Salt and pepper

4 ounces collard greens,
   stemmed and sliced thin
   (2 cups)

4 ounces jícama, peeled and cut
   into 2-inch-long matchsticks

4 radishes, trimmed and cut into
   1-inch-long matchsticks

½ small red onion, halved and
   sliced thin

¼ cup fresh cilantro leaves

1½ teaspoons chili powder

4 (4- to 6-ounce) skin-on
   wild-caught salmon fillets,
   1 inch thick

1 tablespoon expeller-pressed
   canola oil (see page 35)

1 recipe Avocado Crema
   (page 152)

12 (6-inch) corn tortillas, warmed
   Hot sauce

why this recipe works • *California-style fish tacos generally feature deep-fried fish, a tangy cabbage slaw, and a creamy sauce that binds everything together. We wanted to boost the nutrition of each element for a supercharged take on tacos. Since we were forgoing the frying, we opted for wild salmon, which is richer than the more typically used cod or other white fish. A flavorful spice rub gave the fillets a nice crust without the need for frying batter. For a slaw that would stand up to the salmon, we wondered if we could incorporate nutrient-rich dark leafy greens, and collards proved just the ticket. When thinly sliced, they required no precooking. Combined with crunchy radishes, cooling jícama, red onion, cilantro, and lime, they perfectly complemented the fish. For our crema, in lieu of sour cream, we processed avocado with lime juice, yogurt, and cilantro. Skin-on salmon fillets hold together better during cooking, and the skin helps keep the fish moist. If your salmon is less than 1 inch thick, start checking for doneness early. If using farmed salmon, cook until thickest part of fillet registers 125 degrees. You can substitute 2 cups thinly sliced purple cabbage for the collards if desired.*

1 Whisk lime zest and juice, and ¼ teaspoon salt together in large bowl. Add collards, jícama, radishes, onion, and cilantro and toss to combine.

2 Combine chili powder, ¾ teaspoon salt, and ¼ teaspoon pepper in small bowl. Pat salmon dry with paper towels and sprinkle evenly with spice mixture. Heat oil in 12-inch nonstick skillet over medium-high heat until shimmering. Cook salmon, skin side up, until well browned, 3 to 5 minutes. Flip and continue to cook until salmon is still translucent when checked with tip of paring knife and registers 120 degrees (for medium-rare), 3 to 5 minutes. Transfer salmon to plate and let cool slightly, about 2 minutes. Using 2 forks, flake fish into 2-inch pieces, discarding skin.

3 Divide fish, collard slaw, and avocado crema evenly among tortillas, and drizzle with hot sauce to taste. Serve.

PER SERVING (2 TACOS)
Cal 310; Total Fat 14g, Sat Fat 1.5g;
Chol 40mg; Sodium 450mg; Total
Carbs 29g, Fiber 6g, Total Sugar 1g,
Added Sugar 0g; Protein 18g

EXCELLENT SOURCE OF
Protein, Fiber, Vitamin A, Riboflavin,
Niacin, Vitamin B6, Vitamin B12,
Vitamin C, Vitamin K, Selenium

main dishes

serves 4

2 tablespoons plus 1 teaspoon cold-pressed extra-virgin olive oil (see page 35)

12 ounces Swiss chard, stemmed, ½ cup stems chopped fine, leaves cut into 2-inch pieces

1 small onion, chopped fine

2 garlic cloves, minced

4 sprigs fresh thyme
Salt and pepper

2 cups homemade or low-sodium chicken or vegetable broth (see page 36)

1 cup lentilles du Puy, picked over and rinsed

4 (4- to 6-ounce) skin-on wild-caught salmon fillets, 1 inch thick

2 tablespoons pomegranate molasses

½ cup pomegranate seeds

PER SERVING
Cal 460; Total Fat 17g, Sat Fat 2.5g; Chol 60mg; Sodium 510mg; Total Carbs 41g, Fiber 10g, Total Sugar 9g, Added Sugar 0g; Protein 37g

EXCELLENT SOURCE OF
Protein, Fiber, Vitamin A, Thiamine, Riboflavin, Niacin, Pantothenic Acid, Vitamin B6, Vitamin B12, Vitamin C, Vitamin K, Copper, Iron, Magnesium, Phosphorus, Potassium, Selenium

why this recipe works • *Sweet-tart pomegranate brightens the flavors of salmon and earthy lentils; add Swiss chard and you have a satisfying meal with a varied nutritional profile. While chard stems are often discarded, they have great flavor, so we softened them with aromatics before simmering with our lentils, stirring in the leaves near the end of cooking. For the salmon, we wanted sweetness without a sugary glaze, so we painted it with pomegranate molasses. Fresh pomegranate seeds tied the dish together. Skin-on salmon holds together best during cooking, and the skin helps keep the fish moist. If your salmon is less than 1 inch thick, start checking for doneness early. If using farmed salmon, cook until thickest part registers 125 degrees. Lentilles du Puy, also called French green lentils, are our first choice, but brown, black, or regular green lentils will work (cooking times will vary). Pomegranate molasses can be found in the international aisle of well-stocked supermarkets; if you can't find it, substitute 1 tablespoon lemon juice plus 1 tablespoon mild molasses.*

1 Heat 1 tablespoon oil in large saucepan over medium-high heat until shimmering. Add chard stems, onion, garlic, thyme, and ¼ teaspoon salt and cook, stirring frequently, until softened, about 5 minutes. Stir in broth and lentils and bring to boil. Reduce heat to low, cover, and simmer, stirring occasionally, until lentils are mostly tender, 45 to 50 minutes.

2 Adjust oven rack to lowest position, place aluminum foil–lined rimmed baking sheet on rack, and heat oven to 500 degrees. Uncover lentils and stir in chard leaves. Increase heat to medium-low and continue to cook until chard leaves are tender, about 4 minutes. Off heat, discard thyme sprigs, stir in 1 tablespoon oil, and season with salt and pepper to taste; cover to keep warm.

3 Pat salmon dry with paper towels. Brush with remaining 1 teaspoon oil, then brush with 1 tablespoon pomegranate molasses and season with salt and pepper. Once oven reaches 500 degrees, reduce oven temperature to 275 degrees. Remove sheet from oven, carefully place salmon skin-side down on hot sheet. Roast until center is still translucent when checked with tip of paring knife and registers 120 degrees (for medium-rare), 4 to 6 minutes.

4 Brush salmon with remaining 1 tablespoon pomegranate molasses. Slide fish spatula along underside of fillets and transfer to individual plates or serving platter; discard skin. Stir pomegranate seeds into lentil mixture and serve with salmon.

nutritious DELICIOUS

BLACK RICE BOWLS WITH SALMON

serves 4

RICE AND DRESSING

1½ cups black rice
   Salt and pepper
¼ cup rice vinegar
¼ cup mirin
1 tablespoon white miso
1 teaspoon grated fresh ginger
½ teaspoon grated lime zest plus
   2 tablespoons juice

SALMON AND VEGETABLES

4 (4- to 6-ounce) skin-on
   wild-caught salmon fillets,
   1 inch thick
1 teaspoon expeller-pressed
   canola oil (see page 35)
   Salt and pepper
1 (8- by 7½-inch) sheet nori,
   crumbled (optional)
4 radishes, trimmed, halved,
   and sliced thin
1 avocado, halved, pitted,
   and sliced thin
1 cucumber, halved lengthwise,
   seeded, and sliced thin
2 scallions, sliced thin

PER SERVING
Cal 540; Total Fat 18g, Sat Fat 2.5g;
Chol 60mg; Sodium 410mg; Total
Carbs 64g, Fiber 9g, Total Sugar 7g,
Added Sugar 0g; Protein 31g

EXCELLENT SOURCE OF
Protein, Fiber, Thiamine, Riboflavin,
Niacin, Pantothenic Acid,
Vitamin B6, Folate, Vitamin B12,
Vitamin C, Vitamin K, Copper,
Phosphorus, Potassium, Selenium

why this recipe works • *Black rice is an ancient grain that was once reserved for the emperors of China. Its dark color signifies the presence of anthocyanins, and it contains more protein, fiber, and iron than other rice varieties. We decided to use it in a Japanese-style rice bowl. To ensure well-seasoned grains with a bit of chew, we boiled the rice like pasta, and then drizzled it with a mix of rice vinegar, mirin, miso, and ginger. We roasted wild salmon fillets until medium-rare and then arranged them atop the rice before garnishing our bowls with radishes, avocado, cucumber, nori, and scallions. Skin-on salmon fillets hold together best during cooking, and the skin helps keep the fish moist. If your salmon is less than 1 inch thick, start checking for doneness early. If using farmed salmon, cook until thickest part registers 125 degrees. Nori is seaweed that has been dried and pressed into sheets for rolling sushi; you can find it in the international foods aisle of the supermarket.*

1 **FOR THE RICE AND DRESSING** Bring 4 quarts water to boil in Dutch oven over medium-high heat. Add rice and 1 teaspoon salt and cook until rice is tender, 20 to 25 minutes. Drain rice and transfer to large bowl.

2 Whisk vinegar, mirin, miso, ginger, and lime zest and juice together in small bowl until miso is fully incorporated. Season with salt and pepper to taste. Measure out ¼ cup vinegar mixture and drizzle over rice. Let rice cool to room temperature, tossing occasionally, about 20 minutes. Set remaining dressing aside for serving.

3 **FOR THE SALMON AND VEGETABLES** While rice is cooking, adjust oven rack to lowest position, place aluminum foil–lined rimmed baking sheet on rack, and heat oven to 500 degrees. Pat salmon dry with paper towels, rub with oil, and season with salt and pepper.

4 Once oven reaches 500 degrees, reduce oven temperature to 275 degrees. Remove sheet from oven and carefully place salmon skin-side down on hot sheet. Roast until center is still translucent when checked with tip of paring knife and registers 120 degrees (for medium-rare), 4 to 6 minutes.

5 Portion rice into 4 individual serving bowls and sprinkle with some of nori, if using. Flake salmon into large 3-inch pieces. Top rice with salmon, radishes, avocado, and cucumber. Sprinkle with scallions and drizzle with reserved dressing. Serve, passing remaining nori separately.

main dishes

NUT-CRUSTED COD FILLETS

serves 4

½ cup shelled pistachios

2 tablespoons expeller-pressed canola oil (see page 35)

1 large shallot, minced
Salt and pepper

1 garlic clove, minced

1 teaspoon minced fresh thyme or ¼ teaspoon dried

½ cup 100 percent whole-wheat panko bread crumbs

2 tablespoons minced fresh parsley

1 tablespoon organic plain low-fat yogurt

1 large organic egg yolk

½ teaspoon grated lemon zest, plus lemon wedges for serving

4 (4- to 6-ounce) skinless cod fillets, 1 to 1½ inches thick

PER SERVING
Cal 310; Total Fat 16g, Sat Fat 2g; Chol 95mg; Sodium 370mg; Total Carbs 14g, Fiber 3g, Total Sugar 3g, Added Sugar 0g; Protein 26g

EXCELLENT SOURCE OF
Protein, Niacin, Vitamin B6, Vitamin K, Phosphorus, Potassium, Selenium

why this recipe works • *Breaded and fried fish is undeniably delicious when done right, but we wanted a more nutritious path to moist, delicate fish with a crunchy coating, not to mention avoiding the hassle of deep frying. Baking instead of frying was an obvious starting point, but we also wanted to rework the coating. We replaced half the bread crumbs with ground pistachios, which offered more nutrients as well as richness and fragrance. We skipped traditional bread crumbs, which are prone to sogginess, and opted for whole-wheat panko. Toasting the two components together with aromatics brought out their flavors and ensured the topping would remain extra crisp. To help the coating adhere to the fillets, we brushed the vitamin B–rich fish with a mixture of yogurt, egg yolk, and lemon zest before pressing on the crumbs. Because our crust was so flavorful, we only needed to coat the tops of the fillets, making them easy to bake without crumbs falling off the sides or getting soggy underneath. Baking the fillets on a wire rack set in a sheet pan ensured even cooking. You can substitute haddock or halibut for the cod. Any nut will work for the topping, but we particularly liked pistachios and hazelnuts.*

1 Adjust oven rack to middle position and heat oven to 300 degrees. Set wire rack in rimmed baking sheet and spray with canola oil spray. Process pistachios in food processor until finely chopped, 20 to 30 seconds. Heat oil in 12-inch nonstick skillet over medium heat until shimmering. Add shallot and ¼ teaspoon salt and cook until softened, about 3 minutes. Stir in garlic and thyme and cook until fragrant, about 30 seconds. Reduce heat to medium-low, add pistachios, panko, and ¼ teaspoon pepper and cook, stirring frequently, until well browned and crisp, about 8 minutes. Transfer nut mixture to shallow dish and let cool for 10 minutes. Stir in parsley.

2 Whisk yogurt, egg yolk, and lemon zest together in bowl. Pat cod dry with paper towels and season with salt and pepper. Brush tops of fillets evenly with yogurt mixture. Working with 1 fillet at a time, dredge coated side in nut mixture, pressing gently to adhere.

3 Transfer cod, crumb side up, to prepared rack and bake until fish flakes apart when gently prodded with paring knife and registers 140 degrees, 20 to 25 minutes, rotating sheet halfway through baking. Serve with lemon wedges.

serves 4

- 1 tablespoon expeller-pressed canola oil (see page 35)
- 1 leek, white and light green parts only, halved lengthwise, sliced thin, and washed thoroughly
  Salt and pepper
- 4 garlic cloves, minced
- 1 tablespoon grated fresh ginger
- 1 cup water
- 2 carrots, peeled and cut into 2-inch-long matchsticks
- 1 10-inch stalk lemon grass, tough outer leaves removed and bruised with back of knife
- 4 (4- to 6-ounce) skinless cod fillets, 1 to 1½ inches thick
- ⅓ cup canned coconut milk
- 1 tablespoon lime juice, plus lime wedges for serving
- 1 teaspoon fish sauce
- 2 tablespoons chopped dry-roasted peanuts
- 2 tablespoons fresh cilantro leaves
- 1 serrano chile, stemmed and sliced thin

why this recipe works • *Mild, flaky cod is often served "New England style," cloaked in a velvety sauce made from cream and butter. We liked the idea of bathing this lean white, mineral-rich fish in a flavorful liquid but could do without all the butter. A Thai-style approach drew upon the flavors of coconut soup to build a lush, aromatic broth seasoned with lemon grass, ginger, garlic, fish sauce, and lime. Poaching the cod in this broth ensured the flavors infused the fish and allowed it to cook gently and evenly. Mild leeks and sweet carrots complemented the delicate cod, a little coconut milk added richness, and a garnish of peanuts, cilantro, and a serrano chile added welcome color, aroma, and crunch. Best of all, this dish came together quickly and in just one pan, making it an elegant but weeknight-friendly meal. If you can't find a serrano chile, substitute a red Fresno chile. You can use light coconut milk, but the broth will be noticeably thinner and less rich. You can substitute haddock or halibut for the cod.*

1 Heat oil in 12-inch nonstick skillet over medium heat until shimmering. Add leek and ½ teaspoon salt and cook, stirring occasionally, until lightly browned, 4 to 6 minutes. Stir in garlic and ginger and cook uncovered until fragrant, about 30 seconds.

2 Stir in water, carrots, and lemon grass and bring to simmer. Pat cod dry with paper towels and season with salt and pepper. Nestle fish into skillet and bring to simmer. Cover, reduce heat to low, and cook until fish flakes apart when gently prodded with paring knife and registers 140 degrees, 8 to 12 minutes.

3 Carefully transfer fish to individual shallow bowls. Discard lemon grass. Using slotted spoon, divide leeks and carrots evenly among bowls. Off heat, whisk coconut milk, lime juice, and fish sauce into broth and season with salt and pepper to taste. Ladle broth over fish. Sprinkle with peanuts, cilantro, and chile. Serve with lime wedges.

PER SERVING
Cal 230; Total Fat 11g, Sat Fat 4.5g; Chol 50mg; Sodium 470mg; Total Carbs 11g, Fiber 2g, Total Sugar 3g, Added Sugar 0g; Protein 23g

EXCELLENT SOURCE OF
Protein, Vitamin A, Niacin, Vitamin B6, Vitamin K, Manganese, Phosphorus, Potassium, Selenium

nutritious DELICIOUS

BAKED STUFFED TROUT WITH RED PEPPER AND PRESERVED LEMON

serves 4

3 tablespoons cold-pressed extra-virgin olive oil (see page 35)
1 red bell pepper, stemmed, seeded, and chopped fine
1 red onion, chopped fine
½ preserved lemon, pulp and white pith removed, rind rinsed and minced (2 tablespoons)
⅓ cup pitted brine-cured green olives, chopped
1 tablespoon minced fresh parsley
Salt and pepper
4 (8- to 10-ounce) whole trout, gutted, fins snipped off with scissors
Lemon wedges

why this recipe works • *Like salmon, trout is a supremely healthy protein thanks to its abundance of omega-3 fatty acids, vitamins, and minerals. Since we wanted to eat this oily fish more often, we needed a different method than the typical pan-frying, which doesn't add much nutritionally. Instead, we baked the fish whole for a dramatic presentation. Spacing them out on a rimmed baking sheet permitted good air circulation, which allowed the exterior to crisp without retaining too many juices that would cause the fish to steam. Trout has a rich taste that works best with other potent flavors, so we stuffed the fish with a mixture of fragrant preserved lemon, sweet vitamin C–packed red pepper, and briny green olives. If you cannot find preserved lemons, you can make a quick substitute: Mince eight 2-inch strips lemon zest and combine with 2 teaspoons lemon juice, 1 teaspoon water, ½ teaspoon sugar, and ½ teaspoon salt in bowl. Microwave mixture at 50 percent power until liquid evaporates, about 2 minutes, stirring and mashing lemon with back of spoon every 30 seconds. You can substitute mackerel for the trout, if desired. The trout heads can be removed before serving, if desired.*

1 Adjust oven rack to middle position and heat oven to 500 degrees. Heat 2 tablespoons oil in 12-inch skillet over medium-high heat until shimmering. Add bell pepper and onion and cook until vegetables are softened and well browned, 8 to 10 minutes. Stir in preserved lemon and cook until fragrant, about 30 seconds. Off heat, stir in olives and parsley and season with salt and pepper to taste.

2 Grease rimmed baking sheet with remaining 1 tablespoon oil. Rinse each trout under cold running water and pat dry with paper towels inside and out. Open cavity of each trout, season flesh with salt and pepper, and spoon one-quarter of filling into opening. Place trout on prepared sheet, spaced at least 2 inches apart. Bake until thickest part of trout registers 130 to 135 degrees, 10 to 12 minutes. Carefully transfer trout to serving platter and let rest for 5 minutes. Serve with lemon wedges.

PER SERVING
Cal 300; Total Fat 20g, Sat Fat 3g; Chol 65mg; Sodium 510mg; Total Carbs 6g, Fiber 1g, Total Sugar 3g, Added Sugar 0g; Protein 24g

EXCELLENT SOURCE OF
Protein, Vitamin A, Thiamine, Riboflavin, Niacin, Pantothenic Acid, Vitamin B12, Vitamin C, Vitamin D, Vitamin K, Manganese, Phosphorus, Selenium

main dishes

POACHED CHICKEN WITH WARM TOMATO-GINGER VINAIGRETTE

serves 4

CHICKEN

4 (4- to 6-ounce) organic boneless, skinless chicken breasts, trimmed of all visible fat

½ cup low-sodium soy sauce

¼ cup salt

2 tablespoons sugar

6 garlic cloves, smashed and peeled

VINAIGRETTE

2 tablespoons cold-pressed extra-virgin olive oil (see page 35)

1 small shallot, minced

1 teaspoon grated fresh ginger
Pinch ground cumin
Pinch ground fennel

6 ounces cherry tomatoes, halved
Salt and pepper

1½ teaspoons red wine vinegar

½ teaspoon packed light brown sugar

1 tablespoon chopped fresh cilantro

PER SERVING
Cal 220; Total Fat 10g, Sat Fat 1.5g; Chol 85mg; Sodium 360mg; Total Carbs 4g, Fiber 1g, Total Sugar 3g, Added Sugar 1g; Protein 26g

EXCELLENT SOURCE OF
Protein, Niacin, Vitamin B6, Phosphorus, Selenium

why this recipe works • *We love chicken breasts because they're a quick-cooking lean source of protein, but those qualities can lead to dry, stringy results if you aren't careful, especially when sautéing, broiling, or grilling. Poaching, by contrast, is forgiving. Though it may conjure images of bland spa cuisine, we created a super-flavorful poaching liquid, which we used to brine the breasts for added juiciness. Allowing the chicken to gently poach in the residual heat, elevated in a steamer basket, ensured even cooking and guaranteed moist, savory breasts, ready to be paired with a bold sauce or added to salads or sandwiches. Parsley may be substituted for the cilantro in the vinaigrette. You can omit the Warm Tomato-Ginger vinaigrette and instead serve with any of the sauces on pages 152–153.*

1 **FOR THE CHICKEN** Cover chicken breasts with plastic wrap and pound thick ends gently with meat pounder until ¾ inch thick. Whisk 4 quarts water, soy sauce, salt, sugar, and garlic together in Dutch oven until salt and sugar are dissolved. Arrange breasts, skinned side up, in steamer basket, making sure not to overlap them. Submerge steamer basket in brine and let sit at room temperature for 30 minutes.

2 Heat pot over medium heat, stirring liquid occasionally to even out hot spots, until water registers 175 degrees, 15 to 20 minutes. Turn off heat, cover pot, remove from burner, and let stand until meat registers 160 degrees, 17 to 22 minutes.

3 Transfer breasts to carving board, cover tightly with aluminum foil, and let rest for 5 minutes.

4 **FOR THE VINAIGRETTE** While chicken rests, heat 1 tablespoon oil in 10-inch nonstick skillet over medium heat until shimmering. Add shallot, ginger, cumin, and fennel and cook until fragrant, about 15 seconds. Stir in tomatoes and ⅛ teaspoon salt and cook, stirring frequently, until tomatoes have softened, 3 to 5 minutes. Off heat, stir in vinegar and sugar and season with salt and pepper to taste; cover to keep warm.

5 Slice each chicken breast on bias into ¼-inch-thick slices and transfer to serving platter or individual plates. Stir cilantro and remaining 1 tablespoon oil into vinaigrette and serve with the sliced chicken.

EASY SAUCES

Sauces are powerful in their ability to elevate a relatively mild dish and bring it to an entirely new level. Whether it's spooned over a simple chicken or turkey breast, topping a pizza, or dolloped atop a taco, a sauce of just a few ingredients mixed together can transform a meal. However, sauces are often butter or mayo-based and high in saturated fat, and we often turn to convenient store-bought condiments that are loaded with sodium and sugar. We opt to make our own, allowing us to control the type of fat (healthy, unsaturated oils) and amount of sugar and salt. Instead, we pack our homemade sauces with nutrient-dense, flavorful ingredients like fresh herbs, seeds, and yogurt.

GARLIC AÏOLI
makes about ¾ cup

A combination of canola oil and extra-virgin olive oil is crucial to the flavor of the aïoli. A rasp-style grater makes quick work of turning the garlic into a paste.

- 2 large organic egg yolks
- 4 teaspoons lemon juice
- 1 garlic clove, minced to a paste
  Salt and white pepper
- ½ cup expeller-pressed canola oil (see page 35)
- ¼ cup cold-pressed extra-virgin olive oil (see page 35)

Whisk egg yolks, lemon juice, garlic, and ¼ teaspoon salt together in bowl. Whisking constantly, slowly drizzle in oils until emulsified. Season with salt and pepper to taste. (Aïoli can be refrigerated for up to 3 days.)

VARIATION

SRIRACHA AÏOLI
Substitute 2 teaspoons lime juice for lemon juice and add 2 tablespoons Sriracha to egg yolk mixture.

AVOCADO CREMA
makes about ½ cup

Serve with tacos, nachos, or your favorite chili.

- ½ avocado, pitted and chopped coarse
- ¼ cup chopped fresh cilantro
- 3 tablespoons water
- 1 tablespoon lime juice
- 1 tablespoon organic plain low-fat yogurt
  Salt and pepper

Process all ingredients in food processor until completely smooth, about 1 minute, scraping down sides of bowl as needed. Season with salt and pepper to taste. Serve. (Crema can be refrigerated with plastic wrap pressed flush to surface for up to 2 days.)

LEMON-YOGURT SAUCE
makes about 1 cup

This creamy sauce adds bright tang to savory dishes such as our Mushroom and Artichoke Hash with Parmesan Croutons (page 78).

- 1 cup organic plain 2 percent Greek yogurt
- 1 teaspoon grated lemon zest plus 2 tablespoons juice
- 1 garlic clove, minced
  Salt and pepper

nutritious delicious

Whisk yogurt, lemon zest and juice, and garlic together in bowl until combined. Let sit until flavors meld, about 30 minutes. Season with salt and pepper to taste and serve. (Sauce can be refrigerated for up to 4 days.)

TAHINI YOGURT SAUCE
makes about 1¼ cups

This sauce pairs well with grilled or roasted vegetables or poultry.

- ⅓ cup tahini
- ⅓ cup organic plain 2 percent Greek yogurt
- ¼ cup water
- 3 tablespoons lemon juice
- 1 garlic clove, minced
  Salt and pepper

Whisk tahini, yogurt, water, lemon juice, garlic, and ¾ teaspoon salt together in bowl until combined. Season with salt and pepper to taste. Let sit until flavors meld, about 30 minutes. Serve. (Sauce can be refrigerated for up to 4 days.)

CHIMICHURRI SAUCE
makes about ½ cup

Serve with lean grilled meat, poultry, or fish.

- 1 cup fresh parsley leaves
- ¼ cup cold-pressed extra-virgin olive oil (see page 35)
- 1 tablespoon red wine vinegar
- 2 garlic cloves, minced
- ½ teaspoon dried oregano
- ¼ teaspoon red pepper flakes
  Salt and pepper

Pulse all ingredients in food processor until coarsely chopped, about 10 pulses, scraping down sides of bowl as needed. Season with salt and pepper to taste and serve. (Sauce can be refrigerated for up to 24 hours.)

CHERMOULA SAUCE
makes about ½ cup

Serve with lean grilled meat, poultry, fish, or vegetables.

- ¾ cup fresh cilantro leaves
- ¼ cup cold-pressed extra-virgin olive oil (see page 35)
- 2 tablespoons lemon juice
- 4 garlic cloves, minced
- ½ teaspoon ground cumin
- ½ teaspoon paprika
- ⅛ teaspoon cayenne pepper
  Salt and pepper

Pulse all ingredients in food processor until smooth, about 10 pulses, scraping down sides of bowl as needed. Season with salt and pepper to taste and serve. (Sauce can be refrigerated for up to 24 hours.)

KALE AND SUNFLOWER SEED PESTO
makes about 1½ cups

Toss with pasta or whole grains, such as farro, to coat.

- 2½ ounces curly kale, stemmed and chopped (1½ cups)
- 1 cup fresh basil leaves
- 1 cup baby spinach
- ⅓ cup roasted sunflower seeds
- 3 tablespoons water
- 3 garlic cloves, minced
  Salt and pepper
- ½ cup cold-pressed extra-virgin olive oil (see page 35)
- 1 ounce grated Parmesan cheese (½ cup)

Process kale, basil, spinach, sunflower seeds, water, garlic, and ¼ teaspoon salt in food processor until smooth, about 30 seconds, scraping down sides of bowl as needed. With processor running, slowly add oil until incorporated. Transfer mixture to bowl, stir in Parmesan, and season with salt and pepper to taste. Serve. (Pesto can be refrigerated with plastic wrap pressed flush to surface for up to 3 days.)

serves 4

- ½ cup cold-pressed extra-virgin olive oil (see page 35)
- 2 tablespoons minced fresh sage
- 2 teaspoons honey
  Salt and pepper
- ¾ cup organic plain low-fat yogurt
- 1 tablespoon water
- 7 garlic cloves, peeled (6 whole, 1 minced)
- 1 teaspoon grated orange zest
- 8 ounces kale, stemmed and cut into 2-inch pieces
- 2 pounds butternut squash, peeled, seeded, and cut into 1-inch pieces (6 cups)
- 8 shallots, peeled and halved
- ½ cup dried cranberries
- 2 teaspoons paprika
- 4 (8- to 10-ounce) organic bone-in split chicken breasts, trimmed of all visible fat and halved crosswise

PER SERVING
Cal 730; Total Fat 34g, Sat Fat 5g; Chol 135mg; Sodium 580mg; Total Carbs 61g, Fiber 9g, Total Sugar 30g, Added Sugar 3g; Protein 49g

EXCELLENT SOURCE OF
Protein, Fiber, Vitamin A, Thiamine, Riboflavin, Niacin, Pantothenic Acid, Vitamin B6, Folate, Vitamin C, Vitamin E, Vitamin K, Calcium, Copper, Iron, Magnesium, Manganese, Phosphorus, Potassium, Selenium

why this recipe works • *A sheet pan full of roast chicken, kale, and butternut squash promised a satisfying, nutritious meal with minimal cleanup. However, in order to combine sturdy squash, dark leafy greens, and chicken in a single pan, we'd need to get them to cook at the same rate. We used bone-in split chicken breasts, which contain less fat than a whole chicken and wouldn't smother the vegetables underneath and cause them to steam. Halving the breasts assisted in even cooking. A simple sage marinade seasoned both the chicken and vegetables. In just 25 minutes, we had crisp-skinned chicken, tender but not mushy squash, and lightly crispy kale. A sprinkling of dried cranberries added fiber and a sweet-tart chew to the mix. We topped our chicken with a drizzle of light, creamy yogurt sauce accented with orange zest and garlic to bring the dish into harmony. Both curly and Lacinato kale will work.*

1 Adjust oven rack to upper-middle position and heat oven to 475 degrees. Whisk oil, sage, honey, ¾ teaspoon salt, and ½ teaspoon pepper together in large bowl until well combined. In separate bowl whisk together yogurt, water, minced garlic, orange zest, and 1 tablespoon oil mixture, then season with salt and pepper to taste; set aside.

2 Vigorously squeeze and massage kale with hands in large bowl until leaves are uniformly darkened and slightly wilted, about 1 minute. Add squash, shallots, cranberries, whole garlic cloves, and ¼ cup oil mixture and toss to combine. Whisk paprika into remaining oil mixture, then add chicken to oil mixture and toss to coat.

3 Spread vegetable mixture in single layer on rimmed baking sheet, then place chicken, skin side up, on top of vegetables. Bake until chicken registers 160 degrees, 25 to 35 minutes, rotating sheet halfway through baking.

4 Remove skin from chicken and discard if desired. Transfer chicken to serving platter, tent with aluminum foil, and let rest for 5 to 10 minutes. Toss vegetables with any accumulated chicken juices and transfer to platter with chicken. Drizzle ¼ cup yogurt sauce over chicken and vegetables and serve, passing remaining yogurt sauce separately.

nutritious DELICIOUS

PARMESAN CHICKEN WITH WARM ARUGULA, RADICCHIO, AND FENNEL SALAD

2 (6- to 8-ounce) organic boneless, skinless chicken breasts, trimmed, halved horizontally, and pounded ½ inch thick
Salt and pepper
½ cup whole-wheat flour
2 large organic eggs
½ cup 100 percent whole-wheat panko bread crumbs
1 ounce Parmesan cheese, grated (½ cup)
½ teaspoon garlic powder
½ teaspoon dried oregano
5 tablespoons cold-pressed extra-virgin olive oil (see page 35)
1 tablespoon white wine vinegar
1½ teaspoons minced shallot
½ teaspoon Dijon mustard
1 fennel bulb, stalks discarded, bulb halved, cored, and sliced thin
12 ounces cherry tomatoes, halved
½ head radicchio (5 ounces), cored and sliced thin
2 ounces (2 cups) baby arugula

PER SERVING
Cal 460; Total Fat 25g, Sat Fat 5g; Chol 160mg; Sodium 710mg; Total Carbs 28g, Fiber 5g, Total Sugar 6g, Added Sugar 0g; Protein 31g

EXCELLENT SOURCE OF
Protein, Fiber, Vitamin A, Riboflavin, Niacin, Pantothenic Acid, Vitamin B6, Folate, Vitamin C, Vitamin E, Vitamin K, Phosphorus, Potassium, Selenium

why this recipe works • *Chicken Parmesan is often found dripping with oil, smothered with cheese, and served over a mountain of pasta. For a modern, healthier twist, we served our flavorful cutlets with a fresh salad. Instead of a layer of cheese, we added a smaller amount of grated Parmesan to our whole-wheat breading, boosting the flavor with Italian seasonings. Using a nonstick skillet helped us use a moderate amount of oil while still browning the cutlets perfectly. To bring some tomato flavor, we then used our skillet to soften fennel and cherry tomatoes before tossing them with radicchio and baby arugula in a simple vinaigrette for a warm, gently wilted salad. The slight bitterness of the greens paired well with the sweet fennel and juicy chicken.*

1 Adjust oven rack to middle position and heat oven to 200 degrees. Sprinkle each cutlet all over with ⅛ teaspoon salt; let stand at room temperature for 20 minutes.

2 Spread flour in shallow dish. Beat eggs in second shallow dish. Combine panko, Parmesan, garlic powder, and oregano in third shallow dish. Pat chicken dry with paper towels. Working with 1 cutlet at a time, dredge in flour, dip in egg, then coat with panko mixture, pressing gently to adhere.

3 Heat 3 tablespoons oil in 12-inch nonstick skillet over medium heat until shimmering. Add 2 cutlets and cook until chicken is tender, golden brown, and crisp, 3 to 4 minutes per side. Transfer to paper towel–lined plate and place in oven to keep warm. Repeat with remaining 2 cutlets.

4 Whisk vinegar, shallot, mustard, ¼ teaspoon salt, and pinch pepper together in large bowl. Whisking constantly, slowly drizzle in 1 tablespoon oil until emulsified.

5 Wipe out skillet with paper towels. Heat remaining 1 tablespoon oil in now-empty skillet over medium heat until shimmering. Add fennel and cook until softened and just beginning to brown, about 5 minutes; transfer to bowl with vinaigrette.

6 Add tomatoes to now-empty skillet and cook until softened, about 2 minutes; transfer to bowl with fennel. Add radicchio and arugula to bowl and gently toss to combine. Season with salt and pepper to taste and serve with chicken.

main dishes

CRISPY SKILLET TURKEY BURGERS

- 1 pound organic 93 percent lean ground turkey
- 1 cup 100 percent whole-wheat panko bread crumbs
- 2 ounces Monterey jack cheese, shredded (½ cup)
- ½ cup oil-packed sun-dried tomatoes, rinsed, patted dry, and chopped coarse
- ¼ cup organic plain low-fat yogurt
- ¼ cup chopped fresh basil
  Salt and pepper
- 1 tablespoon expeller-pressed canola oil (page 35)
- 4 100 percent whole-wheat hamburger buns, toasted
- 1 tomato, sliced
- 2 ounces (2 cups) baby arugula

why this recipe works • *We love a good burger, and wanted a juicy but nutritious version that we could feel good about eating regularly. Ground turkey, a great lean source of protein, B vitamins, and other nutrients, seemed like a good starting point, but turkey burgers often wind up like dense, dry hockey pucks. We found that mixing in a bit of Monterey Jack cheese went a long way in keeping the burgers moist, and the cheese bits crisped around their edges, creating a flavorful crust. Adding whole-wheat panko and a little yogurt provided structure and kept the burgers from becoming too dense. To perk up the flavor, we liked the sweet tanginess of sun-dried tomatoes and fresh basil—a natural pairing. We cooked the burgers on the stovetop, making them an easy dinner option year-round. Be sure to use 93 percent lean ground turkey, not 99 percent fat-free ground turkey breast, or the burgers will be tough. Serve with Garlic Aïoli (page 152).*

1 Combine turkey, panko, Monterey Jack, sun-dried tomatoes, yogurt, basil, ½ teaspoon salt, and ½ teaspoon pepper in bowl. Using your hands, gently knead mixture until just combined. Pat turkey mixture into four ¾-inch-thick patties, about 4 inches in diameter, and season with salt and pepper.

2 Heat oil in 12-inch nonstick skillet over medium-low heat until shimmering. Add patties and cook until well browned on first side, 5 to 7 minutes. Flip burgers, and continue to cook until second side is well browned and meat registers 160 degrees, 6 to 9 minutes, flipping as needed to ensure even browning. Place burgers on buns, top with tomato and arugula, and serve.

PER BURGER
Cal 500; Total Fat 22g, Sat Fat 6g; Chol 100mg; Sodium 720mg; Total Carbs 42g, Fiber 6g, Total Sugar 5g, Added Sugar 0g; Protein 30g

EXCELLENT SOURCE OF
Protein, Fiber, Vitamin A, Riboflavin, Niacin, Vitamin B6, Vitamin B12, Vitamin C, Vitamin K, Calcium, Iron, Magnesium, Phosphorus, Selenium, Zinc

main dishes

SPICE-RUBBED TURKEY BREAST WITH SOUR ORANGE SAUCE

serves 12

TURKEY

Salt and pepper

2 tablespoons expeller-pressed canola oil (see page 35)

2 teaspoons five-spice powder

1½ teaspoons ground cumin

1 teaspoon garlic powder

¼ teaspoon cayenne pepper

¼ teaspoon ground cardamom

1 (6-pound) organic bone-in whole turkey breast, trimmed of all visible fat

SOUR ORANGE SAUCE

1 tablespoon expeller-pressed canola oil (see page 35)

1 shallot, minced

1 garlic clove, minced

2 cups homemade or low-sodium chicken broth (see page 36)

2 cups orange juice (4 oranges)

2 tablespoons white wine vinegar

1 tablespoon cornstarch

1 tablespoon water

2 teaspoons chopped fresh tarragon

PER SERVING

Cal 320; Total Fat 7g, Sat Fat 1g; Chol 130mg; Sodium 640mg; Total Carbs 6g, Fiber 0g, Total Sugar 4g, Added Sugar 0g; Protein 54g

EXCELLENT SOURCE OF

Protein, Riboflavin, Niacin, Vitamin B6, Vitamin B12, Vitamin C, Phosphorus, Selenium, Zinc

why this recipe works • *As far as roasts go, a bone-in turkey breast is a relatively inexpensive, versatile cut. For a nutritious change of pace from standard gravy and potatoes, we rubbed our turkey with a potent spice paste that provided mellow heat and deep flavor. To crisp skin without drying out meat, we browned the turkey in a Dutch oven before transferring it to roast in a low oven. Instead of building a sauce from drippings, we simmered a bright, sweet-sour sauce using fruit juice, vinegar, and tarragon. Many supermarkets are now selling "hotel-cut" turkey breasts, which still have the wings and rib cage attached. If this is the only type of breast you can find, you will need to remove the wings and cut away the rib cage with kitchen shears before proceeding.*

1 **FOR THE TURKEY** Combine 1½ teaspoons salt, 1 teaspoon pepper, 1 tablespoon oil, five-spice powder, cumin, garlic powder, cayenne, and cardamom in bowl. Using your fingers, gently loosen skin covering breast. Rub paste evenly under skin. Place turkey on large plate, cover with plastic wrap, and refrigerate for at least 6 hours or up to 24 hours.

2 Adjust oven rack to middle position and heat oven to 325 degrees. Heat remaining 1 tablespoon oil in Dutch oven over medium heat until just smoking. Place turkey, skin side down, in Dutch oven and cook, turning breast on its sides as needed, until lightly browned, 8 to 10 minutes.

3 Rotate turkey skin side up and transfer pot to oven. Roast until turkey registers 160 degrees, about 1½ hours. Transfer turkey to carving board, tent with aluminum foil, and let rest for 20 minutes.

4 **FOR THE SOUR ORANGE SAUCE** Meanwhile, heat oil in large saucepan over medium heat until shimmering. Add shallot and cook until softened, about 3 minutes. Add garlic and cook until fragrant, about 30 seconds. Stir in broth, orange juice, and vinegar, increase heat to high, and bring to boil. Cook, stirring occasionally, until sauce is reduced to 1¼ cups, about 20 minutes.

5 Whisk cornstarch and water together in small bowl, then whisk mixture into sauce and cook until thickened, about 1 minute; remove from heat and cover to keep warm.

6 Stir 1 tablespoon turkey pan drippings and tarragon into orange sauce. Season with salt, pepper, and additional vinegar to taste. Remove skin if desired, carve turkey, and serve with sauce.

main dishes

TURKEY CUTLETS WITH BARLEY AND SWISS CHARD

serves 4

> 3 tablespoons cold-pressed
>   extra-virgin olive oil
>   (see page 35)
> ¼ cup finely chopped onion
> 12 ounces Swiss chard, 1 cup
>   chopped stems, leaves cut into
>   1-inch pieces
> 1½ cups pearl barley, rinsed
> 2 garlic cloves, minced
> 2½ cups homemade or low-sodium
>   chicken broth (see page 36)
> 1 teaspoon grated lemon zest,
>   plus 1 lemon, halved and
>   seeded
> 1 ounce Parmesan cheese,
>   grated (½ cup)
>   Salt and pepper
> 6 (4-ounce) organic turkey
>   cutlets, trimmed of all
>   visible fat

why this recipe works • *Seeking to bring more grains into our week-night routine, we wanted to update the traditional chicken-and-rice formula by pairing quick-cooking turkey cutlets with rustic, fiber-packed barley and iron-rich Swiss chard. Since the cutlets cook so quickly, we prepared our barley first, simmering it with aromatics and the chard stems before folding in the chard leaves. To give the turkey bright flavor, we employed a simple trick: We caramelized lemon halves in the cooking oil, infusing it (and thus the cutlets) with flavor. A hint of lemon zest in the barley complemented the lemony oil. And just a half cup of Parmesan added a salty richness, tying the dish together. Do not substitute hulled, hull-less, quick-cooking, or presteamed barley for the pearl barley in this recipe.*

1 Heat 2 tablespoons oil in large saucepan over medium-high heat until shimmering. Add onion and chard stems and cook until softened, about 5 minutes. Stir in barley and garlic and cook until barley is lightly toasted and fragrant, about 3 minutes.

2 Stir in broth and bring to simmer. Reduce heat to low, cover, and simmer until barley is tender and broth is absorbed, 20 to 40 minutes.

3 Fold chard leaves and lemon zest into barley, increase heat to medium-high, and cook, uncovered, stirring gently, until chard is wilted, about 2 minutes. Off heat, stir in ¼ cup Parmesan and season with salt and pepper to taste. Cover to keep warm.

4 Pat cutlets dry with paper towels and season with salt and pepper. Heat 1 teaspoon oil in 12-inch nonstick skillet over medium-high heat until shimmering. Add lemon halves, cut side down, and cook until browned, about 2 minutes; set aside. Heat remaining 2 teaspoons oil in now-empty skillet until shimmering. Add cutlets to skillet and cook until well browned and tender, about 2 minutes per side. Off heat, squeeze lemon halves over cutlets. Serve with barley mixture, sprinkling individual portions with remaining ¼ cup Parmesan.

PER SERVING
Cal 610; Total Fat 15g, Sat Fat 2.5g;
Chol 75mg; Sodium 780mg; Total
Carbs 63g, Fiber 14g, Total Sugar 1g,
Added Sugar 0g; Protein 57g

EXCELLENT SOURCE OF
Protein, Fiber, Vitamin A,
Vitamin C, Vitamin K, Iron

TURKEY SHEPHERD'S PIE

serves 6

3 tablespoons cold-pressed
  extra-virgin olive oil
  (see page 35)
1 large head cauliflower
  (3 pounds), cored and cut
  into ½-inch pieces
½ cup plus 2 tablespoons water
  Salt and pepper
1 large organic egg, lightly
  beaten
3 tablespoons minced fresh
  chives
1 pound organic 93 percent lean
  ground turkey
¼ teaspoon baking soda
8 ounces cremini mushrooms,
  trimmed and chopped
1 onion, chopped
1 tablespoon tomato paste
2 garlic cloves, minced
¾ cup homemade or low-sodium
  chicken broth (see page 36)
2 carrots, peeled and chopped
2 sprigs fresh thyme
1 tablespoon Worcestershire
  sauce
1 tablespoon cornstarch

PER SERVING
Cal 250; Total Fat 10g, Sat Fat 3g;
Chol 60mg; Sodium 710mg; Total
Carbs 19g, Fiber 6g, Total Sugar 8g,
Added Sugar 0g; Protein 26g

EXCELLENT SOURCE OF
Protein, Fiber, Vitamin A,
Riboflavin, Pantothenic Acid,
Vitamin B6, Folate, Vitamin C,
Vitamin K, Manganese, Potassium

why this recipe works • *We wanted to refashion shepherd's pie into a high-nutrient dinner while keeping its hearty comforts. Ground turkey promised a healthy start, but keeping it tender required refraining from browning it. Instead, we browned mushrooms and onions, ensuring a rich gravy. For a nutrient-dense topping, swapping mashed russet potatoes for sweet seemed smart, but overwhelmed tasters. Mild, vitamin-packed cauliflower proved a better choice. We cooked a head of chopped florets until soft and pureed them until velvety smooth. Then we gently bound the mixture with an egg and stirred in chives for flavor. Be sure to use 93 percent lean ground turkey, not 99 percent fat-free ground turkey breast, or the filling will be tough. You will need a 10-inch broiler-safe skillet.*

1 Heat 2 tablespoons oil in Dutch oven over medium-low heat until shimmering. Add cauliflower and cook, stirring occasionally, until softened and beginning to brown, 10 to 12 minutes. Stir in ½ cup water and ¾ teaspoon salt, cover, and cook until cauliflower falls apart easily when poked with fork, about 10 minutes.

2 Transfer cauliflower and any remaining liquid to food processor and let cool for 5 minutes. Process until smooth, about 45 seconds. Transfer to large bowl and stir in beaten egg and chives; set aside.

3 Meanwhile, toss turkey, 1 tablespoon water, ¼ teaspoon salt, ¼ teaspoon pepper, and baking soda in bowl until thoroughly combined. Set aside for 20 minutes.

4 Heat remaining 1 tablespoon oil in broiler-safe 10-inch skillet over medium heat until shimmering. Add mushrooms and onion and cook, stirring occasionally, until liquid has evaporated and fond begins to form on bottom of skillet, 10 to 12 minutes. Stir in tomato paste and garlic and cook until bottom of skillet is dark brown, about 2 minutes.

5 Add broth, carrots, thyme, and Worcestershire and bring to simmer, scraping up any browned bits. Reduce heat to medium-low, pinch off turkey in ½-inch pieces and add to skillet, and bring to gentle simmer. Cover and cook until turkey is cooked through, 8 to 10 minutes, stirring and breaking up meat halfway through cooking.

6 Whisk cornstarch and remaining 1 tablespoon water together in small bowl, then stir mixture into filling and continue to simmer until thickened, about 1 minute. Discard thyme sprigs and season with salt and pepper to taste.

7 Adjust oven rack 5 inches from broiler element and heat broiler. Transfer cauliflower mixture to large zipper-lock bag. Using scissors, snip 1-inch off filled corner. Squeezing bag, pipe mixture in even layer over filling, making sure to cover entire surface. Smooth mixture with back of spoon, then use tines of fork to make ridges over surface. Place skillet on aluminum foil–lined rimmed baking sheet and broil until topping is golden brown and crusty and filling is bubbly, 10 to 15 minutes. Let cool for 10 minutes before serving.

TURKEY MEATBALLS WITH LEMONY BROWN RICE AND SUN-DRIED TOMATOES

serves 4

- 1 slice hearty 100 percent whole-wheat sandwich bread, torn into 1-inch pieces
- 1 pound organic 93 percent lean ground turkey
- 1 large organic egg
- 4 scallions, white and green parts separated and sliced thin
- ¼ cup chopped fresh parsley
- 2 teaspoons grated lemon zest plus 2 tablespoons juice
  Salt and pepper
- 2 tablespoons cold-pressed extra-virgin olive oil (see page 35)
- 1 cup long-grain brown rice, rinsed
- 3 garlic cloves, minced
- 4 cups homemade or low-sodium chicken broth (see page 36)
- ½ cup oil-packed sun-dried tomatoes, rinsed, patted dry, and sliced thin
- ¼ cup grated Parmesan cheese

PER SERVING
Cal 480; Total Fat 14g, Sat Fat 4.5g; Chol 95mg; Sodium 790mg; Total Carbs 46g, Fiber 4g, Total Sugar 2g, Added Sugar 0g; Protein 41g

EXCELLENT SOURCE OF
Protein, Thiamine, Niacin, Vitamin C, Vitamin K, Manganese, Phosphorus

why this recipe works • *A skillet of meatballs and rice makes for a simple, hearty meal, and using ground turkey and brown rice ensures it delivers plenty of nutrients. To perk up the flavor of these mild-mannered ingredients, we used a heavy dose of lemon, garlic, scallions, and parsley. Cooking the brown rice in chicken broth instead of water intensified its richness, adding a meaty backbone to the dish. We scattered sliced sun-dried tomatoes atop the finished dish to add a beautiful pop of red and a sweet, chewy bite. A mere ¼ cup of Parmesan cheese contributed a salty, umami finish. Be sure to use 93 percent lean ground turkey, not 99 percent fat-free ground turkey breast, or the meatballs will be tough. You will need a 12-inch nonstick skillet with a tight-fitting lid.*

1 Pulse bread in food processor to fine crumbs, 10 to 15 pulses; transfer to large bowl. Add turkey, egg, 3 tablespoons scallion greens, 2 tablespoons parsley, 1½ teaspoons lemon zest, ½ teaspoon salt, and ½ teaspoon pepper to bowl and using your hands, gently knead mixture until combined. Using wet hands, roll heaping tablespoons of meat mixture into meatballs and transfer to baking sheet. (You should have 20 meatballs.) Cover with greased plastic wrap and refrigerate for 15 minutes.

2 Heat oil in 12-inch nonstick skillet over medium-high heat until shimmering. Add meatballs and cook until well browned all over, 5 to 7 minutes. Transfer meatballs to paper towel–lined plate.

3 Return now-empty skillet to medium-high heat. Stir in rice and cook until edges of rice begin to turn translucent, about 1 minute. Add scallion whites and garlic and cook until fragrant, about 1 minute. Stir in broth and remaining ½ teaspoon lemon zest and juice and bring to boil.

4 Reduce heat to medium-low, cover, and cook for 15 minutes. Return meatballs to skillet, cover, and cook until rice is tender and meatballs are cooked through, about 15 minutes.

5 Off heat, scatter sun-dried tomatoes over rice and let sit, covered, for 5 minutes. Sprinkle with Parmesan, remaining scallion greens, and remaining 2 tablespoons parsley. Serve.

main dishes

PUMPKIN TURKEY CHILI

serves 8

1 pound organic 93 percent lean ground turkey

2 cups plus 1 tablespoon water
  Salt and pepper

¼ teaspoon baking soda

4 dried ancho chiles, stemmed, seeded, and torn into 1-inch pieces

1½ tablespoons ground cumin

1½ teaspoons ground coriander

1½ teaspoons dried oregano

1½ teaspoons paprika

1 (28-ounce) can whole peeled tomatoes

2 tablespoons cold-pressed extra-virgin olive oil (see page 35)

2 onions, chopped fine

2 red bell peppers, stemmed, seeded, and cut into ½-inch pieces

6 garlic cloves, minced

1 cup canned unsweetened pumpkin puree

2 (15-ounce) cans black beans, rinsed

why this recipe works • *Beef chili can turn out heavy and greasy, but lighter turkey chilis often lack depth and richness. We wanted a nutrient-filled turkey chili that wouldn't leave us missing the beef. To safeguard against rubbery turkey, we treated the meat with salt and baking soda, which helped it hold onto moisture. To give our dish a smoky, aromatic backbone, we made our own chili powder by grinding toasted ancho chiles, cumin, coriander, paprika, and oregano. We loaded the chili with red bell peppers (full of vitamin C) and black beans for fiber and protein. Still, our chili needed more richness. We found the answer in a unique ingredient—pumpkin puree. Folding this into the chili gave it a rich, silky texture and subtle squash-y flavor, along with a big dose of vitamin A, without being overly sweet. Be sure to use 93 percent lean ground turkey, not 99 percent fat-free ground turkey breast, or the turkey will be tough. Serve with low-fat Greek yogurt, lime wedges, avocado, cilantro, and toasted pepitas.*

1 Toss turkey, 1 tablespoon water, ¼ teaspoon salt, and baking soda in bowl until thoroughly combined. Set aside for 20 minutes.

2 Meanwhile, toast anchos in Dutch oven over medium-high heat, stirring frequently, until fragrant, 4 to 6 minutes, reducing heat if anchos begin to smoke. Transfer to food processor and let cool about 5 minutes.

3 Add cumin, coriander, oregano, paprika, and 1 teaspoon pepper to food processor with anchos and process until finely ground, about 2 minutes; transfer mixture to bowl. Process tomatoes and their juice in now-empty food processor until smooth, about 30 seconds.

4 Heat oil in now-empty pot over medium heat until shimmering. Add onions, bell peppers, and ½ teaspoon salt and cook until softened, 8 to 10 minutes. Increase heat to medium-high, add turkey, and cook, breaking up meat with wooden spoon, until no pink remains, 4 to 6 minutes. Stir in spice mixture and garlic and cook until fragrant, about 30 seconds. Stir in pureed tomatoes, pumpkin, and remaining 2 cups water, and bring to simmer. Reduce heat to low, cover, and simmer gently, stirring occasionally, for 1 hour.

5 Stir in beans, cover, and continue to cook until slightly thickened, about 45 minutes. (If chili begins to stick to bottom of pot or looks too thick, stir in extra water as needed.) Season with salt to taste. Serve.

PER SERVING
Cal 230; Total Fat 6g, Sat Fat 1.5g; Chol 20mg; Sodium 700mg; Total Carbs 26g, Fiber 8g, Total Sugar 6g, Added Sugar 0g; Protein 21g

EXCELLENT SOURCE OF
Protein, Fiber, Vitamin A, Vitamin B6, Vitamin C, Iron

main dishes

PULLED BBQ TURKEY WITH RED CABBAGE SLAW

Salt and pepper

1 (1¾- to 2-pound) organic boneless, skinless split turkey breast, trimmed of all visible fat and quartered

2 tablespoons cold-pressed extra-virgin olive oil (see page 35)

1 onion, chopped fine

1 garlic clove, minced

1 teaspoon chili powder

¼ teaspoon cayenne pepper

1 cup ketchup

¼ cup cider vinegar

2 tablespoons Worcestershire sauce

2 tablespoons Dijon mustard

1 tablespoon molasses

1 teaspoon hot sauce

3 cups shredded red cabbage

1 carrot, peeled and shredded

2 tablespoons chopped fresh parsley

why this recipe works • *Slow barbecuing might work well for fatty cuts like pork shoulder, but for tender pull-apart lean turkey breast, we'd need some new tricks. First we pulled together a homemade tangy ketchup and vinegar barbecue sauce that allowed us to control the sugar; a splash of Worcestershire helped to boost the umami factor. To keep our turkey moist, we brined it and gently braised it in our sauce, which made the meat more flavorful. A quick slaw of bright, crunchy red cabbage and carrot provided great color and textural contrast, not to mention vitamins A and C. If using a kosher turkey breast, do not brine in step 1; simply season with salt after patting turkey dry. Serve with pickles on toasted 100 percent whole-wheat hamburger buns.*

1 Dissolve 6 tablespoons salt in 3 quarts cold water in large container. Submerge turkey in brine, cover, and refrigerate for 30 minutes. Remove turkey from brine; pat dry with paper towels.

2 Adjust oven rack to lower-middle position and heat oven to 325 degrees. Heat 1 tablespoon oil in Dutch oven over medium heat until shimmering. Add onion and cook until softened, about 5 minutes. Stir in garlic, chili powder, and cayenne and cook until fragrant, about 30 seconds. Whisk in ketchup, 1 tablespoon vinegar, Worcestershire, mustard, molasses, and hot sauce and bring to simmer. Add turkey to sauce in pot and turn to coat. Cover pot, transfer to oven, and cook until turkey registers 160 degrees, 22 to 28 minutes.

3 Transfer turkey to cutting board and let cool slightly, about 5 minutes. Using two forks, shred turkey into bite-size pieces. Meanwhile, bring sauce to gentle simmer over medium heat and cook, stirring often, until sauce is slightly thickened and measures 1¾ cups, about 5 minutes.

4 Stir shredded turkey and any accumulated juices into sauce and cook until heated through, about 1 minute. Season with salt and pepper to taste.

5 Whisk remaining 3 tablespoons vinegar and remaining 1 tablespoon oil together in bowl. Add cabbage, carrot, and parsley and toss to combine. Season with salt and pepper to taste. Serve pulled turkey with cabbage slaw.

PER SERVING (WITHOUT BUN)
Cal 210; Total Fat 5g, Sat Fat 1g; Chol 55mg; Sodium 750mg; Total Carbs 15g, Fiber 1g, Total Sugar 13g, Added Sugar 2g; Protein 24g

EXCELLENT SOURCE OF
Protein, Vitamin A, Niacin, Vitamin B6, Vitamin C, Vitamin K, Phosphorus, Selenium

nutritious DELICIOUS

GRILLED FLANK STEAK WITH TOMATO, ORANGE, AND AVOCADO

serves 6

1 orange
1 avocado, halved, pitted, and cut into ½-inch pieces
6 ounces cherry tomatoes, quartered
1 shallot, halved and sliced thin
2 tablespoons minced fresh cilantro
1 serrano chile, stemmed, seeded, and minced
4 teaspoons lime juice
Salt and pepper
1 (1½-pound) grass-fed flank steak, trimmed of all visible fat
¼ teaspoon cayenne pepper

why this recipe works • *Most of us eat more red meat than we need to, but that doesn't mean it's not a great source of protein and nutrients, including hard-to-get vitamin B12. We like flank steak because it's lean, tender, and quick-cooking, and we opted for grass-fed meat, which is especially lean (and has a fat makeup that is higher in omega-3 fatty acids). For a perfectly grilled steak, we used a modified two-level fire, a high-heat grilling method that charred the beef and gave it plenty of grill flavor, but kept the inside medium-rare and juicy. For a topping, we assembled a quick salsa-like mixture of oranges and tomatoes (both high in vitamin C and antioxidants) for sweetness and acidity, balanced with rich, buttery avocado. A serrano chile added pleasant heat, while fresh cilantro, shallot, and lime juice tied the salsa together. Grass-fed beef is leaner than conventional grain-fed beef and is prone to overcooking, so be sure to start checking for doneness early.*

1 Cut away peel and pith from orange. Quarter orange, then slice crosswise into ½-inch-thick pieces. Combine orange, avocado, tomatoes, shallot, cilantro, and serrano in bowl. Add lime juice and ¼ teaspoon salt and gently toss to combine; cover and set aside.

2A FOR A CHARCOAL GRILL Open bottom vent completely. Light large chimney starter filled with charcoal briquettes (6 quarts). When top coals are partially covered with ash, pour evenly over half of grill. Set cooking grate in place, cover, and open lid vent completely. Heat grill until hot, about 5 minutes.

2B FOR A GAS GRILL Turn all burners to high, cover, and heat grill until hot, about 15 minutes. Leave primary burner on high and turn off other burner(s).

3 Clean and oil cooking grate. Pat steak dry with paper towels, season with salt and pepper, then sprinkle evenly with cayenne. Place steak over hot part of grill and cook until beginning to char and beads of moisture appear on outer edges of meat, 5 to 6 minutes. Flip steak and continue to cook on second side until charred and meat registers 120 to 125 degrees (for medium-rare), about 5 minutes. Transfer steak to cutting board, tent loosely with aluminum foil, and let rest for 10 minutes. Slice steak thin against grain. Serve with tomato mixture.

PER SERVING
Cal 260; Total Fat 14g, Sat Fat 4.5g; Chol 75mg; Sodium 360mg; Total Carbs 8g, Fiber 3g, Total Sugar 4g, Added Sugar 0g; Protein 25g

EXCELLENT SOURCE OF
Protein, Niacin, Vitamin B6, Vitamin B12, Vitamin C, Phosphorus, Selenium, Zinc

nutritious DELICIOUS

BEEF STIR-FRY WITH BOK CHOY AND GREEN BEANS

serves 6

¼ cup plus 1 tablespoon water
¼ teaspoon baking soda
1 pound grass-fed flank steak, trimmed of all visible fat, cut with grain into 2-inch strips, each strip cut crosswise against grain into ¼-inch-thick slices
3 tablespoons dry sherry or Chinese rice wine
2 tablespoons low-sodium soy sauce
1 tablespoon cornstarch
2 tablespoons expeller-pressed canola oil (see page 35)
3 garlic cloves, minced
1 tablespoon grated fresh ginger
1 tablespoon oyster sauce
2 teaspoons rice vinegar
2 teaspoons coarsely ground pepper
1½ teaspoons expeller-pressed toasted sesame oil (see page 35)
1 pound bok choy, stalks and greens separated, stalks cut on bias into ¼-inch slices and greens cut into ½-inch strips
8 ounces green beans, trimmed and cut into 2-inch pieces
1 carrot, peeled and shredded

PER SERVING
Cal 210; Total Fat 11g, Sat Fat 2.5g; Chol 50mg; Sodium 410mg; Total Carbs 8g, Fiber 2g, Total Sugar 3g, Added Sugar 0g; Protein 19g

EXCELLENT SOURCE OF
Protein, Vitamin A, Niacin, Vitamin B6, Vitamin C, Vitamin K, Phosphorus, Selenium, Zinc

why this recipe works • *Chinese restaurant stir-fries are beloved for their thin strips of meat in succulent sauce, but all too often the meat is chewy, the sauce is loaded with sodium, and the vegetables are few and far between. To boost the nutritional profile of beef stir-fry, we first used more vegetables than meat: vitamin K–rich bok choy, carrots, and green beans provided color, crispness, and a little sweetness. Lean grass-fed flank steak delivered plenty of protein, great beef flavor, and a moderate chew. To tenderize it, we soaked the meat briefly in a mild baking soda solution. Cornstarch worked double duty, preventing the meat from drying out and thickening the sauce. Serve with steamed brown rice.*

1 Combine 1 tablespoon water and baking soda in large bowl. Add beef, tossing to coat, and set aside for 5 minutes.

2 Whisk 1 tablespoon sherry, 1 tablespoon soy sauce, and 1½ teaspoons cornstarch together in small bowl. Add soy sauce mixture to beef, tossing to coat, and set aside for 15 to 30 minutes. Combine 2 teaspoons canola oil, garlic, and ginger in small bowl.

3 Whisk remaining ¼ cup water, remaining 2 tablespoons sherry, remaining 1 tablespoon soy sauce, remaining 1½ teaspoons cornstarch, oyster sauce, vinegar, pepper, and sesame oil together in separate bowl.

4 Heat 1 teaspoon canola oil in 12-inch nonstick skillet over high heat until just smoking. Add half of beef in single layer and cook without stirring for 1 minute. Continue to cook, stirring occasionally, until spotty brown on both sides, about 1 minute longer; transfer to clean bowl. Repeat with remaining beef and 1 teaspoon canola oil.

5 Heat remaining 2 teaspoons canola oil in now-empty skillet over high heat until just smoking. Add bok choy stalks and green beans and cook, stirring occasionally, until vegetables are spotty brown and crisp-tender, about 5 minutes. Push vegetables to sides of skillet. Add garlic mixture to center and cook, mashing mixture into skillet, until fragrant, 30 to 60 seconds. Stir mixture into vegetables. Stir bok choy greens, carrot, and browned beef into vegetable mixture in skillet.

6 Whisk sauce to recombine, then add to skillet and cook, stirring constantly, until sauce has thickened, about 30 seconds. Serve immediately.

main dishes

175

THAI GRILLED-STEAK SALAD

serves 6

- 1 teaspoon paprika
- 1 teaspoon cayenne pepper
- 1 tablespoon white rice
- 3 tablespoons lime juice (2 limes)
- 2 tablespoons fish sauce
- 2 tablespoons water
- ½ teaspoon sugar
- 1 (1½-pound) grass-fed flank steak, trimmed of all visible fat
  Salt and coarsely ground white pepper
- 1½ cups fresh mint leaves, torn
- 1½ cups fresh cilantro leaves
- 4 shallots, sliced thin
- 1 Thai chile, stemmed and sliced into thin rounds
- 1 seedless English cucumber, sliced ¼ inch thick on bias

PER SERVING
Cal 220; Total Fat 8g, Sat Fat 3g; Chol 80mg; Sodium 500mg; Total Carbs 11g, Fiber 3g, Total Sugar 3g, Added Sugar 0g; Protein 27g

EXCELLENT SOURCE OF
Protein, Vitamin A, Niacin, Vitamin B6, Vitamin B12, Vitamin K, Iron, Manganese, Phosphorus, Selenium, Zinc

why this recipe works • *A steak salad is a great way to enjoy a smaller amount of meat at dinner. We were inspired by Thai grilled beef salad, which combines charred steak with nutrient-rich herbs and a bright, bracing dressing. We grilled flank steak over a modified two-level fire, which charred the beef but kept the inside juicy. We also made our own toasted rice powder, a traditional ingredient that gave the salad a fuller body. It's integral to the texture and flavor of the dish. Toasted rice powder (kao kua) can also be found in many Asian markets; substitute 1 tablespoon of rice powder for the white rice. If a fresh Thai chile is unavailable, substitute half of a serrano chile. Grass-fed beef is leaner than conventional grain-fed beef and is prone to overcooking, so be sure to start checking for doneness early. Serve this salad with brown rice if desired.*

1 Heat paprika and cayenne in 8-inch skillet over medium heat; cook, shaking pan, until fragrant, about 1 minute. Transfer to small bowl. Return now-empty skillet to medium-high heat, add rice, and toast, stirring frequently, until deep golden brown, about 5 minutes. Transfer to second small bowl and let cool for 5 minutes. Grind rice with spice grinder, mini food processor, or mortar and pestle until it resembles fine meal, 10 to 30 seconds (you should have about 1 tablespoon rice powder).

2 Whisk lime juice, fish sauce, water, sugar, and ¼ teaspoon toasted paprika mixture together in large bowl; set aside.

3A **FOR A CHARCOAL GRILL** Open bottom vent completely. Light large chimney starter filled with charcoal briquettes (6 quarts). When top coals are partially covered with ash, pour evenly over half of grill. Set cooking grate in place, cover, and open lid vent completely. Heat grill until hot, about 5 minutes.

3B **FOR A GAS GRILL** Turn all burners to high, cover, and heat grill until hot, about 15 minutes. Leave primary burner on high and turn off other burner(s).

4 Clean and oil cooking grate. Pat steak dry with paper towels, then season with salt and white pepper. Place steak over hot part of grill and cook until beginning to char and beads of moisture appear on outer edges of meat, 5 to 6 minutes. Flip steak and continue to cook on second side until charred and meat registers 120 to 125 degrees (for medium-rare), about 5 minutes. Transfer steak to cutting board, tent loosely with aluminum foil, and let rest for 10 minutes (or let cool completely, about 1 hour).

5 Slice steak about ¼ inch thick against grain on bias. Transfer steak to bowl with lime juice mixture. Add mint, cilantro, shallots, chile, and half of rice powder; toss to combine. Line platter with cucumber slices. Place steak mixture on top of cucumber and serve, passing remaining toasted paprika mixture and remaining rice powder separately.

THAI RED CURRY WITH LENTILS AND TOFU

serves 4

14 ounces extra-firm tofu, cut into ½-inch pieces
   Salt and pepper
1 tablespoon expeller-pressed canola oil (see page 35)
1 tablespoon Thai red curry paste
2½ cups water
2 tablespoons fish sauce
1 cup lentilles du Puy, picked over and rinsed
½ cup canned coconut milk
1 red bell pepper, stemmed, seeded, and cut into ¼-inch strips
4 ounces snow peas, strings removed and halved crosswise
½ cup coarsely chopped fresh basil
1 tablespoon lime juice
2 scallions, sliced thin

why this recipe works • *Thai curries embrace a delicate balance of flavors, textures, temperatures, and colors to produce lively, satisfying meals. Though fresh tasting (thanks to potent herbs and aromatics), restaurant renditions can be high in saturated fat due to hefty amounts of coconut milk, especially when made with red meat. We wanted to create a Thai-style red curry that wasn't swimming in coconut milk and featured fiber-rich lentils and tofu instead. We started by cooking the lentils in an aromatic red curry broth. When the lentils were tender but still slightly al dente and had absorbed most of the liquid, we incorporated a bit of coconut milk to create a rich, fragrant sauce. To contrast the nutty earthiness of the lentils, we added vibrant red bell pepper slices, snow peas, and cubes of tofu at the very end, simply warming them through to maintain the vegetables' color and crisp-fresh texture. A generous handful of fresh basil and a sprinkle of scallions gave the dish a brisk, heady finish. Lentilles du Puy, also called French green lentils, are our first choice, but brown, black, or regular green lentils are fine, too (cooking times will vary). Do not use light coconut milk. You will need a 12-inch skillet with a tight-fitting lid.*

1 Spread tofu on paper towel–lined baking sheet and let drain for 20 minutes. Gently press dry with paper towels and season with salt and pepper.

2 Heat oil in 12-inch skillet over medium heat until shimmering. Add curry paste and cook, stirring constantly, until fragrant, about 1 minute. Stir in water, fish sauce, and lentils and bring to simmer. Cover, reduce heat to low, and simmer gently, stirring occasionally, until lentils are tender and about two-thirds of liquid has been absorbed, 30 to 35 minutes.

3 Stir in coconut milk until well combined. Add tofu, bell pepper, and snow peas, and increase heat to medium-high. Cover and cook, stirring occasionally, until tofu is warmed through and vegetables are crisp-tender, about 2 minutes.

4 Off heat, stir in basil and lime juice. Season with salt to taste and sprinkle with scallions. Serve.

STIR-FRIED TEMPEH WITH ORANGE SAUCE

serves 4

SAUCE

- ¼ cup dry sherry or Chinese rice wine
- ¼ cup water
- 2 tablespoons low-sodium soy sauce
- 1 tablespoon cornstarch
- 1 tablespoon grated fresh ginger
- 3 garlic cloves, minced
- 1½ teaspoons expeller-pressed toasted sesame oil (see page 35)
- ¼ teaspoon grated orange zest, plus ¾ cup juice (2 oranges)

STIR-FRY

- 2 tablespoons expeller-pressed canola oil (see page 35)
- 12 ounces tempeh, cut into ½-inch pieces
- 2 tablespoons low-sodium soy sauce
- 1 pound broccoli, florets cut into ½-inch pieces, stalks peeled, halved, and sliced thin
- 1 red bell pepper, stemmed, seeded, and cut into ¼-inch-wide strips
- 6 scallions, sliced thin on bias

PER SERVING

Cal 340; Total Fat 19g, Sat Fat 3g; Chol 0mg; Sodium 580mg; Total Carbs 25g, Fiber 4g, Total Sugar 7g, Added Sugar 0g; Protein 23g

EXCELLENT SOURCE OF

Protein, Vitamin A, Riboflavin, Niacin, Vitamin B6, Folate, Vitamin C, Vitamin K, Copper, Iron, Magnesium, Manganese, Phosphorus, Potassium

why this recipe works • *The stir-fry skillet is a place to get creative. Pick a protein and your favorite vegetables; practically any combo you can dream up will work if you cook each component properly. Unfortunately, when we dreamed up a nutritious-sounding tempeh and vegetable stir-fry, we got pale chunks of tempeh amidst mushy veggies. Not exactly our vision of golden-brown tempeh and crisp vegetables in a tangy-sweet sauce. First we perfected the tempeh, a nutrient-dense, meat-free protein option, searing it in a hot skillet with soy sauce to give it a flavor boost and a crisp brown crust. We added red bell pepper for sweetness and crunch—not to mention plenty of vitamin C. Iron-rich broccoli florets also stood up well to the quick, high heat. As for the sauce, we knew we needed a sweeter sauce to stand up to the slightly bitter tempeh but were wary of adding sugar. A full-bodied sweet-and-sour sauce made with orange juice tamed the tempeh and contributed just enough sweetness. Sliced scallions gave our stir-fry a mild bite. Serve with brown rice and toasted sesame seeds.*

1 **FOR THE SAUCE** Whisk all ingredients together in bowl.

2 **FOR THE STIR-FRY** Heat 1 tablespoon oil in 12-inch nonstick skillet over high heat until just smoking. Add tempeh and soy sauce, and cook, stirring occasionally, until well browned, 4 to 6 minutes; transfer to plate.

3 Return now-empty skillet to high heat, add remaining 1 tablespoon oil, and heat until just smoking. Add broccoli and bell pepper, and cook, stirring occasionally, until vegetables are spotty brown and crisp-tender, about 4 minutes.

4 Stir in browned tempeh. Whisk sauce to recombine, then add to skillet and cook, stirring constantly, until sauce is thickened, about 30 seconds. Off heat, sprinkle with scallions and serve.

VEGETABLE LASAGNA

serves 12

TOMATO SAUCE

- 1 (28-ounce) can crushed tomatoes
- 1 (14.5-ounce) can diced tomatoes, drained
- ¼ cup fresh basil leaves
- 1 tablespoon cold-pressed extra-virgin olive oil (see page 35)
- 2 garlic cloves, minced
- ½ teaspoon salt

LASAGNA

- 12 100 percent whole-wheat lasagna noodles
  Salt and pepper
- 8 ounces (8 cups) baby spinach
- ⅓ cup fresh basil leaves, plus 2 tablespoons chopped
- 2 tablespoons cold-pressed extra-virgin olive oil (see page 35)
- 8 ounces (1 cup) part-skim ricotta cheese
- 1 large organic egg
- 1 ounce Parmesan cheese, grated (½ cup)
- 2 pounds eggplant, peeled and cut into ½-inch pieces
- 1½ pounds cremini mushrooms, trimmed and sliced thin
- 4 garlic cloves, minced
- 4 ounces whole-milk mozzarella cheese, shredded (1 cup)

why this recipe works • *Lasagna is a comfort food classic, but with layers of white pasta, cheese, and ground meat, it's not the most nutritious of dishes. We wanted to make over this Italian favorite with a stronger nutrient profile. We started with a base of vegetables—eggplant and mushrooms; a combination of microwaving and sautéing eliminated excess moisture and deepened flavors. Swapping white lasagna noodles for whole-wheat gave us additional fiber. To keep our sauce simple, we pureed canned tomatoes with basil and garlic. We didn't want to lose the cheesy layers that make lasagna so appealing, but we also wanted to cut back on saturated fat. So in lieu of the standard mozzarella layer, we blitzed part-skim ricotta with spinach and basil in a food processor to get a bright green, soufflé-like filling. A mix of mozzarella and Parmesan made the perfect topping. Our winning whole-wheat lasagna noodles, Bionaturae Organic 100% Whole-Wheat, require cooking in batches. Be sure to follow box instructions carefully.*

1 **FOR THE TOMATO SAUCE** Process all ingredients in food processor until smooth, about 30 seconds. Transfer to bowl and set aside. (Sauce can be refrigerated for up to 1 day).

2 **FOR THE LASAGNA** Bring 4 quarts water to boil in large pot. Add lasagna noodles and 1 tablespoon salt and cook, stirring often, until just tender. Drain noodles and set aside. Pulse spinach, basil leaves, and 1 tablespoon oil together in clean, dry food processor bowl until finely chopped, scraping down sides of bowl as needed, about 6 pulses. Add ricotta, egg, ¼ cup Parmesan, ½ teaspoon salt, and ¼ teaspoon pepper and pulse until just combined, about 6 pulses; transfer to bowl and set aside.

3 Adjust oven rack to middle position and heat oven to 375 degrees. Line large plate with double layer of coffee filters and spray with canola oil spray. Toss eggplant with ½ teaspoon salt and spread evenly over coffee filters. Microwave eggplant, uncovered, until dry to touch and slightly shriveled, 10 to 12 minutes, tossing once halfway through cooking.

4 Heat remaining 1 tablespoon oil in 12-inch nonstick skillet over medium-high heat until shimmering. Add mushrooms and ¼ teaspoon salt, and cook, covered, until mushrooms release their liquid, 6 to 8 minutes. Uncover, increase heat to high, stir in eggplant, and cook until vegetables are lightly browned, 8 to 10 minutes. Stir in garlic and cook until fragrant, about 30 seconds; remove skillet from heat.

5 Spread 1½ cups tomato sauce evenly over bottom of broiler-safe 13 by 9-inch baking dish. Arrange 4 noodles on top of sauce (noodles will overlap). Spread half of ricotta mixture over noodles in even layer. Spread half of eggplant mixture over ricotta. Repeat layering with 1 cup sauce, 4 noodles, remaining half of ricotta and remaining half of eggplant mixture. For final layer, arrange remaining 4 noodles on top and cover completely with remaining 1½ cups tomato sauce. Sprinkle with mozzarella and remaining ¼ cup Parmesan.

6 Cover dish tightly with greased aluminum foil and bake until edges are just bubbling, about 35 minutes, rotating dish halfway through baking. Uncover baking dish and heat broiler. Broil lasagna until cheese is golden brown, 4 to 6 minutes. Let lasagna cool for 20 minutes, then sprinkle with remaining 2 tablespoons basil. Serve.

PER SERVING
Cal 230; Total Fat 9g, Sat Fat 3.5g; Chol 30mg; Sodium 700mg; Total Carbs 27g, Fiber 7g, Total Sugar 7g, Added Sugar 0g; Protein 12g

EXCELLENT SOURCE OF
Protein, Fiber, Vitamin A, Riboflavin, Niacin, Vitamin C, Vitamin K, Calcium, Manganese, Selenium

main dishes

SWISS CHARD MACARONI AND CHEESE

serves 4

- ¼ cup 100 percent whole-wheat panko bread crumbs
- 2 tablespoons expeller-pressed canola oil (see page 35)
- ⅛ teaspoon cayenne pepper
- 2 tablespoons grated Parmesan cheese
- 12 ounces Swiss chard, stemmed and cut into 1-inch pieces
- 8 ounces 100 percent whole-wheat elbow macaroni
  Salt and pepper
- 1 tablespoon all-purpose flour
- ¾ teaspoon dry mustard
- 2 cups organic 1 percent low-fat milk
- 4 ounces Gruyère cheese, shredded (1 cup)
- 2 ounces cream cheese, softened

PER SERVING

Cal 530; Total Fat 25g, Sat Fat 10g; Chol 45mg; Sodium 730mg; Total Carbs 56g, Fiber 7g, Total Sugar 9g, Added Sugar 0g; Protein 25g

EXCELLENT SOURCE OF

Protein, Fiber, Vitamin A, Thiamine, Riboflavin, Niacin, Vitamin C, Vitamin K, Calcium, Copper, Iron, Magnesium, Manganese, Phosphorus, Potassium, Selenium, Zinc

why this recipe works • *It's hard to eat healthy all the time, especially when a craving strikes for something comforting and a little decadent—such as macaroni and cheese. Unfortunately, most nutritious riffs on the cheesy classic are simply blander versions of the original. We vowed to create a macaroni and cheese we'd actually enjoy eating that also delivered good nutritional benefits. Switching from white pasta and panko bread crumbs to whole-wheat versions was a simple start that provided more fiber and protein. We toasted the panko to crisp it up before combining it with Parmesan to make a crunchy, savory topping. We also cooked a hearty 12 ounces of vitamin K–rich Swiss chard and stirred it in just before serving to bulk up the meal. As for our cheese sauce, simply switching to 1 percent low-fat milk led to a chalky sauce, but we found that stirring in a couple ounces of cream cheese turned it velvety and ultra-creamy. Our macaroni and cheese delivered more greens than pasta but tasted comforting and rich, and it was packed with plenty of nutrients. We love the nutty flavor of Gruyère in this recipe, but if you prefer a milder cheese sauce, you can substitute sharp cheddar.*

1 Stir panko, 1 teaspoon oil, and pinch cayenne together in 8-inch nonstick skillet until combined. Cook over medium heat, stirring frequently, until fragrant and crisp, about 3 minutes. Off heat, transfer panko to bowl and stir in Parmesan.

2 Heat 2 teaspoons oil in large saucepan over medium heat until shimmering. Add Swiss chard and cook until wilted, about 4 minutes; transfer to bowl. Bring 2 quarts water to boil in now-empty pot. Add macaroni and 1½ teaspoons salt and cook, stirring often, until tender; drain macaroni and wipe pot dry with paper towels.

3 Heat remaining 1 tablespoon oil in now-empty pot over medium-high heat until shimmering. Add flour, mustard, remaining pinch cayenne, and ¼ teaspoon salt and cook, whisking constantly, until fragrant and mixture darkens slightly, about 1 minute. Gradually whisk in milk. Bring mixture to boil, whisking constantly. Reduce heat to medium and simmer vigorously, whisking occasionally, until thickened to consistency of heavy cream, about 6 minutes.

4 Off heat, gradually whisk in Gruyère and cream cheese until completely melted and smooth. Stir in macaroni and wilted Swiss chard and cook over medium-low heat until warmed through, about 2 minutes. Season with salt and pepper to taste and sprinkle with panko mixture. Serve.

main dishes

185

MUSHROOM BOURGUIGNON

serves 8

½ cup cold-pressed extra-virgin olive oil (see page 35)

5 pounds portobello mushroom caps, quartered

1½ cups frozen pearl onions, thawed

Salt and pepper

⅓ cup all-purpose flour

4 cups homemade or low-sodium chicken or vegetable broth (see page 36)

1 (750-ml) bottle red wine

2 tablespoons unflavored gelatin

2 tablespoons tomato paste

1 tablespoon anchovy paste

2 onions, chopped coarse

2 carrots, peeled and chopped

1 garlic head, cloves separated (unpeeled), and smashed

1 ounce dried porcini mushrooms, rinsed

10 sprigs fresh parsley, plus 3 tablespoons minced

6 sprigs fresh thyme

2 bay leaves

½ teaspoon black peppercorns

PER SERVING
Cal 310; Total Fat 15g, Sat Fat 2g; Chol 0mg; Sodium 480mg; Total Carbs 20g, Fiber 4g, Total Sugar 10g, Added Sugar 0g; Protein 9g

EXCELLENT SOURCE OF
Riboflavin, Niacin, Pantothenic Acid, Vitamin B6, Folate, Copper, Phosphorus, Potassium, Selenium

why this recipe works • *Boeuf bourguignon is a traditional French dish of luscious braised beef with mushrooms, garlic, red wine, and pearl onions. We wanted to translate the dish's wonderful complexity to a meat-free version starring chunks of portobello mushrooms napped in a silky sauce. Without the meat, we needed to "beef up" the flavor with umami enhancers. Anchovy paste and porcini mushrooms gave us great depth of flavor, but our sauce lacked the dish's signature velvety consistency. Typically, a lengthy braising breaks down the collagen in meat to give the sauce body. Instead, we simply stirred in powdered gelatin to get a silky-smooth sauce, cutting the cooking time by almost half. You can substitute agar agar flakes for the gelatin and omit the anchovies to make this recipe vegetarian. Use a good-quality medium-bodied red wine, such as a Burgundy or Pinot Noir, for this stew. If the pearl onions have a papery outer coating, remove by rinsing the onions in warm water and gently squeezing individual onions between your fingertips. Serve over whole-wheat pasta or grains, Butternut Squash Polenta (page 247), or Cauliflower Puree (page 221).*

1 Heat 3 tablespoons oil in Dutch oven over medium-high heat until shimmering. Add half of portobello mushrooms, half of pearl onions, ¼ teaspoon salt, and ⅛ teaspoon pepper, cover, and cook, stirring occasionally, until mushrooms have released their moisture, 8 to 10 minutes.

2 Uncover and continue to cook, stirring occasionally and scraping bottom of pot, until mushrooms are tender and pan is dry, 12 to 15 minutes. Transfer vegetables to bowl, cover, and set aside. Repeat with 3 tablespoons oil, remaining portobello mushrooms, remaining pearl onions, ¼ teaspoon salt, and ⅛ teaspoon pepper.

3 Add remaining 2 tablespoons oil and flour to now-empty pot and whisk until no dry flour remains. Whisk in broth, 2 cups wine, gelatin, tomato paste, and anchovy paste until combined and no lumps remain, scraping up any browned bits. Stir in chopped onions, carrots, garlic, porcini mushrooms, parsley sprigs, thyme sprigs, bay leaves, and peppercorns. Bring to boil and cook, stirring occasionally, until liquid is slightly thickened and onions are translucent and softened, about 15 minutes.

4 Strain liquid through fine-mesh strainer set over large bowl, pressing on solids to extract as much liquid as possible; discard solids. Return liquid to now-empty pot, and stir in remaining wine.

5 Bring mixture to boil over medium-high heat. Cook, stirring occasionally, until sauce has thickened to consistency of heavy cream, 5 to 7 minutes. Reduce heat to medium-low, stir in reserved portobello-onion mixture, and cook until just heated through, 3 to 5 minutes. Stir in minced parsley and serve.

BEET BARLEY RISOTTO

serves 6

- 3 cups homemade or low-sodium chicken or vegetable broth (see page 36)
- 3 cups water
- 2 tablespoons cold-pressed extra-virgin olive oil (see page 35)
- 1 pound beets with greens attached, beets peeled and grated, greens stemmed and cut into 1-inch pieces (2 cups)
- 1 onion, chopped
  Salt and pepper
- 1½ cups pearl barley
- 4 garlic cloves, minced
- 1 teaspoon minced fresh thyme or ¼ teaspoon dried
- 1 cup dry white wine
- 1 ounce Parmesan cheese, grated (½ cup)
- 2 tablespoons chopped fresh parsley

why this recipe works • *A good risotto might seem to depend upon refined white rice for its texture, since the release of the exposed starch is what produces the dish's hallmark creaminess (usually aided by butter and cheese). However, we found a more nutrient-dense grain that yields similar results: pearl barley. This form of barley is not processed like other refined grains: while the starchy interior is exposed, it may retain some of its bran. As a result, it created a supple, velvety sauce when simmered while delivering a boost of vitamins and minerals. To complement the hearty grain and give the risotto a vibrant hue, we added sweet, earthy beets, making sure to save the beet greens to stir in at the end. Pre-cooking the beets was unnecessary; we simply grated them raw and stirred them into the grains—half at the beginning for a base of flavor, and half at the end for freshness and color. To balance their flavor, we stirred in a little Parmesan cheese, thyme, and parsley. Do not substitute hulled, hull-less, quick-cooking, or presteamed barley for the pearl barley. If you can't find beets with their greens attached or the greens aren't in good shape, use 10 ounces of beets and 2 cups stemmed and chopped Swiss chard. You might not need to use all of the broth when cooking the risotto. You can use a box grater or the shredding disk on a food processor to shred the beets.*

1 Bring broth and water to simmer in medium saucepan. Reduce heat to lowest setting and cover to keep warm.

2 Heat oil in large saucepan over medium heat until shimmering. Add half of grated beets, onion, and ¾ teaspoon salt and cook until vegetables are softened, 5 to 7 minutes. Stir in barley and cook, stirring often, until aromatic, about 4 minutes. Stir in garlic and thyme and cook until fragrant, about 30 seconds. Stir in wine and cook until fully absorbed, about 2 minutes.

3 Stir in 3 cups warm broth. Simmer, stirring occasionally, until liquid is absorbed and bottom of pan is dry, 22 to 25 minutes. Stir in 2 cups warm broth and simmer, stirring occasionally, until liquid is absorbed and bottom of pan is dry, 15 to 18 minutes.

4 Add beet greens and continue to cook, stirring often and adding remaining broth as needed to prevent pan bottom from becoming dry, until greens are softened and barley is cooked through but still somewhat firm in center, 5 to 10 minutes. Off heat, stir in remaining grated beets and Parmesan. Season with salt and pepper to taste and sprinkle with parsley. Serve.

PER SERVING
Cal 330; Total Fat 7g, Sat Fat 1.5g; Chol 5mg; Sodium 640mg; Total Carbs 51g, Fiber 12g, Total Sugar 6g, Added Sugar 0g; Protein 11g

EXCELLENT SOURCE OF
Protein, Fiber, Vitamin A, Folate, Vitamin C, Vitamin K, Manganese

main dishes

SWEET POTATO, POBLANO, AND BLACK BEAN TACOS

serves 6

3 tablespoons cold-pressed extra-virgin olive oil (see page 35)

3 garlic cloves, minced

1½ teaspoons ground cumin

1½ teaspoons ground coriander

1 teaspoon minced fresh oregano or ¼ teaspoon dried
Salt and pepper

1 pound sweet potatoes, peeled and cut into ½-inch pieces

4 poblano chiles, stemmed, seeded, and cut into ½-inch-wide strips

1 large onion, halved and sliced ½ inch thick

1 (15-ounce) can black beans, rinsed

¼ cup chopped fresh cilantro

12 (6-inch) corn tortillas, warmed

1 recipe Avocado Crema (page 152)

1 recipe Quick Sweet-and-Spicy Pickled Onions (page 64) (optional)

why this recipe works • *Tacos are often focused on rich meats, but we wanted a delicious version that was all about vegetables. Our favorite combination turned out to be sweet potatoes and poblano chiles, which we seasoned with fragrant garlic, cumin, coriander, and oregano. Roasting produced caramelized exteriors and tender interiors. Adding black beans turned the tacos into a satiating meal packed with vitamins and fiber. Instead of topping the tacos with queso fresco or sour cream, we made an avocado crema. For a tangy, spicy finish, we sprinkled the tacos with our Quick Sweet-and-Spicy Pickled Red Onions.*

1 Adjust oven racks to upper-middle and lower-middle positions and heat oven to 450 degrees. Whisk oil, garlic, cumin, coriander, oregano, 1 teaspoon salt, and ½ teaspoon pepper together in large bowl. Add potatoes, poblanos, and onion to oil mixture and toss to coat.

2 Spread vegetable mixture in even layer over 2 foil-lined rimmed baking sheets. Roast vegetables until tender and golden brown, about 30 minutes, stirring vegetables and switching and rotating sheets halfway through baking.

3 Return vegetables to now-empty bowl, add black beans and cilantro, and gently toss to combine. Divide vegetables evenly among warm tortillas and top with avocado crema and pickled onions. Serve.

PER SERVING
Cal 350; Total Fat 12g, Sat Fat 1.5g; Chol 0mg; Sodium 590mg; Total Carbs 55g, Fiber 10g, Total Sugar 10g, Added Sugar 0g; Protein 8g

EXCELLENT SOURCE OF
Fiber, Vitamin A, Vitamin C

SWISS CHARD ENCHILADAS

serves 6

¼ cup expeller-pressed canola oil (see page 35)

2 onions, chopped fine

3 tablespoons chili powder

6 garlic cloves, minced

2 teaspoons ground cumin

2 teaspoons sugar

2 (8-ounce) cans tomato sauce

½ cup water
   Salt and pepper

1 pound Swiss chard, stemmed and sliced into ½-inch-wide strips

2 green bell peppers, stemmed, seeded, and cut into ½-inch pieces

1 (15-ounce) can pinto beans, rinsed

12 (6-inch) corn tortillas, warmed

4 ounces Monterey Jack cheese, shredded (1 cup)

¼ cup fresh cilantro leaves
   Lime wedges

PER SERVING
Cal 390; Total Fat 18g, Sat Fat 4.5g; Chol 15mg; Sodium 930mg; Total Carbs 48g, Fiber 9g, Total Sugar 7g, Added Sugar 1g; Protein 13g

EXCELLENT SOURCE OF
Protein, Fiber, Vitamin A, Vitamin C, Vitamin E, Vitamin K, Calcium, Manganese, Potassium

why this recipe works • *Traditionally, enchiladas consist of fried tortillas filled with meat, cheese, and more, all topped with sauce and more cheese. We wanted hearty, delicious vegetable enchiladas with less saturated fat but tons of flavor. We wilted nutrient-rich Swiss chard and green peppers with garlic and onions. To add creamy cohesiveness and protein, we mashed half a can of pinto beans and mixed in our greens; we stirred in the rest of the beans whole for contrasting texture. This filling needed a robust sauce to round out the flavors; a quick simmer of canned tomato sauce with aromatics and spices did the trick. Instead of frying the tortillas, we found that brushing them with oil and microwaving worked just as well—and without the mess.*

1 Adjust oven rack to middle position and heat oven to 450 degrees. Heat 1 tablespoon oil in large saucepan over medium heat until shimmering. Add half of onions and cook until softened, about 5 minutes. Stir in chili powder, half of garlic, cumin, and sugar, and cook until fragrant, about 30 seconds. Stir in tomato sauce and water, bring to simmer, and cook until slightly thickened, about 7 minutes. Season with salt and pepper to taste; set sauce aside.

2 Meanwhile, heat 1 tablespoon oil in Dutch oven over medium heat until shimmering. Add remaining onions and cook until softened and just beginning to brown, 5 to 7 minutes. Add remaining garlic and cook until fragrant, about 30 seconds. Add chard and bell peppers, cover, and cook until chard is tender, 6 to 8 minutes. Using potato masher, coarsely mash half of beans in large bowl. Stir in chard-pepper mixture, ¼ cup sauce, and remaining whole beans. Season filling with salt and pepper to taste.

3 Spread ½ cup sauce over bottom of 13 by 9-inch baking dish. Brush both sides of tortillas with remaining 2 tablespoons oil. Stack tortillas, wrap in damp dish towel, and place on plate; microwave until warm and pliable, about 1 minute. Working with 1 warm tortilla at a time, spread ¼ cup chard filling across center. Roll tortilla tightly around filling and place seam side down in baking dish; arrange enchiladas in 2 columns across width of dish. Cover completely with remaining sauce and sprinkle evenly with Monterey Jack.

4 Cover dish tightly with greased aluminum foil and bake until enchiladas are heated through and cheese is melted, 15 to 20 minutes. Let enchiladas cool for 10 minutes. Sprinkle with cilantro and serve with lime wedges.

main dishes

CAULIFLOWER STEAKS

serves 4

2 heads cauliflower
(2 pounds each)

¼ cup cold-pressed extra-virgin
olive oil (see page 35)
Salt and pepper

1 recipe Chermoula Sauce
(page 153)
Lemon wedges

why this recipe works • *A steak doesn't have to be meat, or even a protein; it could be a vegetable. And given that most of us eat enough protein, but not nearly enough vegetables, putting plants at the center of the plate from time to time isn't such a bad idea. Enter cauliflower steaks. When you roast thick planks of cauliflower, they develop a meaty texture and become nutty, sweet, and caramelized. Many recipes, however, are fussy, involving transitions between stovetop and oven. We wanted a simpler method that produced four perfectly cooked cauliflower steaks simultaneously, so we opted for a rimmed baking sheet and a scorching oven. Steaming the cauliflower briefly under foil followed by high-heat uncovered roasting produced well-caramelized steaks with tender interiors. To elevate the cauliflower to centerpiece status, we paired it with a vibrant Chermoula Sauce—a pungent Moroccan blend of herbs and spices. We brushed the hot steaks with the bright sauce so they'd soak up its robust flavor. Look for fresh, firm, bright white heads of cauliflower that feel heavy for their size and are free of blemishes or soft spots; florets are more likely to separate from older heads of cauliflower.*

1 Adjust oven rack to lowest position and heat oven to 500 degrees. Working with 1 head cauliflower at a time, discard outer leaves and trim stem flush with bottom florets. Halve cauliflower lengthwise through core. Cut one 1½-inch-thick slab lengthwise from each half, trimming any florets not connected to core. Repeat with remaining cauliflower. (You should have 4 steaks; reserve remaining cauliflower for another use.)

2 Place steaks on rimmed baking sheet and drizzle with 2 tablespoons oil. Sprinkle with ¼ teaspoon salt and ⅛ teaspoon pepper and rub to distribute. Flip steaks and repeat.

3 Cover baking sheet tightly with foil and roast for 5 minutes. Remove foil and continue to roast until bottoms of steaks are well browned, 8 to 10 minutes. Gently flip and continue to roast until tender and second sides are well browned, 6 to 8 minutes.

4 Transfer steaks to platter and brush tops evenly with ¼ cup chermoula sauce. Serve with lemon wedges and remaining chermoula.

PER SERVING
Cal 340; Total Fat 29g, Sat Fat 4.5g; Chol 0mg; Sodium 240mg; Total Carbs 17g, Fiber 6g, Total Sugar 6g, Added Sugar 0g; Protein 6g

EXCELLENT SOURCE OF
Fiber, Pantothenic Acid, Vitamin B6, Folate, Vitamin C, Vitamin K, Manganese, Potassium

nutritious DELICIOUS

WHOLE-WHEAT PIZZA WITH KALE AND SUNFLOWER SEED PESTO

DOUGH

- 1½ cups (8¼ ounces) whole-wheat flour
- 1 cup (5½ ounces) bread flour
- 2 teaspoons honey
- ¾ teaspoon instant or rapid-rise yeast
- 1¼ cups ice water
- 2 tablespoons cold-pressed extra-virgin olive oil (see page 35)
- 1¾ teaspoons salt

TOPPINGS

- 5½ ounces curly kale, stemmed and cut into 1½-inch pieces (3½ cups)
- 1 tablespoon cold-pressed extra-virgin olive oil (see page 35), plus extra for drizzling
  Salt and pepper
- 1 cup Kale and Sunflower Seed Pesto (page 153)
- 6 ounces cherry tomatoes, quartered
- 1 ounce Parmesan cheese, shaved

PER SLICE
Cal 210; Total Fat 12g, Sat Fat 2g; Chol 5mg; Sodium 400 mg; Total Carbs 21g, Fiber 3g, Total Sugar 1g, Added Sugar 1g; Protein 6g

EXCELLENT SOURCE OF
Vitamin A, Vitamin C, Vitamin K, Manganese

why this recipe works • *"Healthy" pizzas often taste like cardboard. We set out to develop a recipe to satisfy any pizza craving while delivering plenty of nutrients. For starters, we replaced over half of the bread flour with whole-wheat flour, which required making an extra-wet dough for optimal chew. For a sauce, we used our power-house Kale and Sunflower Seed Pesto. Cherry tomatoes provided bursts of sweetness and acidity to balance the earthy pesto underneath. We topped the pizza with even more kale, which crisped in the oven. A few shavings of Parmesan completed the picture. The pizza dough needs to proof for at least 18 hours before baking. If you do not have a baking stone, you can use a preheated rimless (or inverted rimmed) baking sheet, however the crust will be less crisp. Shape the second dough ball while the first pizza bakes, but don't top the pizza until right before you bake it. We prefer to use our pizza dough, but you can substitute 2 pounds store-bought whole-wheat pizza dough (1 pound of dough per pizza).*

1 **FOR THE DOUGH** Process whole-wheat flour, bread flour, honey, and yeast in food processor until combined, about 2 seconds. With processor running, add ice water and process until dough is just combined and no dry flour remains, about 10 seconds. Let dough sit for 10 minutes.

2 Add oil and salt to dough and process until it forms satiny, sticky ball that clears sides of bowl, 45 to 60 seconds. Remove from bowl and knead on oiled counter until smooth, about 1 minute. Divide dough in half, shape each half into a tight ball, and place each in lightly oiled bowl. Cover tightly with plastic wrap and refrigerate for at least 18 hours or up to 2 days.

3 One hour before baking pizza, adjust oven rack to middle position, set pizza stone on rack, and heat oven to 500 degrees. Remove dough from refrigerator and let sit until dough springs back minimally when poked gently with your knuckle, at least 1 hour.

4 **FOR THE TOPPINGS** Combine kale, oil, and ¼ teaspoon salt in bowl and massage lightly to coat leaves evenly. Heat broiler for 10 minutes. Meanwhile, coat 1 ball of dough generously with flour and place on well-floured counter. Using your fingertips, gently flatten into 8-inch disk, leaving 1 inch of outer edge slightly thicker than center. Lift edge of dough and, using back of your hands and knuckles, gently stretch disk into 12-inch round, working along edges and giving disk quarter turns as you stretch. Transfer dough to well-floured pizza peel and stretch into 13-inch round.

5 Spread ½ cup pesto over surface of dough, leaving ½-inch border around edge. Scatter half of tomatoes and half of kale mixture over pizza. Slide pizza carefully onto stone, return oven to 500 degrees, and bake until crust is well browned and edges of kale leaves are crisp and brown, 8 to 10 minutes. Remove pizza, place on wire rack, and let pizza rest for 5 minutes. Drizzle with additional oil to taste and sprinkle with half of Parmesan. Slice pizza into 8 slices and serve.

6 Heat broiler for 10 minutes. Repeat process of stretching, topping, and baking with remaining dough and toppings, returning oven to 500 degrees when pizza is placed on stone.

CAULIFLOWER-CHICKPEA FLATBREAD WITH ROMESCO

1 head cauliflower (2 pounds),
  cored and cut into ¾-inch
  florets (about 7 cups)

1 cup chickpea flour

2 large organic eggs

½ cup cold-pressed extra-virgin
  olive oil (see page 35),
  plus extra for drizzling

3 garlic cloves, minced

2 teaspoons chopped fresh
  oregano or ¾ teaspoon dried
  Salt

6 ounces Parmesan cheese,
  grated (3 cups)

1¼ cups fresh parsley leaves

⅔ cup jarred roasted red peppers,
  rinsed, patted dry, and
  chopped

¼ cup walnuts, toasted

1 tablespoon sherry vinegar

6 anchovy fillets, rinsed, patted
  dry, and chopped fine
  (optional)

¼ cup part-skim ricotta cheese

PER SLICE
Cal 180; Total Fat 13g, Sat Fat 3g;
Chol 35mg; Sodium 460mg; Total
Carbs 9g, Fiber 3g, Total Sugar 3g,
Added Sugar 0g; Protein 10g

EXCELLENT SOURCE OF
Folate, Vitamin C, Vitamin K,
Calcium

why this recipe works • *Cauliflower pizza crusts have taken the Internet by storm, and we can understand the appeal of a vegetable-based (and gluten-free) crust. Yet most underdeliver, sticking to pans or crumbling. For a cauliflower crust with better structure, we took a hint from socca, the Italian chickpea pancake, and incorporated chickpea flour. It gave our crust durability, but we wanted crispness. So we stirred in grated Parmesan, which essentially fried in the oven to provide a crisp crust. We topped the crust with a savory red pepper romesco sauce, more cauliflower, anchovies, and parsley, giving us a nutrient-dense flatbread with pizzazz. If you do not have a baking stone, you can use a preheated rimless (or inverted rimmed) baking sheet, however the crust will be less crisp. Don't top the second flatbread until right before you bake it.*

1 One hour before baking, adjust oven rack to upper-middle position, set baking stone on rack, and heat oven to 475 degrees. Process 4 cups cauliflower florets, chickpea flour, eggs, ¼ cup oil, two-thirds of the garlic, oregano, and ¼ teaspoon salt together in food processor until thick, smooth batter forms, about 3 minutes, scraping down sides and bottom of bowl as needed. Transfer batter to large bowl and stir in Parmesan.

2 Line pizza peel with 16- by 12-inch piece of parchment paper with long edge perpendicular to handle and spray parchment well with canola oil spray. Transfer half of batter (about 2 cups) to center of prepared parchment and top with second greased sheet parchment. Gently press batter into 12-inch round (about ¼-inch thick), then discard top piece parchment. Carefully slide round, still on parchment, onto stone and bake until edges are browned and crisp and top is golden, about 12 minutes, rotating halfway through baking (parchment will darken). Transfer crust to wire rack set in rimmed baking sheet and discard bottom parchment. Repeat with remaining batter to make second crust.

3 In clean, dry workbowl, process ¼ cup parsley, red peppers, walnuts, sherry vinegar, remaining garlic, and ¼ teaspoon salt until smooth, about 30 seconds, scraping down sides of bowl as needed. With processor running, slowly add 3 tablespoons oil until incorporated. (Romesco sauce can be refrigerated for up to 3 days.)

4 Heat remaining 1 tablespoon oil in 12-inch nonstick skillet over medium-high heat until shimmering. Add remaining 3 cups cauliflower florets and ½ teaspoon salt and cook, stirring frequently, until florets are spotty brown and crisp-tender, 12 to 15 minutes.

5 Working with 1 crust at a time, spread half of sauce (about ⅓ cup) in thin layer over crust, leaving ¼-inch border around edge. Scatter half of cauliflower and half of anchovies (if using) evenly over top. Place flatbread (still on wire rack on sheet) on stone and bake until warmed through, about 5 minutes.

6 Transfer flatbread to cutting board. Sprinkle evenly with ½ cup parsley, dollop half of ricotta in small spoonfuls evenly over flatbread, and drizzle with oil to taste. Slice into 8 slices and serve immediately. Repeat topping and baking for second flatbread.

VEGETABLES AND SIDES

202 Roasted Artichokes with Lemon Vinaigrette

204 Stir-Fried Asparagus with Shiitakes

207 Beets with Orange and Walnuts

208 Grilled Broccoli with Lemon and Parmesan

211 Broccoli Salad with Almonds and Cranberries

213 Roasted Brussels Sprouts with Walnuts and Lemon

214 Brussels Sprout, Red Cabbage, and Pomegranate Slaw

216 Carrot "Tabbouleh" with Mint, Pistachios, and Pomegranate Seeds

Carrot "Tabbouleh" with Fennel, Orange, and Hazelnuts

218 Slow-Cooked Whole Carrots with Pine Nut Relish

221 Cauliflower Puree

223 Cauliflower Rice

225 Edamame Salad with Arugula and Radishes

226 Stir-Fried Eggplant with Garlic-Basil Sauce

228 Sautéed Green Beans with Mushroom and Dukkah

231 Garlicky Braised Kale

232 Sautéed Spinach with Yogurt and Dukkah

235 Roasted Butternut Squash with Pistachios and Feta

237 Twice-Baked Sweet Potatoes with Hazelnuts

238 Sweet Potato and Swiss Chard Gratin

240 Roasted Spiralized Sweet Potatoes with Walnuts and Feta

243 Lentils with Spinach and Garlic Chips

244 Curried Chickpeas with Garlic and Yogurt

247 Butternut Squash Polenta

249 Quinoa Pilaf with Shiitakes, Edamame, and Ginger

250 Brown Rice Pilaf with Dates and Pistachios

253 Bulgur Pilaf with Cremini Mushrooms

Bulgur Pilaf with Shiitake Mushrooms

ROASTED ARTICHOKES WITH LEMON VINAIGRETTE

serves 4

3 lemons

4 artichokes (8 to 10 ounces each)

9 tablespoons cold-pressed extra-virgin olive oil (see page 35)
Salt and pepper

½ teaspoon garlic, minced to paste

½ teaspoon Dijon mustard

2 teaspoons chopped fresh parsley

why this recipe works • *Though we often stir artichokes into dips laden with sour cream and cheese, they deserve a healthier treatment that pays respect to their unique flavor and strong nutrient makeup, including fiber, minerals, and antioxidants. We trimmed and dropped them in lemon water to prevent oxidation before tossing them with seasoned oil and then roasting them alongside lemon halves. Our vinaigrette included Dijon, garlic, and the nutritious pulp from the roasted lemon halves, which gave it more body. If your artichokes are larger than 8 to 10 ounces, strip away another layer or two of the toughest outer leaves. The tender inner leaves, heart, and stem are entirely edible. To eat the tough outer leaves, use your teeth to scrape the flesh from the underside of each leaf. A rasp-style grater makes quick work of turning the garlic into a paste. These artichokes taste great warm or at room temperature.*

1 Adjust oven rack to lower-middle position and heat oven to 475 degrees. Cut 1 lemon in half, squeeze halves into container filled with 2 quarts water, then add spent halves.

2 Working with 1 artichoke at a time, trim stem to about ¾ inch and cut off top quarter of artichoke. Break off bottom 3 or 4 rows of tough outer leaves by pulling them downward. Using paring knife, trim outer layer of stem and base, removing any dark green parts. Cut artichoke in half lengthwise, then remove fuzzy choke and any tiny inner purple-tinged leaves using small spoon. Submerge prepped artichokes in lemon water.

3 Coat bottom of 13 by 9-inch baking dish with 1 tablespoon oil. Remove artichokes from lemon water and shake off excess water. Toss artichokes with 2 tablespoons oil, ¼ teaspoon salt, and pinch pepper; gently rub oil and seasonings between leaves. Arrange artichokes cut side down in prepared dish. Halve remaining 2 lemons crosswise, and arrange cut side up next to artichokes. Cover tightly with aluminum foil and roast until cut sides of artichokes begin to brown and bases and leaves are tender when poked with tip of paring knife, 25 to 30 minutes.

4 Transfer artichokes to serving platter. Let lemons cool slightly, then squeeze into fine-mesh strainer set over bowl, extracting as much juice and pulp as possible; press firmly on solids to yield 1½ tablespoons juice. Whisk garlic and mustard into juice. Whisking constantly, slowly drizzle in remaining 6 tablespoons oil until emulsified. Whisk in parsley and season with salt and pepper to taste. Serve artichokes with dressing.

PER SERVING
Cal 400; Total Fat 28g, Sat Fat 4g; Chol 0mg; Sodium 590mg; Total Carbs 35g, Fiber 17g, Total Sugar 6g, Added Sugar 0g; Protein 11g

EXCELLENT SOURCE OF
Protein, Fiber, Niacin, Folate, Vitamin C, Vitamin E, Vitamin K, Iron, Magnesium, Manganese, Phosphorus, Potassium

nutritious DELICIOUS

STIR-FRIED ASPARAGUS WITH SHIITAKES

serves 4

2 tablespoons water

1 tablespoon low-sodium soy sauce

1 tablespoon dry sherry

2 teaspoons packed brown sugar

2 teaspoons grated fresh ginger

1 teaspoon expeller-pressed toasted sesame oil (see page 35)

1 tablespoon expeller-pressed canola oil (see page 35)

1 pound asparagus, trimmed and cut on bias into 2-inch lengths

4 ounces shiitake mushrooms, stemmed and sliced thin

2 scallions, green parts only, sliced thin on bias

why this recipe works • *Vegetable stir-fries are a great way to incorporate more veggies into your meals, but most bottled stir-fry sauces are loaded with salt, sugar, and preservatives, and it can be easy to keep pouring and end up with more sauce than vegetables. We wanted a stir-fry method that would produce crisp-tender vegetables with a sauce that complemented but didn't overpower them. Asparagus especially benefits from quick stir-frying, as vitamins can leach out during boiling. Shiitakes complemented the spears with their earthiness and meaty texture. We gave the asparagus time to brown before adding our flavorful stir-fry sauce during the last two minutes—just enough to lightly coat the veggies. To allow it to brown, stir the asparagus only occasionally. Look for spears that are no thicker than ½ inch.*

1 Whisk water, soy sauce, sherry, sugar, ginger, and sesame oil together in bowl.

2 Heat canola oil in 12-inch nonstick skillet over high heat until smoking. Add asparagus and mushrooms and cook, stirring occasionally, until asparagus is spotty brown, about 4 minutes. Add soy sauce mixture and cook, stirring once or twice, until pan is almost dry and asparagus is crisp-tender, about 2 minutes. Transfer to serving platter, sprinkle with scallions, and serve.

PER SERVING
Cal 80; Total Fat 4.5g, Sat Fat 0g; Chol 0mg; Sodium 140mg; Total Carbs 8g, Fiber 2g, Total Sugar 5g, Added Sugar 2g; Protein 3g

EXCELLENT SOURCE OF
Vitamin K, Manganese

nutritious DELICIOUS

BEETS WITH ORANGE AND WALNUTS

serves 6

1½ pounds beets, trimmed and halved crosswise

1¼ cups water
  Salt and pepper

3 tablespoons distilled white vinegar

1 tablespoon packed light brown sugar

1 shallot, sliced thin

1 teaspoon grated orange zest

½ cup walnuts, toasted and chopped

2 tablespoons chopped fresh parsley

1 teaspoon chopped fresh thyme

why this recipe works • *For a simple side of tender beets, instead of boiling and draining away the vitamin-filled water, we used a smaller amount of cooking liquid and transformed it into a glaze. We first simmered halved beets in 1¼ cups of water until just tender. After transferring the beets to a cutting board, we increased the heat, letting the liquid reduce to a syrupy consistency, and added a little brown sugar and white vinegar for a sweet-sour glaze. We then peeled the cooled beets, cut them into wedges, and returned them to the glaze, along with a shallot and pinch of orange zest for brightness. A final sprinkle of toasted walnuts—full of healthy fats—added a nice crunch to the tender beets, while a sprinkle of fresh parsley and thyme complemented their earthiness. To ensure even cooking, we recommend using beets that are of similar size—roughly 2 to 3 inches in diameter. The beets can be served warm or at room temperature. If serving at room temperature, wait to sprinkle with walnuts and herbs until right before serving.*

1 Place beets, cut side down, in single layer in Dutch oven. Add water and ¼ teaspoon salt and bring to simmer over medium-high heat. Cover, reduce heat to low, and simmer until beets are tender and tip of paring knife inserted into beets meets no resistance, 45 to 50 minutes.

2 Transfer beets to cutting board. Increase heat to medium-high and reduce cooking liquid, stirring occasionally, until pan is almost dry, 5 to 6 minutes. Add vinegar and sugar to pot, return to boil, and cook, stirring constantly with rubber spatula, until spatula leaves wide trail when dragged through glaze, about 1 minute. Remove pot from heat.

3 When beets are cool enough to handle, rub off skins with paper towels and cut into ½-inch wedges. Add beets, shallot, orange zest, ½ teaspoon salt, and ¼ teaspoon pepper to glaze in pot and toss to coat. Transfer beets to serving dish. Sprinkle with walnuts, parsley, and thyme and serve.

PER SERVING
Cal 120; Total Fat 6g, Sat Fat 0.5g; Chol 0mg; Sodium 380mg; Total Carbs 15g, Fiber 4g, Total Sugar 11g, Added Sugar 2g; Protein 3g

EXCELLENT SOURCE OF
Folate, Vitamin K, Manganese

GRILLED BROCCOLI WITH LEMON AND PARMESAN

serves 6

¼ cup cold-pressed extra-virgin
  olive oil (see page 35),
  plus extra for serving
1 tablespoon water
  Salt and pepper
2 pounds broccoli
1 lemon, halved
¼ cup shredded Parmesan cheese

why this recipe works • *Broccoli is often paired with gooey cheese sauce, turning this nutrient-packed vegetable into a not-so-healthy side. We wanted a broccoli dish that wasn't overshadowed by a cheesy topping, but still retained some richness from cheese. We turned to Parmesan; just a ¼ cup provided the salty, savory bite we were after. Instead of roasting or steaming, we wanted to grill the broccoli, as its hearty structure would stand up well to this cooking method, which would impart great smoky flavor. To cook the broccoli through without overcharring, we wrapped it in aluminum foil "hobo packs" and let it steam (an ideal cooking method to preserve nutrients) first on the grill. We then removed the spears and placed them directly on the grill. To keep the packs from tearing, use heavy-duty aluminum foil. Use the large holes of a box grater to shred the Parmesan.*

1 Cut two 26- by 12-inch sheets of heavy-duty aluminum foil. Whisk oil, water, ¾ teaspoon salt, and ½ teaspoon pepper together in large bowl.

2 Trim broccoli stalks so each entire head of broccoli measures about 6 inches long. Using vegetable peeler, peel away tough outer layer of broccoli stalks. Cut broccoli in half lengthwise (stalks should be about ½ inch thick and florets about 3 inches wide) and add to oil mixture, tossing to coat.

3 Divide broccoli between sheets of foil, placing cut sides down and alternating direction of florets and stems, arranging broccoli in center of each sheet. Bring short sides of foil together and crimp tightly. Crimp long ends to seal packs tightly.

4A FOR A CHARCOAL GRILL Open bottom vent completely. Light large chimney starter filled with charcoal briquettes (6 quarts). When top coals are partially covered with ash, pour evenly over half of grill. Set cooking grate in place, cover, and open lid vent completely. Heat grill until hot, about 5 minutes.

4B FOR A GAS GRILL Turn all burners to high, cover, and heat grill until hot, about 15 minutes. Turn all burners to medium-high.

5 Clean and oil cooking grate. Place packs on cooking grates (over coals if using charcoal), cover, and cook for 8 minutes, flipping packs halfway through cooking.

PER SERVING
Cal 140; Total Fat 11g, Sat Fat 1.5g; Chol 0mg; Sodium 370mg; Total Carbs 8g, Fiber 4g, Total Sugar 2g, Added Sugar 0g; Protein 6g

EXCELLENT SOURCE OF
Vitamin A, Folate, Vitamin C

nutritious DELICIOUS

6 Transfer packs to rimmed baking sheet and, using scissors, carefully cut open, allowing steam to escape away from you. (Broccoli should be bright green and fork inserted into stems should meet some resistance.)

7 Discard foil and place broccoli and lemon halves cut side down on cooking grates (over coals if using charcoal). Grill (covered if using gas), turning broccoli every 2 minutes, until stems are fork-tender and broccoli and lemons are well charred, 6 to 8 minutes. (Transfer broccoli to now-empty baking sheet as it finishes cooking.)

8 Transfer broccoli to cutting board and cut into 2-inch pieces; transfer to platter. Season with salt and pepper to taste. Squeeze lemon over broccoli to taste, sprinkle with Parmesan, and drizzle with extra oil. Serve.

BROCCOLI SALAD WITH ALMONDS AND CRANBERRIES

serves 6

1½ pounds broccoli, florets cut into 1-inch pieces, stalks peeled, halved lengthwise, and sliced ¼ inch thick
1 avocado, halved, pitted, and cut into ½-inch pieces
2 tablespoons cold-pressed extra-virgin olive oil (see page 35)
1 teaspoon grated lemon zest plus 3 tablespoons juice
1 garlic clove, minced
Salt and pepper
½ cup dried cranberries
½ cup sliced almonds, toasted
1 shallot, sliced thin
1 tablespoon minced fresh tarragon

why this recipe works • *A backyard barbecue favorite, broccoli salad should be a nutritious alternative to potato salad, thanks to its combination of crisp broccoli, dried fruit, and nuts. The problem lies in a heavy hand with mayonnaise (and often sugar), yielding a dressing that overwhelms everything else. We found a more nutritious option in creamy, heart-healthy avocado. Whizzed with lemon juice and zest, a little olive oil, and aromatic garlic, it produced a smooth dressing that let the broccoli shine. Most recipes use raw broccoli, but we got better texture and flavor by quickly steaming and then shocking it in ice water to lock in color and nutrients. Steaming also allowed us to cook the tougher broccoli stalks, leaving nothing to waste. By placing the chopped stalks in a little boiling water and perching the florets atop to steam, we ensured that both became tender at the same time. Drying the broccoli in a salad spinner helped to avoid a watery salad. To finish, we added toasted almonds for crunch and dried cranberries for brightness. A sprinkle of fresh tarragon brought everything together. Be sure to set up the ice water bath before cooking the broccoli stems and florets, as plunging them in the cold water immediately after cooking retains their bright green color and ensures that they don't overcook.*

1 Fill large bowl halfway with ice and water; set aside. Bring 1 inch water to rolling boil in medium saucepan over high heat. Place broccoli in steamer basket. Transfer basket to saucepan. Cover, reduce heat to medium-low, and cook until broccoli is bright green and crisp-tender, 4 to 6 minutes.

2 Drain well and transfer immediately to bowl with ice water to cool, about 10 minutes. Drain again, transfer to salad spinner, and spin dry.

3 Process avocado, oil, lemon zest and juice, garlic, ¾ teaspoon salt, and ¼ teaspoon pepper in food processor until smooth, about 30 seconds, scraping down sides of bowl as needed; transfer to large serving bowl. Add broccoli, cranberries, almonds, shallot, and tarragon and toss to combine. Season with salt and pepper to taste. Serve.

PER SERVING
Cal 230; Total Fat 14g, Sat Fat 1.5g; Chol 0mg; Sodium 330mg; Total Carbs 25g, Fiber 7g, Total Sugar 13g, Added Sugar 0g; Protein 6g

EXCELLENT SOURCE OF
Fiber, Folate, Vitamin C, Vitamin E, Vitamin K, Manganese

vegetables and sides

ROASTED BRUSSELS SPROUTS WITH WALNUTS AND LEMON

serves 8

2 ¼ pounds Brussels sprouts, trimmed and halved

¼ cup cold-pressed extra-virgin olive oil (see page 35)

1 tablespoon water
Salt and pepper

1 tablespoon lemon juice

⅓ cup walnuts, toasted and finely chopped

why this recipe works • *Brussels sprouts and bacon are a classic combination, as the vegetable holds up well to the smoky meat and takes on the savory flavor of the rendered fat. But we were determined to find a more nutritious pairing for this cruciferous vegetable, which is packed with fiber, folate, and vitamin K. Instead of smoked meat, we tossed the sprouts with toasted walnuts for richness and healthy omega-3 fats, and used olive oil as our base. In order to ensure the interior of the sprouts cooked through by the time the exterior caramelized, we added just a tablespoon of water to our oil and seasoning that would coat the sprouts. We then roasted them covered to trap some of their steam and soften them. After 10 minutes, we removed the foil, allowing them to brown and finish cooking through until just tender (and not overcooked). A final toss with lemon juice added brightness. If you are buying loose Brussels sprouts, select those that are about 1 ½ inches long. Quarter Brussels sprouts longer than 2 ½ inches; leave whole sprouts that are shorter than 1 inch.*

1 Adjust oven rack to upper-middle position and heat oven to 500 degrees. Toss Brussels sprouts, 3 tablespoons oil, water, ¾ teaspoon salt, and ¼ teaspoon pepper in large bowl until sprouts are coated. Transfer sprouts to rimmed baking sheet and arrange cut side down in single layer.

2 Cover sheet tightly with aluminum foil and roast for 10 minutes. Remove foil and continue to cook until Brussels sprouts are well browned and tender, 10 to 12 minutes. Transfer to serving platter and toss with remaining 1 tablespoon oil, lemon juice, and walnuts. Season with salt and pepper to taste. Serve.

PER SERVING
Cal 150; Total Fat 11g, Sat Fat 1.5g; Chol 0mg; Sodium 250mg; Total Carbs 12g, Fiber 5g, Total Sugar 3g, Added Sugar 0g; Protein 5g

EXCELLENT SOURCE OF
Fiber, Folate, Vitamin C, Vitamin K, Manganese

BRUSSELS SPROUT, RED CABBAGE, AND POMEGRANATE SLAW

serves 8

¼ cup cider vinegar
1 tablespoon pomegranate molasses
  Salt and pepper
3 tablespoons cold-pressed extra-virgin olive oil (see page 35)
1 pound Brussels sprouts, trimmed, halved, and sliced very thin
3 cups thinly sliced red cabbage
1½ cups pomegranate seeds
½ cup sliced almonds, toasted
2 tablespoons minced fresh mint

why this recipe works • *Shredded cabbage makes a good starting point for a supercharged slaw bursting with colors, textures, and flavors and exploding with nutrients. Our goal was to let the slaw shine without drowning it in a heavy dressing, as is often the case. We started with a base of delicate shredded Brussels sprouts and vibrant red cabbage, liking the visual contrast of the two brassicas, both known for high levels of fiber, vitamins, and minerals, plus the bonus antioxidants found in the red cabbage. To add a bright pop of sweetness, we incorporated a generous amount of antioxidant-rich pomegranate seeds. A handful of toasted sliced almonds provided a nutty foil to the fruit. Instead of a creamy dressing, we made a sweet-tart vinaigrette of apple cider vinegar, pomegranate molasses, and olive oil. A sprinkle of fresh mint added a lively finish. Pomegranate molasses can be found in the international aisle of well-stocked supermarkets; if you can't find it, substitute 2 teaspoons of lemon juice plus 2 teaspoons of mild molasses for the tablespoon of pomegranate molasses. The Brussels sprouts and cabbage can be sliced with a knife or the slicing disk of a food processor. Either way, slice them as thinly as possible.*

1 Whisk vinegar, pomegranate molasses, ¾ teaspoon salt, and ¼ teaspoon pepper together in large bowl until well combined. Whisking constantly, slowly drizzle in oil until combined.

2 Add Brussels sprouts, cabbage, pomegranate seeds, almonds, and mint, and toss well to coat. Season with salt and pepper to taste. Serve.

PER SERVING
Cal 150; Total Fat 9g, Sat Fat 1g; Chol 0mg; Sodium 240mg; Total Carbs 16g, Fiber 5g, Total Sugar 8g, Added Sugar 0g; Protein 4g

EXCELLENT SOURCE OF
Fiber, Vitamin C, Vitamin K, Manganese

CARROT "TABBOULEH" WITH MINT, PISTACHIOS, AND POMEGRANATE SEEDS

serves 6

- ¾ cup shelled pistachios, toasted
- ¼ cup cold-pressed extra-virgin olive oil (see page 35)
- 3 tablespoons lemon juice
- 1 tablespoon honey
- ½ teaspoon smoked paprika
- ⅛ teaspoon cayenne pepper
  Salt and pepper
- 1 pound carrots, unpeeled, trimmed and cut into 1-inch pieces
- 2 cups minced fresh mint leaves
- 1 cup pomegranate seeds

why this recipe works • *We love finding new and exciting ways to eat more vegetables, particularly when they can stand in for starchier carbohydrates and provide more variety. We've used beets to make colorful noodles and cauliflower to make fluffy rice; as it turns out, beta-carotene-loaded carrots can be transformed into a vibrant tabbouleh-like salad. We took advantage of our food processor, using it first to chop rich pistachios and two bunches of fragrant mint. After emptying the bowl, we gave our carrots a whir, grinding them to a grain-like size. We then tossed them with a simple dressing enlivened with honey and paprika, stirred in the mint and pistachios, and added antioxidant-rich pomegranate seeds for a pop of color and juicy, tart sweetness. We prefer the convenience and the hint of bitterness that unpeeled carrots lend to this salad; just be sure to scrub the carrots well before using.*

Pulse pistachios in food processor until coarsely chopped, 10 to 12 pulses. Transfer to bowl. Whisk oil, lemon juice, honey, paprika, cayenne, 1 teaspoon salt, and ½ teaspoon black pepper in large bowl until combined. Process carrots in now-empty food processor until finely chopped, 10 to 20 seconds, scraping down sides of bowl as needed. Transfer carrots to bowl with dressing, add mint, half of pomegranate seeds, and half of pistachios and toss to combine. Season with salt to taste. Transfer to serving platter, sprinkle with remaining pomegranate seeds and pistachios, and serve.

VARIATION

CARROT "TABBOULEH" WITH FENNEL, ORANGE, AND HAZELNUTS
Omit smoked paprika and cayenne. Substitute toasted, skinned, and chopped hazelnuts for pistachios, 1 halved and cored fennel bulb cut into 1-inch pieces for mint, and orange juice for lemon juice. Add ¼ teaspoon orange zest and 2 tablespoons white wine vinegar to mixture with carrots. Substitute ½ cup minced fresh chives for pomegranate seeds.

PER SERVING
Cal 250; Total Fat 17g, Sat Fat 2.5g; Chol 0mg; Sodium 440mg; Total Carbs 21g, Fiber 6g, Total Sugar 12g, Added Sugar 3g; Protein 5g

EXCELLENT SOURCE OF
Fiber, Vitamin A, Vitamin B6, Vitamin C, Vitamin K, Manganese

nutritious DELICIOUS

SLOW-COOKED WHOLE CARROTS WITH PINE NUT RELISH

serves 6

⅓ cup pine nuts, toasted

1 shallot, minced

1 tablespoon sherry vinegar

1 tablespoon minced fresh parsley

1 teaspoon honey

½ teaspoon minced fresh rosemary

¼ teaspoon smoked paprika
 Salt
 Pinch cayenne pepper

3 cups water

1 tablespoon cold-pressed extra-virgin olive oil (see page 35)

1½ pounds carrots, trimmed and peeled

why this recipe works • *Glazed carrots are a dinnertime staple, but the carrots often simmer in what amounts to a simple syrup, and they tend to wind up overcooked and mushy. We wanted to utilize the vitamin A–packed roots' natural sweetness while slightly softening them to perfection. Instead of just boiling them, we gently "steeped" the carrots in warm water before cooking to firm up the vegetable's cell walls, making them more resistant to breaking down when cooked at a higher temperature. This activated an enzyme within the carrots that strengthened their pectin. After their brief warm soak, we removed the lid and topped the carrots with a fitted piece of parchment paper, called a* cartouche, *which ensured they cooked evenly from end to end and didn't become mushy. Just a bit of oil in the cooking water provided a slight sheen—no extra sugar necessary. A simple, flavor-packed pine nut relish was the perfect finishing touch. Use carrots that measure ¾ inch to 1¼ inches across at the thickest end. You will need a 12-inch skillet with a tight-fitting lid for this recipe.*

1 Cut parchment paper into 11-inch circle, then cut 1-inch hole in center, folding paper as needed. Combine pine nuts, shallot, sherry vinegar, parsley, honey, rosemary, paprika, ¼ teaspoon salt, and cayenne in small bowl; set aside.

2 Bring water, oil, and ½ teaspoon salt to simmer in 12-inch skillet over high heat. Off heat, add carrots, top with parchment, cover skillet, and let sit for 20 minutes.

3 Uncover, leaving parchment in place, and bring to simmer over high heat. Reduce heat to medium-low and cook until most of water has evaporated and carrots are very tender, about 45 minutes.

4 Discard parchment, increase heat to medium-high, and cook carrots, shaking skillet often, until lightly glazed and no water remains, 2 to 4 minutes. Spoon relish over carrots before serving.

PER SERVING
Cal 120; Total Fat 8g, Sat Fat 0.5g; Chol 0mg; Sodium 360mg; Total Carbs 12g, Fiber 3g, Total Sugar 6g, Added Sugar 1g; Protein 2g

EXCELLENT SOURCE OF
Vitamin A, Vitamin K, Manganese

nutritious DELICIOUS

CAULIFLOWER PUREE

serves 6

- ¼ cup cold-pressed extra-virgin olive oil (see page 35)
- 2 garlic cloves, minced
- 2 teaspoons minced fresh thyme or ¾ teaspoon dried
  Salt and pepper
- ¼ teaspoon white wine vinegar
- 1 large head cauliflower (3 pounds), florets cut into 1-inch pieces, core peeled and sliced ¼ inch thick

why this recipe works • *Most experienced cooks will admit that the key to silky mashed potatoes involves loads of butter and cream. To create a similarly creamy, equally versatile puree without all the saturated fat, we turned to cauliflower. Cauliflower is getting a lot of love these days and it's no wonder why: The crucifer—high in vitamins and potassium—is easy to work with and, thanks to its neutral flavor, makes a great stand-in for potatoes. As a bonus, the low starch content means it purees like a dream. We first tried mashing cauliflower with some potato, but only got wet, sloppy potatoes. But when we ditched the potato (and masher) and pureed steamed cauliflower in the food processor (which would have turned a potato gummy), we got a smooth, velvety texture. To make our puree reminiscent of mashed potatoes, we added thyme and a little garlic sautéed in olive oil. A dash of white wine vinegar balanced all the flavors.*

1 Combine oil and garlic in 8-inch nonstick skillet. Cook over low heat, stirring occasionally, until garlic is pale golden, 9 to 12 minutes. Off heat, stir in thyme, ½ teaspoon salt, and vinegar; transfer to 1-cup liquid measuring cup and set aside to cool.

2 Meanwhile, bring 2½ cups water and ½ teaspoon salt to boil in Dutch oven over high heat. Add cauliflower, cover, and cook until cauliflower is tender, stirring once halfway through, 14 to 16 minutes.

3 Drain cauliflower and transfer to food processor. Add 2 tablespoons water and process cauliflower until mostly smooth, 3 to 4 minutes, scraping down sides of bowl as needed. With processor running, drizzle in oil-garlic mixture and process until completely smooth, about 30 seconds. (If puree is too thick, add hot water, 1 tablespoon at a time, until desired consistency is reached). Transfer to serving bowl and season with salt and pepper to taste. Serve.

PER SERVING
Cal 140; Total Fat 10g, Sat Fat 1.5g; Chol 0mg; Sodium 310mg; Total Carbs 12g, Fiber 5g, Total Sugar 4g, Added Sugar 0g; Protein 4g

EXCELLENT SOURCE OF
Fiber, Vitamin B6, Folate, Vitamin C, Vitamin K, Potassium

vegetables and sides

CAULIFLOWER RICE

serves 4

- 1 head cauliflower (2 pounds), cored and cut into 1-inch florets (6 cups)
- 1 tablespoon cold-pressed extra-virgin olive oil (see page 35)
- 1 shallot, minced
- ½ cup homemade or low-sodium chicken or vegetable broth (see page 36)
  Salt and pepper
- 2 tablespoons minced fresh parsley

why this recipe works • *Cauliflower doesn't just stand in for mashed potatoes. This shape-shifter of a vegetable also approximates cooked white rice surprisingly well, providing a neutral-flavored but more nutrient-dense companion to all sorts of dishes. We found that the key was to blitz the florets in a food processor until transformed into perfect rice-size granules. To make our cauliflower rice foolproof, we worked in batches, making sure all of the florets broke down evenly. Next, we needed to give our cauliflower a boost in flavor; a shallot and a small amount of broth did the trick. To ensure that the cauliflower was tender but still maintained a rice-like chew, we first steamed the "rice" in a covered pot, then finished cooking it uncovered to evaporate any remaining moisture. Our faux rice cooked up pleasantly fluffy, making it the perfect accompaniment to any meal.*

1 Working in 2 batches, pulse cauliflower in food processor until finely ground into ¼- to ⅛-inch pieces, 6 to 8 pulses, scraping down sides of bowl as needed; transfer to bowl.

2 Heat oil in large saucepan over medium-low heat until shimmering. Add shallot and cook until softened, about 3 minutes. Stir in processed cauliflower, broth, and ¾ teaspoon salt. Cover and cook, stirring occasionally, until cauliflower is tender, 12 to 15 minutes.

3 Uncover and continue to cook, stirring occasionally, until cauliflower rice is almost completely dry, about 3 minutes. Off heat, stir in parsley and season with salt and pepper to taste. Serve.

PER SERVING
Cal 100; Total Fat 4g, Sat Fat 1g; Chol 0mg; Sodium 540mg; Total Carbs 13g, Fiber 5g, Total Sugar 5g, Added Sugar 0g; Protein 5g

EXCELLENT SOURCE OF
Fiber, Vitamin B6, Folate, Vitamin C, Vitamin K, Potassium

EDAMAME SALAD WITH ARUGULA AND RADISHES

serves 6

- 2 tablespoons rice vinegar
- 1 tablespoon honey
- 1 small garlic clove, minced
  Salt and pepper
- 3 tablespoons cold-pressed extra-virgin olive oil (see page 35)
- 20 ounces frozen shelled edamame beans, thawed and patted dry
- 2 ounces (2 cups) baby arugula
- ½ cup shredded fresh basil
- ½ cup chopped fresh mint
- 2 radishes, trimmed, halved, and sliced thin
- 1 shallot, halved and sliced thin
- ¼ cup roasted sunflower seeds

why this recipe works • *We love snacking on edamame steamed in their shells, but to turn these immature soybeans into a more substantial salad, we took advantage of frozen, shelled edamame, a great source of vegetable protein and isoflavones, and tossed them with a vibrant mix of arugula, basil, and mint. The sweetness of the basil and mint complemented the peppery arugula, and the edamame's neutral flavor and satisfying pop of texture paired well with the fragrant greens. Though fresh herbs are often used in minimal amounts for seasoning, we wanted to treat them like salad greens and used a handful of each, ensuring tons of flavor and a host of extra vitamins and minerals. Thinly sliced shallot added mild onion flavor, and just a couple of radishes added crunch and color. For the vinaigrette, we chose to use rice vinegar for its mild acidity, which would complement and not overpower the edamame, and added a little honey for sweetness and to help emulsify the dressing. One small clove of garlic added flavor without taking over the dish. The finishing touch was a sprinkling of roasted sunflower seeds, which added nuttiness and depth to our bright salad.*

1 Whisk vinegar, honey, garlic, and ¾ teaspoon salt together in large bowl. Whisking constantly, drizzle in oil until combined.

2 Add edamame, arugula, basil, mint, radishes, and shallot to bowl and toss to combine. Sprinkle with sunflower seeds and season with salt and pepper to taste. Serve.

PER SERVING
Cal 230; Total Fat 14g, Sat Fat 1.5g; Chol 0mg; Sodium 300mg; Total Carbs 14g, Fiber 6g, Total Sugar 7g, Added Sugar 3g; Protein 13g

EXCELLENT SOURCE OF
Protein, Fiber, Vitamin K, Iron

STIR-FRIED EGGPLANT WITH GARLIC-BASIL SAUCE

serves 6

SAUCE

- ½ cup water
- ¼ cup fish sauce
- 2 tablespoons packed brown sugar
- 2 teaspoons grated lime zest plus 1 tablespoon juice
- 2 teaspoons cornstarch
- ⅛ teaspoon red pepper flakes

VEGETABLES

- 2 tablespoons plus 1 teaspoon expeller-pressed canola oil (see page 35)
- 6 garlic cloves, minced
- 1 tablespoon grated fresh ginger
- 1 pound eggplant, cut into ¾-inch pieces
- 1 red bell pepper, stemmed, seeded, and cut into ¼-inch pieces
- ½ cup fresh basil leaves, torn into rough ½-inch pieces
- 2 scallions, sliced thin

why this recipe works • *We love the versatility of eggplant, but its one downfall is that its flesh acts like a sponge, absorbing copious amounts of oil during cooking. We wanted an Asian-inspired stir-fry that starred eggplant but wasn't weighed down by excessive oil, yet still boasted plenty of flavor. We started by mixing our sauce ingredients, allowing the bright lime zest, savory fish sauce, and spicy pepper flakes to meld together. We used just 2 tablespoons of heart-healthy canola oil and sautéed the eggplant (purposefully leaving the skin on for extra fiber and phytonutrients) with a vitamin C–rich red bell pepper until both softened, letting them brown and take on a deeper, caramelized flavor. We then added the garlic and ginger to the center of the skillet, and let them become fragrant before briefly mingling them with the vegetables. We poured our sauce into the stir-fry and added a final sprinkle of basil and scallions to lend a fresh sweetness to the dish before serving. Do not peel the eggplant: In addition to adding nutrients, leaving the skin on helps it hold together during cooking. Serve with brown rice.*

1 **FOR THE SAUCE** Whisk all ingredients together in bowl.

2 **FOR THE VEGETABLES** Combine 1 teaspoon oil, garlic, and ginger in bowl. Heat remaining 2 tablespoons oil in 12-inch nonstick skillet over high heat until shimmering. Add eggplant and bell pepper and cook, stirring often, until well browned and tender, 8 to 10 minutes.

3 Clear center of skillet, add garlic mixture, and cook, mashing mixture into skillet, until fragrant, about 30 seconds. Stir garlic mixture into vegetables. Whisk sauce to recombine, then add to skillet. Cook, stirring constantly, until sauce is thickened, about 30 seconds. Off heat, stir in basil and scallions and serve.

PER SERVING
Cal 120; Total Fat 6g, Sat Fat 0g; Chol 0mg; Sodium 470mg; Total Carbs 15g, Fiber 3g, Total Sugar 8g, Added Sugar 4g; Protein 3g

EXCELLENT SOURCE OF
Vitamin C, Vitamin K

nutritious DELICIOUS

SAUTÉED GREEN BEANS WITH MUSHROOM AND DUKKAH

serves 4

5 teaspoons cold-pressed
  extra-virgin olive oil
  (see page 35)
1 garlic clove, minced
2 tablespoons minced fresh
  parsley
1 teaspoon grated lemon zest
  plus 2 teaspoons lemon juice
8 ounces cremini mushrooms,
  trimmed and sliced thin
3 shallots, halved and sliced thin
  Salt and pepper
1 pound green beans, trimmed
  and cut into 2-inch lengths
¼ cup water
⅓ cup organic plain low-fat
  yogurt
2 tablespoons Dukkah
  (page 232)

why this recipe works • *A traditional green bean casserole may hold nostalgic appeal, but it doesn't pull much nutritional weight with its limp beans, canned cream of mushroom soup, and processed fried onions. To give this classic an overhaul that even Grandma would happily serve year-round, we took inspiration from Middle Eastern flavors. We traded the casserole dish for a skillet and sautéed meaty cremini mushrooms with shallots until golden brown. Next we sautéed fresh green beans until crisp-tender, which maintained maximum nutritional value as well vibrant color. Adding a simple, bold mixture of lemon zest, garlic, and parsley during the last minutes of cooking brought plenty of flavor, which we brightened with lemon juice. To deliver creaminess without weighing down the vegetables, we drizzled on yogurt. Finally we sprinkled the dish with dukkah, an addictive nutrient-packed Middle Eastern blend of roasted chickpeas, pistachios, sesame seeds, and coriander. It made all the flavors pop and proved to be the perfect crunchy finish to our inventive update. You will need a 12-inch nonstick skillet with a tight-fitting lid. We prefer to use homemade dukkah (page 232), but you can substitute store-bought dukkah if you wish.*

1 Combine 1 tablespoon oil, garlic, parsley, and lemon zest in bowl; set aside. Heat 1 teaspoon oil in 12-inch nonstick skillet over medium heat until shimmering. Add mushrooms, shallots, ½ teaspoon salt, and ⅛ teaspoon pepper, cover, and cook until mushrooms have released their liquid, about 5 minutes. Uncover, increase heat to high, and cook, stirring occasionally, until mushrooms are golden, about 8 minutes. Transfer to clean bowl.

2 Heat remaining 1 teaspoon oil in now-empty skillet over medium heat until shimmering. Add green beans and cook, stirring occasionally, until spotty brown, 4 to 6 minutes. Add water, cover, and cook until green beans are bright green and still crisp, about 2 minutes.

3 Uncover, increase heat to high, and cook until water evaporates, 30 to 60 seconds. Stir in oil-garlic mixture and mushrooms and cook until beans are crisp-tender, 1 to 3 minutes. Off heat, stir in lemon juice and season with salt and pepper to taste. Transfer to platter, drizzle with yogurt, and sprinkle with dukkah. Serve.

PER SERVING
Cal 150; Total Fat 7g, Sat Fat 1g;
Chol 0mg; Sodium 380mg; Total
Carbs 17g, Fiber 5g, Total Sugar 8g,
Added Sugar 0g; Protein 5g

EXCELLENT SOURCE OF
Fiber, Riboflavin, Vitamin C,
Vitamin K, Manganese

nutritious DELICIOUS

GARLICKY BRAISED KALE

3 tablespoons cold-pressed
   extra-virgin olive oil
   (see page 35)
1 onion, chopped fine
5 garlic cloves, minced
⅛ teaspoon red pepper flakes
2 pounds kale, stemmed and
   cut into 3-inch pieces
1 cup homemade or low-sodium
   chicken or vegetable broth
   (see page 36)
1 cup water
   Salt and pepper
2 teaspoons lemon juice

why this recipe works • *Kale is among the most nutrient-dense of all vegetables, but it can be difficult to turn the hearty green tender enough to enjoy. We wanted a simple approach to producing tender kale without overcooking the greens or leaving them awash in liquid, draining away many of the nutrients. We started with a generous 2 pounds of kale. To fit them in the pot, we sautéed half of the greens before adding the rest, then we stirred in a little liquid and covered the pot. In less than half an hour, the greens had almost the tender-firm texture we wanted. We removed the lid to allow the liquid to evaporate as the greens finished cooking. For flavorings, we added a substantial amount of healthful garlic plus chopped onion and a pinch of red pepper flakes for heat. A squeeze of fresh lemon juice balanced the dish. You can substitute collard greens for the kale here. For the best results, be sure the greens are fully cooked and tender in step 1 before moving on to step 2.*

1 Heat 2 tablespoons oil in Dutch oven over medium heat until shimmering. Add onion and cook until softened and beginning to brown, 5 to 7 minutes. Stir in garlic and pepper flakes and cook until fragrant, about 1 minute. Stir in half of kale and cook until beginning to wilt, about 1 minute. Stir in remaining kale, broth, water, and ¼ teaspoon salt. Cover pot, reduce heat to medium-low, and cook, stirring occasionally, until greens are tender, 25 to 35 minutes.

2 Uncover and increase heat to medium-high. Cook, stirring occasionally, until most of liquid has evaporated (bottom of pot will be almost dry and greens will begin to sizzle), 8 to 12 minutes. Off heat, stir in lemon juice and remaining 1 tablespoon oil. Season with salt and pepper to taste. Serve.

PER SERVING
Cal 110; Total Fat 8g, Sat Fat 1g;
Chol 0mg; Sodium 190mg; Total
Carbs 10g, Fiber 3g, Total Sugar 3g,
Added Sugar 0g; Protein 4g

EXCELLENT SOURCE OF
Vitamin A, Folate, Vitamin C,
Vitamin K, Copper, Manganese

vegetables and sides

SAUTÉED SPINACH WITH YOGURT AND DUKKAH

serves 4

½ cup organic plain low-fat
   yogurt
1½ teaspoons lemon zest plus
   1 teaspoon juice
   Salt and pepper
3 tablespoons cold-pressed
   extra-virgin olive oil
   (see page 35)
20 ounces curly-leaf spinach,
   stemmed
2 garlic cloves, minced
¼ cup Dukkah (recipe follows)

why this recipe works • *Creamed spinach is hard to resist, but the healthful benefits of spinach, such as iron and vitamin K, are canceled out by the butter and cream. Seeking a healthier route, we were pleased to find the tanginess of yogurt paired even better with spinach's earthy flavor. To emphasize the yogurt's tang, we added lemon zest and juice and drizzled it over our garlicky spinach. To elevate the flavor, we sprinkled on dukkah, a power-packed Middle Eastern blend of ground roasted chickpeas, nuts, and seeds, which lent a nice textural contrast. Two pounds of flat-leaf spinach (about three bunches) can be substituted for the curly-leaf spinach; do not substitute baby spinach. We prefer to use our homemade dukkah, but you can substitute store-bought dukkah if you wish.*

1 Combine yogurt and lemon zest and juice in bowl, and season with salt and pepper to taste; set aside for serving. Heat 1 tablespoon oil in Dutch oven over high heat until shimmering. Add spinach, 1 handful at a time, and cook, stirring constantly, until wilted, about 1 minute. Transfer spinach to colander and squeeze between tongs to release excess liquid.

2 Wipe pot dry with paper towels. Add remaining 2 tablespoons oil and garlic to now-empty pot and cook over medium heat until fragrant, about 30 seconds. Add spinach and toss to coat, gently separating leaves to evenly coat with garlic oil. Off heat, season with salt and pepper to taste. Transfer spinach to serving platter, drizzle with yogurt sauce, and sprinkle with dukkah. Serve.

DUKKAH
makes 2 cups
Dukkah is traditionally sprinkled on olive oil to use as a dip for bread, but it also makes a crunchy garnish for soup, salads, and vegetables.

1 (15-ounce) can chickpeas, rinsed and patted dry
1 teaspoon cold-pressed extra-virgin olive oil (see page 35)
½ cup shelled pistachios, toasted
⅓ cup black sesame seeds, toasted
2½ tablespoons coriander seeds, toasted
1 tablespoon cumin seeds, toasted
2 teaspoons fennel seeds, toasted
1½ teaspoons pepper
1¼ teaspoons salt

PER SERVING
Cal 180; Total Fat 13g, Sat Fat 2g;
Chol 0mg; Sodium 250mg; Total
Carbs 10g, Fiber 4g, Total Sugar 2g,
Added Sugar 0g; Protein 6g

EXCELLENT SOURCE OF
Vitamin A, Folate, Vitamin C,
Vitamin K, Calcium, Iron,
Magnesium, Manganese

1 Adjust oven rack to middle position and heat oven to 400 degrees. Toss chickpeas with oil and spread in single layer on rimmed baking sheet. Roast until browned and crisp, 40 to 45 minutes, stirring every 5 to 10 minutes; let cool completely.

2 Process chickpeas in food processor until coarsely ground, about 10 seconds; transfer to bowl. Pulse pistachios and sesame seeds in now-empty food processor until coarsely ground, about 15 pulses; transfer to bowl with chickpeas. Process coriander, cumin, and fennel seeds in again-empty food processor until finely ground, 2 to 3 minutes; transfer to bowl with chickpeas. Add pepper and salt and toss until well combined. (Dukkah can be refrigerated for up to 1 month.)

ROASTED BUTTERNUT SQUASH WITH PISTACHIOS AND FETA

serves 6

3 pounds butternut squash
3 tablespoons cold-pressed extra-virgin olive oil (see page 35)
   Salt and pepper
1 tablespoon tahini
1½ teaspoons lemon juice
1 teaspoon honey
1 ounce feta cheese, crumbled (¼ cup)
¼ cup shelled pistachios, toasted and chopped fine
2 tablespoons chopped fresh mint

why this recipe works • *We wanted to kick up the flavor of roasted butternut squash without resorting to a cloyingly sweet or excessively rich treatment. For a more balanced and nutritious approach, we used a light hand with bold-flavored pistachios and briny feta. First, to get perfectly cooked squash, we peeled it to remove not only the tough outer skin, but also the rugged fibrous layer of white flesh just beneath, exposing the vibrant orange, supremely tender flesh full of beta-carotene. To encourage the natural sugars in the squash to caramelize, we used a hot 425-degree oven, placed the squash on the lowest oven rack, and increased the roasting time to evaporate moisture. We added our flavorings: pistachios for crunch and some heart-healthy fat, mint for brightness, and feta for tang and richness. Spiked with a touch of honey and lemon juice, tahini (another good source of healthy fats plus calcium and iron) was the perfect topping and made for a simple, beautiful presentation. This dish can be served warm or at room temperature. For the best texture, be sure to peel the squash thoroughly, removing all of the fibrous flesh just below the skin.*

1 Adjust oven rack to lowest position and heat oven to 425 degrees. Using vegetable peeler or chef's knife, remove squash skin and fibrous threads just below skin (squash should be completely orange with no white flesh). Halve squash lengthwise and scrape out seeds. Place squash cut side down on cutting board and slice crosswise into ½-inch-thick pieces.

2 Toss squash with 2 tablespoons oil, ½ teaspoon salt, and ½ teaspoon pepper and arrange in single layer on rimmed baking sheet. Roast until bottoms of squash toward back of oven are well browned, 25 to 30 minutes. Rotate sheet and continue to roast until bottoms of remaining squash are well browned, 6 to 10 minutes.

3 Flip each squash piece and continue to roast until very tender and bottoms are browned, 10 to 15 minutes.

4 Transfer squash to serving platter. Whisk tahini, lemon juice, honey, remaining 1 tablespoon oil, and pinch salt together in bowl. Drizzle tahini mixture over squash and sprinkle with feta, pistachios, and mint. Serve.

PER SERVING
Cal 210; Total Fat 12g, Sat Fat 2g; Chol 4mg; Sodium 250mg; Total Carbs 25g, Fiber 4g, Total Sugar 6g, Added Sugar 1g; Protein 4g

EXCELLENT SOURCE OF
Vitamin A, Vitamin B6, Vitamin C, Manganese, Potassium

TWICE-BAKED SWEET POTATOES WITH HAZELNUTS

serves 6

- 4 small sweet potatoes (8 ounces each), unpeeled, each lightly pricked with fork in 3 places
- 2 tablespoons cold-pressed extra-virgin olive oil (see page 35)
- 2 shallots, sliced thin
- 2 garlic cloves, minced
- ¼ cup hazelnuts, toasted, skinned, and chopped
- 2 tablespoons chopped fresh parsley
- 2 tablespoons minced fresh chives
- 2 tablespoons grated Parmesan cheese
  Salt and pepper
- 1 large organic egg, lightly beaten
- ¼ cup organic plain 2 percent Greek yogurt

PER SERVING
Cal 210; Total Fat 10g, Sat Fat 1.5g; Chol 35mg; Sodium 220mg; Total Carbs 26g, Fiber 5g, Total Sugar 8g, Added Sugar 0g; Protein 6g

EXCELLENT SOURCE OF
Fiber, Vitamin A, Vitamin C, Vitamin K, Manganese

why this recipe works • *Part baked potato, part casserole, twice-baked potatoes spruce up any meal. Unfortunately, they come loaded with luxurious butter, bacon, cheese, and sour cream. To remake this classic into an elegant, nutritious side, we swapped out starchy russets for sweet potatoes, choosing small potatoes for reasonably sized portions. Keeping the skin on provided extra fiber. Mashing the flesh with an egg, Greek yogurt, and Parmesan produced a filling that was fluffy and just rich enough. To accentuate the earthy potatoes, we topped them with toasted hazelnuts, parsley, and chives and traded sour cream for seasoned Greek yogurt for a creamy finish.*

1 Adjust oven rack to middle position and heat oven to 425 degrees. Place potatoes in shallow baking dish. Microwave until skewer glides easily through flesh, 9 to 12 minutes, flipping potatoes every 3 minutes. Let potatoes cool for 10 minutes.

2 Halve each potato lengthwise. Using spoon, scoop flesh from each half into medium bowl, leaving about ⅛- to ¼-inch thickness of flesh. Place 6 shells cut side up on wire rack set in rimmed baking sheet (discard remaining 2 shells). Bake shells until dry and slightly crispy, about 10 minutes. Remove shells from oven and reduce temperature to 325 degrees.

3 Heat oil in 10-inch skillet over medium heat until shimmering. Add shallots and cook, stirring occasionally, until softened and lightly browned, about 3 minutes. Stir in half of the garlic and cook until fragrant, about 30 seconds. Transfer mixture to second bowl. Add hazelnuts, parsley, chives, 1 tablespoon Parmesan, and ⅛ teaspoon pepper to shallot mixture and toss to combine.

4 Mash potato flesh with ricer, food mill, or potato masher until smooth. Whisk in egg, 1 tablespoon yogurt, remaining garlic, remaining 1 tablespoon Parmesan, and ¼ teaspoon salt until well combined and fluffy.

5 Divide mashed potato mixture evenly among shells. Top each filled shell with shallot-hazelnut mixture and return filled potatoes to wire rack. When oven has reached 325 degrees, bake until topping is spotty golden brown and filling is hot, about 20 minutes.

6 Season remaining 3 tablespoons yogurt with salt and pepper and dollop onto potatoes. Serve.

vegetables and sides

SWEET POTATO AND SWISS CHARD GRATIN

serves 6

- 2 tablespoons cold-pressed extra-virgin olive oil (see page 35)
- 2 shallots, minced
  Salt and pepper
- 2 pounds Swiss chard, stemmed and cut into ½-inch-wide strips
- 3 garlic cloves, minced
- 2 teaspoons minced fresh thyme or ¾ teaspoon dried
- ⅓ cup homemade or low-sodium chicken or vegetable broth (page 36)
- ⅓ cup water
- ⅓ cup dry white wine
- 3 pounds sweet potatoes, peeled and sliced ⅛ inch thick
- 2 ounces Parmesan cheese, grated (1 cup)

why this recipe works • *Potato gratin is a satisfying classic, but we wanted a more nutritious version that wasn't swimming in cream. We first replaced the regular spuds with their sweet, bright-orange relative, a rich source of vitamin A. But sweet potatoes got their name for a reason, so to mitigate some of their sweetness, we turned to earthy, slightly bitter Swiss chard, packed full of vitamin K, which we sautéed with shallots, garlic, and thyme. We shingled half the sliced potatoes along the bottom of a gratin dish, added our chard, then layered on the remaining potatoes. Pouring a mix of broth, water, and wine over the vegetables encouraged the potatoes to cook evenly and imparted a welcome savoriness—no cream necessary. We topped the potatoes with Parmesan; just 2 ounces provided the salty richness we wanted. Covering the gratin dish for the first 20 minutes of baking gave the potatoes enough time to cook through, then we uncovered the dish to ensure the excess liquid could evaporate and the cheesy topping could brown and form the perfect light crust. Slicing the potatoes ⅛ inch thick is crucial for the success of this dish; use a mandoline, a V-slicer, or a food processor fitted with a ⅛-inch-thick slicing blade.*

1 Adjust oven rack to middle position and heat oven to 350 degrees. Heat oil in Dutch oven over medium-high heat until shimmering. Add shallots and ¼ teaspoon salt and cook until shallots are softened, about 2 minutes. Stir in chard and cook until wilted, about 2 minutes. Stir in garlic, thyme, and ¾ teaspoon pepper and cook until fragrant, about 30 seconds; transfer to bowl.

2 Add broth, water, wine, and ¼ teaspoon salt to now-empty pot and bring to simmer over medium-high heat. Remove pot from heat and cover to keep warm.

3 Shingle half of potatoes evenly into 3-quart gratin dish (or 13 by 9-inch baking dish). Spread wilted chard mixture evenly over potatoes, then shingle remaining potatoes over top. Pour broth mixture evenly over top, and sprinkle with Parmesan.

4 Cover dish with aluminum foil and bake for 20 minutes. Uncover, and continue to bake until gratin is golden and feels tender when poked with paring knife, 40 to 50 minutes. Let cool for 10 minutes, season with salt and pepper to taste, and serve.

PER SERVING
Cal 270; Total Fat 8g, Sat Fat 2g; Chol 5mg; Sodium 650mg; Total Carbs 40g, Fiber 8g, Total Sugar 12g, Added Sugar 0g; Protein 9g

EXCELLENT SOURCE OF
Fiber, Vitamin A, Vitamin C, Vitamin K, Calcium, Potassium

nutritious delicious

ROASTED SPIRALIZED SWEET POTATOES WITH WALNUTS AND FETA

serves 4

2 pounds sweet potatoes, peeled
1 tablespoon cold-pressed extra-virgin olive oil (see page 35), plus extra for serving
Salt and pepper
¼ cup walnuts, toasted and chopped coarse
1 ounce feta cheese, crumbled (¼ cup)
2 tablespoons chopped fresh parsley

why this recipe works • *Wanting a simple but more nutrient-packed alternative to roasted white potatoes, we set out to create a quick side dish highlighting sweet potatoes. We decided to use a spiralizer to cut the potatoes into beautiful ⅛-inch-thick noodles which would cook quickly. We found that simply roasting the potatoes in a hot oven, uncovered, for about 12 minutes gave us the result we were after: sweet potatoes that were tender but not mushy, with just a bit of caramelization. To finish the dish, we sprinkled on ¼ cup each of tangy feta and earthy, omega-3-rich walnuts, plus a generous sprinkle of fresh parsley. Sweet potato noodles are quite delicate; be careful when tossing them with the oil and seasonings in step 2, and again when transferring them to the serving platter before serving. Our favorite spiralizer model is the Paderno World Cuisine Tri-Blade Plastic Spiral Vegetable Slicer. If you do not have a spiralizer, you can also use a mandoline or V-slicer fitted with a ⅛-inch julienne attachment. Make sure to position the vegetables on the mandoline vertically so that the resulting noodles are as long as possible. We do not recommend cutting vegetable noodles by hand.*

1 Adjust oven rack to middle position and heat oven to 450 degrees. Using spiralizer, cut sweet potatoes into ⅛-inch-thick noodles, then cut noodles into 12-inch lengths.

2 Toss potato noodles with oil, ¼ teaspoon salt, and ⅛ teaspoon pepper and spread on rimmed baking sheet. Roast until potatoes are just tender, 12 to 14 minutes, stirring once halfway through roasting.

3 Season potatoes with salt and pepper to taste and transfer to serving platter. Sprinkle walnuts, feta, and parsley over top, then drizzle with extra oil to taste. Serve.

PER SERVING
Cal 240; Total Fat 9g, Sat Fat 2g; Chol 5mg; Sodium 320mg; Total Carbs 35g, Fiber 6g, Total Sugar 11g, Added Sugar 0g; Protein 5g

EXCELLENT SOURCE OF
Fiber, Vitamin A, Vitamin C, Vitamin K

LENTILS WITH SPINACH AND GARLIC CHIPS

serves 6

2 tablespoons cold-pressed extra-virgin olive oil (see page 35)
4 garlic cloves, sliced thin
Salt and pepper
1 onion, chopped fine
1 teaspoon ground coriander
1 teaspoon ground cumin
2½ cups water
1 cup green or brown lentils, picked over and rinsed
8 ounces curly-leaf spinach, stemmed and chopped coarse
1 tablespoon red wine vinegar

why this recipe works • *Nutrient-dense and easy to prepare, lentils are not given nearly enough credit. Their relatively neutral flavor makes them adaptable to a range of flavors. To give our lentils, which are packed with fiber, an equally healthy partner, we paired them with fresh spinach, which contributed its own array of vitamins and minerals. We started by sautéing sliced garlic in oil until crisp; the crunchy golden garlic chips added a nice textural contrast and infused the cooking oil with garlic flavor. We then bloomed coriander and cumin in the oil until fragrant before adding our lentils, which would absorb the warm spices as they cooked. Allowing the sturdy curly-leaf spinach to wilt in the pot with the lentils was simple and avoided dirtying extra dishes. For a finishing touch, we stirred in some red wine vinegar for brightness. If you can't find curly-leaf spinach, you can substitute 12 ounces of flat-leaf spinach; do not substitute baby spinach. We prefer green or brown lentils for this recipe, but it will work with any type of lentil except red or yellow (note that cooking times will vary depending on the type used).*

1 Cook oil and garlic in large saucepan over medium-low heat, stirring often, until garlic turns crisp and golden but not brown, about 5 minutes. Using slotted spoon, transfer garlic to paper towel–lined plate and season lightly with salt; set aside.

2 Add onion and ½ teaspoon salt to oil left in saucepan and cook over medium heat until softened and lightly browned, 5 to 7 minutes. Stir in coriander and cumin and cook until fragrant, about 30 seconds.

3 Stir in water and lentils and bring to simmer. Cover, reduce heat to low, and simmer gently, stirring occasionally, until lentils are mostly tender but still intact, 45 to 50 minutes.

4 Stir in spinach, 1 handful at a time. Cook, uncovered, stirring occasionally, until spinach is wilted and lentils are completely tender, about 8 minutes. Stir in vinegar and season with salt and pepper to taste. Sprinkle with toasted garlic and serve.

PER SERVING
Cal 160; Total Fat 5g, Sat Fat 0.5g; Chol 0mg; Sodium 230mg; Total Carbs 22g, Fiber 6g, Total Sugar 1g, Added Sugar 0g; Protein 8g

EXCELLENT SOURCE OF
Fiber, Vitamin A, Vitamin C, Vitamin K, Manganese

vegetables and sides

CURRIED CHICKPEAS WITH GARLIC AND YOGURT

serves 6

¼ cup cold-pressed extra-virgin olive oil (see page 35)
4 garlic cloves, sliced thin
1 onion, chopped fine
Salt and pepper
1 teaspoon curry powder
2 (15-ounce) cans chickpeas, rinsed
1 cup homemade or low-sodium chicken or vegetable broth (page 36)
⅓ cup raisins
2 tablespoons minced fresh parsley
2 teaspoons lime juice
¼ cup organic plain low-fat yogurt

why this recipe works • *Chickpeas are a pantry staple with plenty of fiber, protein, and iron. To get more mileage out of them, we wanted to use them in a simple everyday side dish. We created a flavorful base for our chickpeas by sautéing garlic and onion. We then elevated the humble legume by infusing our oil with fragrant curry powder. In search of other easy kitchen staples to flavor our chickpeas, we reached for chicken or vegetable broth and raisins, which imparted a sweet-savory backbone to the dish without overpowering it, complementing the warm spice of the curry. Keeping the chickpeas whole provided excellent texture. As final touches, we added parsley and lime juice for freshness, along with yogurt, which added a creamy tang to mellow the curry.*

1 Combine 3 tablespoons oil and garlic in 12-inch skillet and cook over medium heat, stirring occasionally, until garlic is light golden, 3 to 5 minutes. Stir in onion and ¼ teaspoon salt and cook until onion is softened and lightly browned, 5 to 7 minutes.

2 Stir in curry powder and cook until fragrant, about 30 seconds. Stir in chickpeas, broth, and raisins and bring to simmer. Cover and cook until chickpeas are warmed through and flavors have melded, about 7 minutes.

3 Uncover, increase heat to high, and simmer until nearly all liquid has evaporated, about 3 minutes. Off heat, stir in parsley and lime juice. Stir in yogurt, season with salt and pepper to taste, and drizzle with remaining 1 tablespoon oil. Serve.

nutritious DELICIOUS

PER SERVING
Cal 210; Total Fat 11g, Sat Fat 1.5g; Chol 0mg; Sodium 380mg; Total Carbs 23g, Fiber 4g, Total Sugar 9g, Added Sugar 0g; Protein 5g

EXCELLENT SOURCE OF
Vitamin K

BUTTERNUT SQUASH POLENTA

serves 8

- 1 small (1½- to 2-pound) butternut squash, halved lengthwise, seeds removed
- 1 tablespoon cold-pressed extra-virgin olive oil, plus extra for serving (see page 35)
  Salt and pepper
- 1 small onion, chopped fine
- 1½ teaspoons minced fresh sage
- ⅛ teaspoon ground nutmeg
- 5 cups water
- 1 bay leaf
  Pinch baking soda
- 1 cup whole-grain coarse-ground cornmeal
- 1 ounce Parmesan cheese, grated (½ cup); plus extra for serving
- 2 tablespoons pepitas, toasted
  Balsamic vinegar

PER SERVING
Cal 140; Total Fat 4.5g, Sat Fat 1g; Chol 3mg; Sodium 380mg; Total Carbs 24g, Fiber 5g, Total Sugar 3g, Added Sugar 0g; Protein 4g

EXCELLENT SOURCE OF
Fiber, Vitamin A, Vitamin C

why this recipe works • *Butternut squash puree transforms polenta into a nutritious side dish while enhancing its rustic appeal. How much squash could we add without overpowering polenta's texture and sweet corn flavor? Turns out, for 1 cup of cornmeal, a whole small squash was perfect. Roasting squash halves and scooping out the creamy flesh kept the process unfussy. For fluffy, creamy polenta, we added a pinch of baking soda, which encouraged the grains to release their starches for a silky consistency with minimal stirring. To round out the flavor, we cooked the polenta with fresh sage and a pinch of nutmeg, then finished with a bit of Parmesan.*

1 Adjust oven rack to middle position and heat oven to 400 degrees. Line rimmed baking sheet with aluminum foil. Brush cut sides of squash with 1½ teaspoons oil, season with ¼ teaspoon salt and ⅛ teaspoon pepper, and place cut sides down on prepared baking sheet. Roast until fork inserted into center meets little resistance and sides touching sheet are deep golden brown, 40 to 50 minutes.

2 Remove squash from oven and let cool for 10 minutes. Scoop flesh of squash into medium bowl and set aside; discard skin.

3 Heat remaining 1½ teaspoons oil in large saucepan over medium heat until shimmering. Add onion and ¾ teaspoon salt and cook until softened and lightly browned, 5 to 7 minutes. Add sage and nutmeg and cook until fragrant, about 30 seconds. Stir in water, bay leaf, ¼ teaspoon pepper, and baking soda and bring to boil. Slowly pour cornmeal into water in steady stream while stirring back and forth with wooden spoon or rubber spatula. Bring mixture to boil, stirring constantly, about 1 minute. Reduce heat to lowest setting and cover.

4 After 5 minutes, whisk polenta to smooth out any lumps that may have formed, about 15 seconds. (Make sure to scrape down sides and bottom of saucepan.) Cover and continue to cook, whisking occasionally, until polenta grains are tender but slightly al dente, about 25 minutes longer.

5 Stir in cooked squash, increase heat to medium-low, and cook, stirring occasionally, until squash is well incorporated, about 5 minutes.

6 Off heat, stir in Parmesan and season with salt and pepper to taste. Cover and let sit for 5 minutes. Serve, topping individual portions with extra Parmesan, pepitas, and a drizzle of balsamic vinegar.

QUINOA PILAF WITH SHIITAKES, EDAMAME, AND GINGER

serves 6

- 1½ cups prewashed white quinoa
- 2 tablespoons expeller-pressed canola oil (see page 35)
- 4 scallions, white parts minced, green parts sliced thin on bias
- 4 ounces shiitake mushrooms, stemmed and sliced thin
- 2 teaspoons grated fresh ginger
  Salt and pepper
- 1¾ cups water
- ½ cup frozen shelled edamame beans, thawed and patted dry
- 4 teaspoons rice vinegar
- 1 tablespoon mirin

why this recipe works • Quinoa cooks quickly and is hands-off, making it ideal for weeknight dinners; plus, the tiny seeds toast up nicely, making it the perfect starting point for a vegetable-full pilaf. We started by toasting the quinoa in a dry skillet to bring out its natural nuttiness. Then we sautéed fragrant scallions, shiitakes, and ginger, letting them soften and become even more aromatic before adding our liquid. Most recipes for quinoa pilaf turn out woefully overcooked because they call for far too much liquid. We cut the water back to ensure tender grains with a satisfying bite. The fresh ginger provided a brightness to the quinoa that paired well with pungent scallions and earthy, vitamin-and-mineral-packed mushrooms. And because they cooked with the quinoa and weren't just mixed in toward the end, their flavors melded thoroughly with the protein-packed seed. If you buy unwashed quinoa (or if you are unsure whether it's washed), be sure to rinse it before cooking to remove its bitter protective coating (called saponin).

1 Toast quinoa in medium saucepan over medium-high heat, stirring frequently, until quinoa is very fragrant and makes continuous popping sound, 5 to 7 minutes. Transfer quinoa to bowl.

2 Return now-empty saucepan to medium-low heat, add oil, and heat until shimmering. Add scallion whites, mushrooms, ginger, and ¾ teaspoon salt and cook, stirring frequently, until softened, 5 to 7 minutes.

3 Increase heat to medium-high, stir in water and toasted quinoa, and bring to simmer. Cover, reduce heat to low, and simmer until grains are just tender and liquid is absorbed, 18 to 20 minutes, stirring once halfway through cooking.

4 Remove pot from heat and stir in edamame. Lay clean folded dish towel underneath lid and let sit, covered, for 10 minutes. Fluff quinoa with fork, stir in scallion greens, vinegar, and mirin, and season with salt and pepper to taste. Serve.

PER SERVING
Cal 230; Total Fat 8g, Sat Fat 0.5g; Chol 0mg; Sodium 300mg; Total Carbs 31g, Fiber 4g, Total Sugar 4g, Added Sugar 0g; Protein 8g

EXCELLENT SOURCE OF
Folate, Vitamin K, Magnesium, Manganese, Phosphorus

BROWN RICE PILAF WITH DATES AND PISTACHIOS

serves 6

1 tablespoon cold-pressed
   extra-virgin olive oil
   (see page 35)
1 onion, chopped fine
   Salt and pepper
3¼ cups homemade or low-sodium
   chicken or vegetable broth
   (see page 36)
1½ cups long-grain brown rice,
   rinsed
1 bay leaf
1½ ounces pitted dates, chopped
   (¼ cup)
⅓ cup shelled pistachios, toasted
   and coarsely chopped
¼ cup minced fresh mint

why this recipe works • *We set out to enrich simple rice pilaf with nutritious add-ins without distracting from its ability to complement any number of dishes. The first order of business was to exchange white rice for brown to build a healthful base for our add-ins. A Middle Eastern–inspired combination of aromatic onions, sweet dates, earthy pistachios, and fresh mint created the flavorful yet mild profile we were after. We knew from previous testing that oven baking brown rice guaranteed the most even and appealing texture. (On the stovetop, the rice on top can become mushy as the rice on the bottom dries out.) In a Dutch oven, we sautéed a base of onions, stirred in broth, rice, and a bay leaf, and baked it all, covered, for about an hour. When the rice was tender, we removed it from the oven, sprinkled chopped dates over the top, covered the pot again, and let it sit for 5 minutes, just enough time for the dates to become plump and tender. After a quick fluff with a fork to incorporate a sprinkling of pistachios and mint, our pilaf was good to go. Medium-grain or short-grain brown rice can be substituted for the long-grain rice.*

1 Adjust oven rack to middle position and heat oven to 375 degrees. Heat oil in Dutch oven over medium heat until shimmering. Add onion and ½ teaspoon salt and cook until softened and lightly browned, 5 to 7 minutes.

2 Stir in broth, cover, and bring to boil. Off heat, stir in rice and bay leaf. Cover, transfer pot to oven, and bake until liquid is absorbed and rice is tender, 55 to 65 minutes.

3 Remove pot from oven. Sprinkle dates over rice and let sit, covered, for 10 minutes. Discard bay leaf. Fluff rice with fork, stir in pistachios and mint, and season with salt and pepper to taste. Serve.

PER SERVING
Cal 270; Total Fat 7g, Sat Fat 1g;
Chol 0mg; Sodium 350mg; Total
Carbs 44g, Fiber 3g, Total Sugar 6g,
Added Sugar 0g; Protein 7g

EXCELLENT SOURCE OF
Thiamine, Niacin, Manganese

BULGUR PILAF WITH CREMINI MUSHROOMS

serves 4

- 2 tablespoons cold-pressed extra-virgin olive oil (see page 35)
- 1 onion, chopped fine
- ¼ ounce dried porcini mushrooms, rinsed and minced
  Salt and pepper
- 8 ounces cremini mushrooms, stemmed and quartered if small or cut into 6 pieces if large
- 2 garlic cloves, minced
- 1 cup medium-grind bulgur, rinsed
- ¾ cup homemade or low-sodium chicken or vegetable broth (see page 36)
- ¾ cup water
- 1 teaspoon low-sodium soy sauce
- ¼ cup minced fresh parsley

why this recipe works • *Brown rice isn't the only whole grain that takes well to the pilaf method. To bring more diversity to our grain sides, we swapped out rice for bulgur, a form of wheat grain that's been parboiled and dried so it cooks fast yet still retains all the benefits of whole grains. Earthy mushrooms paired well with the hearty grain and packed even more of a nutritional punch. For big mushroom flavor, we chose widely available cremini mushrooms plus a ¼ ounce of dried porcini, which added nice depth. Just a dash of soy sauce boosted the mushroom's umami flavor even further and gave the dish a rich mahogany color. We sautéed the mushrooms with an onion, then we added the bulgur and the cooking liquid (a combination of water and broth) and simmered it until tender. After removing the pot from the heat, we placed a dish towel underneath the lid (which helped absorb moisture) and let the bulgur steam gently for 10 minutes, which resulted in perfectly tender, chewy grains. When shopping, don't confuse bulgur with cracked wheat, which has a much longer cooking time and will not work in this recipe.*

1 Heat oil in large saucepan over medium heat until shimmering. Add onion, porcini mushrooms, and ¼ teaspoon salt and cook until onion is softened, about 5 minutes. Stir in cremini mushrooms, increase heat to medium-high, cover, and cook until cremini mushrooms have released their liquid and begin to brown, about 4 minutes.

2 Stir in garlic and cook until fragrant, about 30 seconds. Stir in bulgur, broth, water, and soy sauce and bring to simmer. Cover, reduce heat to low, and simmer until bulgur is tender, 16 to 18 minutes.

3 Remove pot from heat, lay clean folded dish towel underneath lid, and let bulgur sit, covered, for 10 minutes. Fluff bulgur with fork, stir in parsley, and season with salt and pepper to taste. Serve.

PER SERVING
Cal 220; Total Fat 8g, Sat Fat 1g; Chol 0mg; Sodium 280mg; Total Carbs 33g, Fiber 5g, Total Sugar 3g, Added Sugar 0g; Protein 6g

EXCELLENT SOURCE OF
Fiber, Riboflavin, Niacin, Vitamin K, Manganese

VARIATION
BULGUR PILAF WITH SHIITAKE MUSHROOMS
Substitute 8 ounces stemmed and thinly sliced shiitake mushrooms for cremini, and 2 thinly sliced scallions for parsley. Add 1 tablespoon grated fresh ginger to pot with garlic.

SNACKS

256 Beet Muhammara

258 Super Guacamole

261 Sweet Potato Hummus

263 Navy Bean and Artichoke Dip

264 Roasted Tomato Salsa with Black Beans

267 Anchovy Dip

269 Kale Chips

270 Beet Chips

273 Whole-Wheat Seeded Crackers

275 Ultimate Nachos

276 Smoked Trout Deviled Eggs
     Smoked Salmon Deviled Eggs

278 Brown Rice Onigiri with Spinach, Edamame, and Sesame

281 Cherry, Chocolate, and Orange Trail Mix
     Cranberry, Coconut, Chili, and Lime Trail Mix

BEET MUHAMMARA

makes about 2 cups

- 8 ounces beets, trimmed, peeled, and shredded
- 1 cup jarred roasted red peppers, rinsed and patted dry
- 1 cup walnuts, toasted
- 1 scallion, sliced thin
- 2 tablespoons cold-pressed extra-virgin olive oil (see page 35), plus extra for drizzling
- 2 tablespoons pomegranate molasses
- 2 teaspoons lemon juice
- ¾ teaspoon salt
- ½ teaspoon ground cumin
- ⅛ teaspoon cayenne pepper
- 2 tablespoons minced fresh parsley

why this recipe works • *Traditional* muhammara *is a sweet-smoky blend of roasted red peppers, toasted walnuts, pomegranate molasses, and spices popular in Turkish and Syrian cuisine. A true multi-use recipe bursting with flavor, it makes a delicious dip, a spread for sandwiches, and even a sauce for meat and fish. Our simple version incorporates beets, which gives the already nutrient-packed mixture a splendid color, along with a boost of vitamins and minerals. We tested several methods of preparing the beets, steering away from roasting to minimize kitchen time. Some tasters loved the flavor and texture imparted by raw grated beets, but for optimal creaminess we found that microwaving grated beets softened them just enough to blend into the mixture while preserving their bright, fresh flavor as well as their nutrients. Some recipes thicken the dip with bread, but we opted for protein-rich walnuts to do the job. Jarred roasted peppers added smokiness without any hassle. A touch of pomegranate molasses gave the dip its hallmark sweet yet slightly bitter flavor. Pomegranate molasses can be found in the international aisle of well-stocked supermarkets; if you can't find it, substitute 1 tablespoon lemon juice plus 1 tablespoon mild molasses for the 2 tablespoons of pomegranate molasses. You can use the large holes of a box grater or a food processor fitted with a shredding disk to shred the beets. Serve with vegetables, whole-grain crackers, or whole-grain chips.*

1 Microwave beets in covered bowl, stirring often, until beets are tender, about 4 minutes. Transfer beets to fine-mesh strainer set over bowl and let drain for 10 minutes.

2 Process drained beets, peppers, walnuts, scallion, oil, pomegranate molasses, lemon juice, salt, cumin, and cayenne together in food processor until smooth, about 1 minute, scraping down sides of bowl as needed.

3 Transfer mixture to serving bowl. Season with salt to taste. (Muhammara can be refrigerated for up to 3 days; bring to room temperature before serving.) Drizzle with extra oil to taste, and sprinkle with parsley before serving.

PER ¼ CUP
Cal 150; Total Fat 12g, Sat Fat 1.5g; Chol 0mg; Sodium 330mg; Total Carbs 9g, Fiber 2g, Total Sugar 6g, Added Sugar 0g; Protein 2g

EXCELLENT SOURCE OF
Vitamin K, Manganese

SUPER GUACAMOLE

makes about 2 cups

- 3 tablespoons pomegranate seeds
- 2 scallions, sliced thin
- 2 tablespoons roasted pepitas
- 2 tablespoons fresh cilantro leaves plus 2 tablespoons chopped
- 2 tablespoons finely chopped onion
- 1 serrano chile, stemmed, seeded, and chopped fine
- ¼ teaspoon grated lime zest plus 5 teaspoons juice
  Kosher salt
- 3 ripe avocados, halved, pitted, and cut into ½-inch pieces
- 1 plum tomato, cored, seeded, and minced
- 1 teaspoon cold-pressed extra-virgin olive oil (see page 35)

why this recipe works • *Avocados have become food celebrities; everyone loves the buttery fruit that's as healthy as it is rich thanks to its 20 essential nutrients including stores of monounsaturated fats and fiber. And no party is complete without a bowl of guacamole. To prevent this adored dip from ever becoming tired, we incorporated pomegranate seeds and pepitas for a nutritionally supercharged guac sporting a lively interplay of flavors and textures. First, we made the perfect rustic but creamy guacamole by mashing three diced avocados with a whisk until cohesive but still chunky. Mincing our seasonings together ensured the flavors would be evenly distributed. For our topping, we scattered the dip with a mix of pomegranate seeds, pepitas, scallions, and cilantro leaves. The result was a creamy guacamole punctuated with pops of bright fruit and earthy crunch. For more spice, mince the ribs and seeds from the chile with the other ingredients. A mortar and pestle can be used to process the aromatics. To minimize discoloration, do not prepare the avocados until the paste has been made. To dice the avocado, hold pitted half in one hand and use a butter knife to slice through avocado flesh down to peel, spacing cuts ½ inch apart, in crosshatch pattern. Use a large spoon to scoop the flesh into bowl.*

1 Combine pomegranate seeds, scallions, pepitas, and cilantro leaves in bowl.

2 Chop onion, chile, and lime zest with 1 teaspoon salt until very finely minced and homogeneous. Transfer to second bowl and stir in 4½ teaspoons lime juice. Add avocado and, using sturdy whisk, mash and stir mixture until well combined with some ¼- to ½-inch chunks remaining. Stir in tomato and chopped cilantro and season with salt to taste.

3 Toss pomegranate-pepita mixture with oil and remaining ½ teaspoon lime juice. Transfer guacamole to serving bowl and top with pomegranate-pepita mixture. Serve.

PER ¼ CUP
Cal 150; Total Fat 13g, Sat Fat 2g; Chol 0mg; Sodium 150mg; Total Carbs 9g, Fiber 6g, Total Sugar 2g, Added Sugar 0g; Protein 2g

EXCELLENT SOURCE OF
Fiber, Vitamin K

nutritious DELICIOUS

SWEET POTATO HUMMUS

makes about 3½ cups

1 large sweet potato (about 1 pound), unpeeled
¾ cup water
¼ cup lemon juice (2 lemons)
¼ cup tahini
2 tablespoons cold-pressed extra-virgin olive oil (see page 35), plus extra for drizzling
1 (15-ounce) can chickpeas, rinsed
1 small garlic clove, minced
1 teaspoon paprika
1 teaspoon salt
½ teaspoon ground coriander
¼ teaspoon ground cumin
⅛ teaspoon ground cinnamon
⅛ teaspoon cayenne pepper

why this recipe works • *While traditional hummus makes for a healthy snack, this sweet-potato hummus ups the nutritional game by combining creamy chickpeas with earthy, vibrant sweet potato. To bring out the sweet potato's subtle flavor, we tested mixing varying amounts with our classic hummus. One large sweet potato (about 1 pound) gave us just the right balance. We found that microwaving the sweet potato yielded a flavor that was nearly as intense as roasting and a lot faster, which was important for such a simple dish (plus, using the microwave helped preserve nutrients). As for seasonings, tasters preferred less tahini than in traditional hummus, so we used just ¼ cup. To complement the sweet potato, we added warm spices: sweet paprika, coriander, cinnamon, and cumin. A dash of cayenne pepper and a clove of garlic cut the sweetness and accented the hummus well. Serve with vegetables, whole-grain crackers, or vegetable chips.*

1 Prick sweet potato several times with fork, place on plate, and microwave until very soft, about 12 minutes, flipping halfway through microwaving. Slice potato in half lengthwise, let cool, then scrape sweet potato flesh from skin and transfer to food processor; discard skin.

2 Combine water and lemon juice in small bowl. In separate bowl, whisk tahini and oil together.

3 Process sweet potato, chickpeas, garlic, paprika, salt, coriander, cumin, cinnamon, and cayenne in food processor until almost fully ground, about 15 seconds. Scrape down bowl with rubber spatula. With machine running, add lemon juice mixture in steady stream. Scrape down bowl and continue to process for 1 minute. With machine running, add tahini mixture in steady stream and process until hummus is smooth and creamy, about 15 seconds, scraping down bowl as needed.

4 Transfer hummus to serving bowl. Cover with plastic wrap and let sit at room temperature until flavors meld, about 30 minutes. (Hummus can be refrigerated for up to 5 days; bring to room temperature before serving and stir in 1 tablespoon warm water to loosen hummus texture if necessary.) Drizzle with extra olive oil to taste before serving.

PER ½ CUP
Cal 170; Total Fat 9g, Sat Fat 1g; Chol 0mg; Sodium 460mg; Total Carbs 20g, Fiber 4g, Total Sugar 4g, Added Sugar 0g; Protein 4g

EXCELLENT SOURCE OF
Vitamin A, Vitamin C

NAVY BEAN AND ARTICHOKE DIP

makes about 2 cups

- 1 teaspoon grated lemon zest plus 2 tablespoons juice
- 1 small garlic clove, minced
- 1 (15-ounce) can navy beans, 2 tablespoons liquid reserved, beans rinsed
- 1 cup jarred whole artichoke hearts packed in water, rinsed and patted dry, 2 tablespoons chopped
- ¼ cup fresh parsley leaves
- 1 scallion, white and light green parts cut into ½-inch pieces, dark green part sliced thin on bias
  Salt
- ¼ teaspoon ground fennel
  Pinch cayenne pepper
- ¼ cup organic plain 2 percent Greek yogurt
  Cold-pressed extra-virgin olive oil (see page 35)

why this recipe works • *Most artichoke dips could justifiably be called mayonnaise and cheese dips, given what goes into them. To create a more nutritious rendition, we looked to bean dip to provide a creamy base that contributed protein and fiber instead of saturated fat. We thought that the vegetal artichokes (high in vitamins K and C and various minerals) would partner well with the earthy-sweet but mild beans, adding some needed character. We chose navy beans for their velvety texture, rinsing them to remove excess sodium. Using canned beans and jarred artichoke hearts kept the recipe easy. To increase the creaminess of our dip and add a filling burst of protein, we incorporated Greek yogurt. Finally, a healthy dose of lemon juice, garlic, parsley, and scallion added fresh flavor and brightness. Serve with vegetables, whole-grain crackers, or whole-grain chips.*

1 Combine lemon zest and juice and garlic in bowl and let sit for 15 minutes.

2 Pulse garlic–lemon juice mixture, beans, their reserved liquid, whole artichoke hearts, parsley, white and light green scallion pieces, ¾ teaspoon salt, fennel, and cayenne in food processor until finely ground, 5 to 10 pulses, scraping down bowl as needed. Continue to process until uniform paste forms, about 1 minute, scraping down bowl as needed.

3 Add yogurt and continue to process until smooth, about 15 seconds. Transfer to serving bowl, cover, and let stand at room temperature for 30 minutes. (Dip can be refrigerated for up to 1 day; bring to room temperature before serving.) Season with salt to taste. Sprinkle with reserved chopped artichokes and dark green scallion parts, and drizzle with oil to taste before serving.

PER ½ CUP
Cal 120; Total Fat 0.5g; Sat Fat 0g; Chol 0mg; Sodium 840mg; Total Carbs 21g, Fiber 4g, Total Sugar 1g, Added Sugar 0g; Protein 8g

EXCELLENT SOURCE OF
Fiber, Vitamin K

ROASTED TOMATO SALSA WITH BLACK BEANS

makes about 3 cups

1½ pounds tomatoes, halved and cored

1 onion, sliced into ½-inch-thick rounds

1–3 red jalapeño or Fresno chiles, stemmed and halved lengthwise

3 garlic cloves, peeled

2 tablespoons lime juice, plus extra for serving
Salt

½ teaspoon ground cumin

1 (15-ounce) can black beans, rinsed

2 teaspoons chopped fresh cilantro

why this recipe works • *For a heartier take on salsa that would make a simple, wholesome snack, we incorporated fiber-rich black beans. We started by preparing a salsa asada, or "roasted salsa." We broiled tomato and red jalapeño halves with sliced onion and whole garlic cloves until everything was well charred, ensuring deep smoky flavor. A bit of cumin provided an earthy undertone. Cooking our salsa a bit further on the stovetop intensified the flavors and developed a saucier base, guaranteeing that our salsa would be thick and scoopable with chips. Fresh cilantro added a citrusy, bright green pop and the addition of protein-rich, high- fiber black beans made our salsa hearty. For a milder salsa, use 1 chile; for a spicy salsa, use all 3 chiles.*

1 Adjust oven rack 4 inches from broiler element and heat broiler. Line rimmed baking sheet with aluminum foil. Place tomatoes, cut side down, and onion on prepared sheet. Broil until tomatoes and onion are well charred, about 10 minutes; transfer to bowl. Place jalapeños, cut side down, and garlic on now-empty sheet and broil until chiles are well charred, 3 to 5 minutes.

2 Transfer chiles, garlic, half of tomatoes, and half of onions to food processor and process to thick puree, about 10 seconds; transfer to large saucepan. Pulse remaining broiled tomatoes and onions in now-empty food processor into ½-inch pieces, 2 or 3 pulses; transfer to saucepan.

3 Stir in lime juice, 1 teaspoon salt, and cumin and bring to boil over medium-high heat. Cook, stirring often, until salsa has thickened slightly and measures about 2 cups, about 10 minutes.

4 Transfer tomato mixture to bowl and stir in black beans; let cool to room temperature. Cover loosely with plastic wrap and refrigerate until completely cooled, at least 1 hour. Stir in cilantro and season with salt and additional lime juice to taste. Serve.

PER ½ CUP
Cal 70; Total Fat 0.5g, Sat Fat 0g; Chol 0mg; Sodium 540mg; Total Carbs 14g, Fiber 4g, Total Sugar 4g, Added Sugar 0g; Protein 4g

EXCELLENT SOURCE OF
Vitamin A, Vitamin C

nutritious DELICIOUS

ANCHOVY DIP

makes about 1½ cups

¾ cup whole blanched almonds

20 anchovy fillets (1½ ounces), rinsed, patted dry, and minced

¼ cup water

2 tablespoons raisins

2 tablespoons lemon juice, plus extra for serving

1 garlic clove, minced

1 teaspoon Dijon mustard
  Salt and pepper

¼ cup cold-pressed extra-virgin olive oil (see page 35), plus extra for serving

1 tablespoon minced fresh chives

why this recipe works • *A potently flavorful mixture of anchovies, olive oil, and garlic, this Provençal dip can be slathered on crackers or served with crudités. We loved the idea of a dip centered on umami-rich anchovies, among the most nutrient-rich fish because of their omega-3 fatty acids. But many versions can be unappealingly oily or overrun with ingredients that drown out the anchovy flavor. To make a smooth, anchovy-focused dip, we started by creating a creamy, neutral base with blanched almonds, another great source of healthy fats. When boiled and pureed, the nuts took on a smooth consistency that helped to keep our dip cohesive and provided richness without being greasy. We discovered that boiling and then rinsing the blanched almonds also ensured that the dip wouldn't turn out grainy. We added 20 anchovy fillets to the softened almonds, along with raisins for subtle sweetness and a few savory ingredients to round out the flavor. Because extra-virgin olive oil can become bitter if overprocessed, we waited until the dip was mostly smooth before slowly drizzling it in. Fresh chives and a final drizzle of olive oil were all this dip needed for a refined presentation to match its sophisticated anchovy flavor. Our favorite brand of anchovies is King Oscar Anchovies-Flat Fillets in Olive Oil. Serve with vegetables, whole-grain crackers, or whole-grain chips.*

1 Bring 4 cups water to boil in medium saucepan over medium-high heat. Add almonds and cook until softened, about 20 minutes. Drain and rinse well.

2 Process drained almonds, anchovies, water, raisins, lemon juice, garlic, mustard, ¼ teaspoon pepper, and ⅛ teaspoon salt in food processor to mostly smooth paste, about 2 minutes, scraping down sides of bowl as needed. With processor running, slowly add oil and process to smooth puree, about 2 minutes.

3 Transfer mixture to bowl, stir in 2 teaspoons chives, and season with salt and extra lemon juice to taste. (Dip can be refrigerated for up to 2 days; bring to room temperature before serving.) Sprinkle with remaining 1 teaspoon chives and drizzle with extra oil to taste before serving.

PER 3 TABLESPOONS
Cal 160; Total Fat 15g, Sat Fat 1.5g; Chol 5mg; Sodium 250mg; Total Carbs 5g, Fiber 1g, Total Sugar 3g, Added Sugar 0g; Protein 5g

EXCELLENT SOURCE OF
Vitamin E

snacks

KALE CHIPS

serves 4

12 ounces Lacinato kale, stemmed and torn into 3-inch pieces
1 tablespoon cold-pressed extra-virgin olive oil (see page 35)
½ teaspoon kosher salt

why this recipe works • *A nutritious alternative to potato chips, kale chips have recently become all the rage. But store-bought versions are often deep fried and loaded with salt, and homemade ones never turn out crispy enough. We wanted a light-as-air, earthy kale chip that remained crispy. We discovered three keys to getting kale chips to the perfect texture. First, we lengthened the cooking time and lowered the oven temperature to mimic the effects of a dehydrator. Next, we baked the kale on wire racks to allow the oven air to circulate above and beneath the leaves. Finally, we started with completely dry leaves—we blotted them between two dish towels to make sure no water was left clinging. Tossed with olive oil and seasoned lightly with crunchy kosher salt, these ultracrisp kale chips were a supersatisfying snack. We prefer to use Lacinato (Tuscan) kale in this recipe, but curly-leaf kale can be substituted; chips made with curly-leaf kale will taste a bit chewy at the edges and won't keep as well. We prefer the larger crystal size of kosher salt here; if using table salt, reduce the amount by half.*

1 Adjust oven racks to upper-middle and lower-middle positions and heat oven to 200 degrees. Set wire racks in 2 rimmed baking sheets. Dry kale thoroughly between dish towels, transfer to large bowl, and toss with oil and salt.

2 Arrange kale on prepared racks, making sure leaves overlap as little as possible. Bake kale until very crisp, 45 to 60 minutes, switching and rotating sheets halfway through baking. Let kale chips cool completely before serving. (Kale chips can be stored in paper towel–lined airtight container for up to 1 day.)

PER SERVING
Cal 60; Total Fat 4g, Sat Fat 0.5g; Chol 0mg; Sodium 160mg; Total Carbs 5g, Fiber 2g, Total Sugar 1g, Added Sugar 0g; Protein 3g

EXCELLENT SOURCE OF
Vitamin A, Folate, Vitamin C, Vitamin K, Copper, Manganese

snacks

BEET CHIPS

serves 2

1 pound beets, peeled, trimmed, and sliced 1/16 inch thick
½ teaspoon salt

why this recipe works • *A snackable chip made from beets has become another popular alternative to potato chips. Beet chips sounded delightful, but we were skeptical about getting truly crisp results without any special equipment. Indeed, many of the recipes we tested produced chips that were leathery and floppy, or overcooked and bitter. We knew that crispness depended on extracting as much moisture as possible from the beets. To do this without overcooking the chips, we tried lightly salting them to draw out some water—and it worked, extracting almost 2 tablespoons before cooking. We then tried microwaving the beets, which is a popular alternative to frying, but the process was inconsistent at best; the difference between perfection and burnt was mere seconds. So we took a cue from our kale chip method and slow-baked our beets in a 200-degree oven. It took a couple of hours but produced chips with a concentrated beet flavor, light crunch, and deep color. Be careful to not let the beet chips turn brown, as they will become bitter. Thinly sliced beets are key to crispy beet chips—use a mandoline, V-slicer, or the slicing disk on a food processor.*

1 Adjust oven racks to upper-middle and lower-middle positions and heat oven to 200 degrees. Set wire racks in 2 rimmed baking sheets and spray with canola oil spray. Combine beets and salt in colander set over bowl and let drain for 25 minutes. Pat beets dry with paper towels.

2 Arrange beet slices on prepared racks, making sure slices overlap as little as possible. Bake beets until shrunken slightly and crisp throughout, 2 to 3 hours, switching and rotating sheets halfway through baking. Let beet chips cool completely before serving (beets will continue to crisp as they cool). (Beet chips can be stored in paper towel–lined airtight container for up to 2 weeks.)

PER SERVING
Cal 100; Total Fat 0g, Sat Fat 0g; Chol 0mg; Sodium 320mg; Total Carbs 22g, Fiber 6g, Total Sugar 15g, Added Sugar 0g; Protein 4g

EXCELLENT SOURCE OF
Fiber, Folate, Manganese, Potassium

nutritious DELICIOUS

WHOLE-WHEAT SEEDED CRACKERS

serves 12

- 3 cups (16½ ounces) whole-wheat flour
- 2 tablespoons ground golden flaxseeds
- 2 tablespoons sesame seeds
- 1 teaspoon ground turmeric
  Salt and pepper
- 1 cup warm water
- ⅓ cup cold-pressed extra-virgin olive oil (see page 35), plus extra for brushing
- 1 large organic egg, lightly beaten
- 2 tablespoons chia seeds
- 2 teaspoons flake sea salt or kosher salt

why this recipe works • *Our goal was a crisp, flavorful cracker without all the added sugars, saturated fats, and preservatives found in many store-bought crackers. Our starting point was the Mediterranean lavash cracker, typically made with a mix of white, wheat, and semolina flours. We preferred using all whole-wheat flour, which boosted nutrition. To give them texture, we added omega-3-rich flaxseeds and sesame seeds to the dough along with a touch of turmeric for its mild, warm flavor. After mixing the dough, we let it rest for an hour which made it easier to roll out, then rolled it between sheets of parchment paper. We pricked it all over with a fork to prevent air bubbles, brushed it with egg, and sprinkled it with chia seeds, sea salt, and pepper. Finally, we baked the crackers until deep golden brown and let them cool before breaking them up. We prefer golden flaxseeds for their milder flavor, but brown flaxseeds can be used. We prefer the larger crystal size of sea salt or kosher salt for sprinkling on the crackers; if using table salt, reduce the amount by half.*

1 Using stand mixer fitted with dough hook, mix whole-wheat flour, ground flaxseeds, sesame seeds, turmeric, and ¾ teaspoon salt together on low speed. Gradually add water and oil and knead until dough is smooth and elastic, 7 to 9 minutes. Turn dough out onto lightly floured counter and knead by hand to form smooth, round ball. Divide dough into 4 equal pieces, brush with oil, and cover with plastic wrap. Let rest at room temperature for 1 hour.

2 Adjust oven racks to upper-middle and lower-middle positions and heat oven to 400 degrees. Working with 1 piece of dough (keep remaining dough covered with plastic), roll between 2 large sheets of parchment paper into 15 by 11-inch rectangle (about ⅛ inch thick). Remove top sheet of parchment and slide parchment with dough onto baking sheet. Repeat with second piece of dough and second baking sheet.

3 Using fork, poke holes in doughs at 2-inch intervals. Brush doughs with beaten egg, then sprinkle each with 1½ teaspoons chia seeds, ½ teaspoon sea salt, and pepper to taste. Press gently on seeds and seasonings to help them adhere.

4 Bake crackers until golden brown, 15 to 18 minutes, switching and rotating sheets halfway through baking. Transfer crackers to wire rack and let cool completely. Let baking sheets cool completely before rolling out and baking remaining 2 pieces of dough. Break cooled crackers into large pieces and serve. (Crackers can be stored at room temperature for up to 2 weeks.)

PER SERVING
Cal 220; Total Fat 9g, Sat Fat 1.5g; Chol 15mg; Sodium 340mg; Total Carbs 30g, Fiber 5g, Total Sugar 0g, Added Sugar 0g; Protein 7g

EXCELLENT SOURCE OF
Fiber, Manganese

snacks

ULTIMATE NACHOS

serves 8

TOMATO SALSA
- ½ cup chopped fresh cilantro
- 1 small red onion, chopped
- 1 jalapeño chile, stemmed, seeded, and chopped coarse
- 1 small garlic clove, minced
- 1½ pounds tomatoes, cored, quartered, and seeded
- ½ teaspoon salt
- 1 tablespoon lime juice

NACHOS
- 1 tablespoon cold-pressed extra-virgin olive oil (see page 35)
- 1 onion, chopped fine
- 1 pound Swiss chard, 1 cup stems chopped fine, leaves sliced into ½-inch-wide strips
- 1 poblano chile, stemmed, seeded, and chopped
  Salt and pepper
- 4 garlic cloves, minced
- 1 (15-ounce) can black beans, rinsed
- 8 ounces whole-grain tortilla chips
- 4 ounces Monterey Jack cheese, shredded (1 cup)
- 1 jalapeño chile, stemmed and sliced thin
- ½ cup organic plain 2 percent Greek yogurt

PER SERVING
Cal 290; Total Fat 14g, Sat Fat 3.5g; Chol 15mg; Sodium 540mg; Total Carbs 33g, Fiber 6g, Total Sugar 6g, Added Sugar 0g; Protein 11g

EXCELLENT SOURCE OF
Protein, Fiber, Vitamin A, Vitamin C, Vitamin K

why this recipe works • *To overhaul the standard formula of chips smothered with cheese, we set out to construct a vegetable-focused nacho platter that would satisfy even the most old-line nacho fans. We first prepared a simple tomato salsa. Next, we created a vibrant greens-and-beans filling, sautéing aromatics with a pound of vitamin-packed Swiss chard, garlic, and black beans. We layered the filling and half the salsa between whole-grain tortilla chips, adding just a bit of Monterey Jack cheese and some sliced fresh jalapeños. After baking the nachos, we topped them with the remaining salsa and dollops of Greek yogurt. We had good luck using Food Should Taste Good Multigrain Tortilla Chips, but you can use any whole-grain tortilla chip. Store-bought fresh tomato salsa (pico de gallo) can be substituted for homemade; you will need 3 cups. Drain it in a fine-mesh strainer for 5 minutes before using. Serve with lime wedges.*

1 **FOR THE TOMATO SALSA** Pulse cilantro, red onion, jalapeño, and garlic in food processor until finely chopped, about 10 pulses, scraping down sides of bowl as needed. Add tomatoes and salt and pulse until tomatoes are coarsely chopped, about 8 pulses. Transfer to fine-mesh strainer set over bowl and let drain for 30 minutes. Transfer tomato mixture to clean bowl and stir in lime juice; set aside.

2 **FOR THE NACHOS** Meanwhile, adjust oven rack to middle position and heat oven to 400 degrees. Heat oil in 12-inch skillet over medium heat until shimmering. Stir in onion, chard stems, poblano, and ¼ teaspoon salt and cook until softened and lightly browned, 5 to 7 minutes. Stir in garlic and cook until fragrant, about 30 seconds. Increase heat to high, add chard leaves, 1 handful at a time, and cook until wilted, about 2 minutes.

3 Stir in beans and continue to cook, stirring often, until chard is tender and beans are slightly softened, about 2 minutes. Off heat, season with salt and pepper to taste.

4 Spread half of tortilla chips evenly in 13 by 9-inch baking dish. Sprinkle ⅓ cup cheese evenly over chips, then top evenly with half of chard-bean mixture, followed by half of tomato salsa, and, finally, half of jalapeño slices. Then layer with remaining chips, ⅓ cup cheese, and remaining chard-bean mixture. Sprinkle with remaining ⅓ cup cheese and remaining jalapeño slices. Bake until cheese is melted and just beginning to brown, 7 to 10 minutes.

5 Let nachos cool for 2 minutes, then top with remaining salsa and dollop with yogurt. Serve immediately.

snacks

SMOKED TROUT DEVILED EGGS

serves 6

- 7 large organic eggs
- 2½ ounces smoked trout, skin removed (2 ounces chopped fine, ½ ounce flaked)
- 1 tablespoon capers, rinsed and chopped fine
- 1 tablespoon chopped fresh chives
- 3 tablespoons organic plain low-fat yogurt
- 2 teaspoons mayonnaise
- 1½ teaspoons lemon juice
- ¾ teaspoon whole-grain mustard
- ¼ teaspoon ground turmeric

why this recipe works • *Deviled eggs may not project healthfulness, but we saw the nutritious potential in a snack based on cooked egg whites. The filling just needed an update. We kept the yolks, which get a bad rap but contain much of the egg's nutrition, including fat-soluble vitamins A and D, as well as folate and choline. We mashed the yolks with smoked trout (high in omega-3 fatty acids). Fresh chives and briny capers tamed the fish's smokiness, creating a bold filling. For creaminess, we added yogurt and a touch of mayonnaise to ensure richness. Lemon juice and whole-grain mustard accented our filling, and a hint of turmeric boosted the yellow color. We flaked a half ounce of fish over the tops before garnishing with additional chives. If you don't have a steamer basket, use a spoon or tongs to gently place the eggs in the water. It doesn't matter if the eggs are above the water or partially submerged. You can double the recipe, as long as you use a pot and steamer basket large enough to hold the eggs in a single layer. If you prefer, use a pastry bag fitted with a large plain or star tip to fill the eggs halves.*

1 Bring 1 inch water to rolling boil in medium saucepan over high heat. Place eggs in steamer basket in single layer. Transfer basket to saucepan. Cover, reduce heat to medium-low, and cook eggs for 11 minutes.

2 When eggs are almost finished cooking, fill medium bowl halfway with ice and water. Using slotted spoon, transfer eggs to bowl of ice water and let sit for 15 minutes to cool.

3 Peel eggs and halve lengthwise. Transfer egg yolks to bowl. Arrange whites on serving platter, discarding two worst-looking halves. Mash yolks with fork until no large lumps remain. Stir in chopped trout, capers, 2 teaspoons chives, yogurt, mayonnaise, lemon juice, mustard, and turmeric, mashing mixture against side of bowl until well incorporated.

4 Transfer yolk mixture to small, heavy-duty plastic bag. Press mixture into one corner and twist top of bag. Using scissors, snip ½ inch off filled corner. Squeezing bag, distribute yolk mixture evenly among egg white halves, mounding filling above flat surface of whites. Top each egg with piece of flaked trout and sprinkle with remaining 1 teaspoon chives. Serve immediately.

VARIATION

SMOKED SALMON DEVILED EGGS
Substitute smoked salmon for trout and dill for chives.

PER 2 HALVES
Cal 120; Total Fat 8g, Sat Fat 2.5g; Chol 225mg; Sodium 140mg; Total Carbs 1g, Fiber 0g, Total Sugar 1g, Added Sugar 0g; Protein 11g

EXCELLENT SOURCE OF
Protein

nutritious DELICIOUS

BROWN RICE ONIGIRI WITH SPINACH, EDAMAME, AND SESAME

makes 24 onigiri, serves 6

¼ cup low-sodium soy sauce

2 tablespoons rice vinegar

2 tablespoons mirin

1¾ cups plus 2 tablespoons water

3 scallions, sliced thin

2½ teaspoons expeller-pressed toasted sesame oil (see page 35)

1 cup short-grain brown rice

1 cup baby spinach

¾ cup frozen shelled edamame beans, thawed and patted dry

2 (8 by 7½-inch) sheets nori, crumbled

¼ cup sesame seeds, toasted

2 teaspoons grated fresh ginger

½ teaspoon salt

why this recipe works • *A Japanese bento box staple, traditional onigiri are adorable little bundles of white sushi rice stuffed with morsels of fish, pickled plums, sea vegetables, or other ingredients. To rework these snacks so they'd pack more of a nutritional punch, we first swapped out white rice for short-grain brown rice. Since brown rice is less sticky than white, we skipped the standard rinsing to preserve as much starch as possible. Our next change was more dramatic: Instead of stuffing tidbits of spinach and edamame filling into balls of rice, we pulsed them up with the rice in the food processor. This enabled us to incorporate far more filling into each onigiri (it also made our job simpler). Slightly processing the rice released more starch, making the mixture easier to shape. We scooped out portions of the rice mixture and, with lightly moistened hands, pressed each into a petite disk, which we found less delicate than the traditional ball shape. We rolled the edges in toasted sesame seeds, which added a crunchy, nutty contrast to the rice. A simple soy dipping sauce made a tasty accompaniment.*

1 Combine soy sauce, rice vinegar, mirin, 2 tablespoons water, one-third of the scallions, and ½ teaspoon sesame oil in small bowl; set aside.

2 Bring remaining 1¾ cups water and rice to simmer in large saucepan over high heat. Reduce heat to low, cover, and simmer gently until rice is tender and water is absorbed, 40 to 45 minutes. Off heat, lay clean dish towel underneath lid, and let sit for 10 minutes. Fluff rice with fork and cover.

3 Pulse spinach, edamame, nori, 2 tablespoons sesame seeds, ginger, salt, remaining scallions, and remaining 2 teaspoons sesame oil in food processor until mixture is finely ground (it should not be smooth), about 10 pulses. Add rice and pulse until rice is coarsely chopped and mixture is well combined, about 8 pulses.

4 Divide rice mixture into 24 portions (about 1½ tablespoons each) and arrange on parchment-lined baking sheet. Using lightly moistened hands, roll each into ball, then press into disk about 1½ inches wide and ¾ inch thick. Spread remaining 2 tablespoons sesame seeds onto plate. Gently roll sides of disks in sesame seeds, pressing lightly to adhere, and transfer to serving platter. Serve with soy dipping sauce. (Onigiri can be covered and refrigerated up to 24 hours; bring to room temperature before serving.)

PER 3 ONIGIRI
Cal 200; Total Fat 7g, Sat Fat 0.5g; Chol 0mg; Sodium 560mg; Total Carbs 30g, Fiber 5g, Total Sugar 3g, Added Sugar 0g; Protein 7g

EXCELLENT SOURCE OF
Fiber, Vitamin K

CHERRY, CHOCOLATE, AND ORANGE TRAIL MIX

makes about 3 cups

- 1 cup whole raw almonds
- 1 cup raw walnuts, chopped coarse
- ½ cup raw pepitas
- 2 tablespoons grated orange zest
- ¼ teaspoon ground cinnamon
- ⅛ teaspoon salt
- ½ cup dried unsweetened tart cherries
- ⅓ cup 70 percent dark chocolate chips

why this recipe works • *Free from filler ingredients and preservatives found in packaged trail mixes, this mixture of nuts, seeds, dried fruit, and dark chocolate is an easy-to-make and easy-to-pack power snack. The options for trail mix are endless, but we loved the combination of fragrant almonds, meaty walnuts, and crisp pepitas—a nutrient-dense base for the exquisite pairing of dried cherries and dark chocolate. To tie everything together, we seasoned our mix with a hefty dose of orange zest, plus a touch of cinnamon to highlight the chocolate. Many packaged mixes will add cheap oil to help the seasonings adhere, but we found that stirring the seasonings into the mixture toward the end of roasting worked perfectly: the nuts and seeds came out of the oven marvelously fragrant, infused with the natural oils of the orange zest. (The variation employs lime zest and chili powder to similar effect.) You can substitute pistachios, cashews, peanuts, or hazelnuts for the almonds and/or walnuts, and dried cranberries for the cherries. Make sure the nuts and pepitas have cooled completely before adding the cherries and chocolate in step 3. We prefer the flavor of 70 percent dark chocolate chips in this recipe, though higher cacao percentages will also work (see page 31).*

1 Adjust oven rack to middle position and heat oven to 350 degrees. Line rimmed baking sheet with parchment paper. Spread almonds and walnuts evenly over prepared sheet and bake until just fragrant, about 6 minutes. Meanwhile, toss pepitas, orange zest, cinnamon, and salt together in bowl.

2 Remove sheet from oven, stir pepita mixture into almonds and walnuts, and continue to bake until nuts and pepitas are golden and fragrant, about 3 minutes. Transfer nut mixture to large bowl and let cool completely, about 20 minutes.

3 Add dried cherries and chocolate chips to cooled nut mixture and toss to combine. (Trail mix can be stored for up to 2 weeks.)

PER ⅓ CUP
Cal 260; Total Fat 22g, Sat Fat 3.5g; Chol 0mg; Sodium 35mg; Total Carbs 14g, Fiber 4g, Total Sugar 6g, Added Sugar 0g; Protein 8g

EXCELLENT SOURCE OF
Vitamin E, Copper, Magnesium, Manganese, Phosphorus

VARIATION
CRANBERRY, COCONUT, CHILI, AND LIME TRAIL MIX
Substitute lime zest for orange zest, cayenne pepper for cinnamon, and dried cranberries for dried cherries. Omit chocolate and add ⅓ cup unsweetened flaked coconut to pepita mixture in step 1.

DESSERT

284 Oatmeal Cookies with Chocolate and Goji Berries

286 Pumpkin–Cream Cheese Brownies

288 Beet-Chocolate Cupcakes
Beet "Sprinkles"

290 Carrot Snack Cake
Yogurt–Cream Cheese Frosting

293 Cranberry-Apple Crisp

294 Skillet-Roasted Apples with Dried Figs, Walnuts, and Maple Yogurt

297 Peaches, Blackberries, and Strawberries with Basil and Pepper

298 Chocolate-Avocado Pudding

301 Chocolate Bark with Pepitas and Dried Goji Berries
Chocolate Bark with Almonds and Cherries

OATMEAL COOKIES WITH CHOCOLATE AND GOJI BERRIES

makes 24 cookies

- 1 cup (5 ounces) all-purpose flour
- ¾ teaspoon salt
- ½ teaspoon baking soda
- 1 cup packed (7 ounces) dark brown sugar
- ⅔ cup expeller-pressed canola oil (see page 35)
- 1 tablespoon water
- 1 teaspoon vanilla extract
- 1 large organic egg plus 1 large yolk
- 3 cups (9 ounces) old-fashioned rolled oats
- 1 cup goji berries (see page 34)
- 3½ ounces 70 percent dark chocolate, chopped into ¼-inch pieces

why this recipe works • *Few desserts are more appealing than warm cookies straight from the oven. Instead of depriving ourselves of this treat, we sought to create a "better for you" cookie that emphasized whole grains. As we love the soft chew and heartiness of the oatmeal-raisin variety, we used that as our starting point. A hefty 3 cups of fiber-rich rolled oats would ensure plenty of whole-grain benefits. We initially tried to solely use oat flour, but this resulted in a crumbly, difficult-to-work-with dough, so we ultimately stuck with all-purpose flour to provide the necessary structure. We wanted to increase the nutritious mix-ins as much as possible, so for an antioxidant boost, we stirred chopped dark chocolate and a full cup of chewy, sweet-tart goji berries into the dough. Heart-healthy canola oil kept the cookies dense and chewy. A bit of salt complemented the oats and brought out their sweet-nuttiness, and a tablespoon of water helped the cookies spread to the perfect size. Do not use quick, instant, or thick-cut oats in this recipe. If you can't find goji berries, you can substitute dried unsweetened tart cherries or dried cranberries. We prefer the flavor of 70 percent dark chocolate in this recipe, though higher cacao percentages will also work (see page 31).*

1 Adjust oven rack to middle position and heat oven to 375 degrees. Line 2 rimmed baking sheets with parchment paper. Whisk flour, salt, and baking soda together in bowl; set aside.

2 Whisk sugar, oil, water, and vanilla together in large bowl until well combined. Add egg and yolk and whisk until smooth. Using rubber spatula, stir in flour mixture until fully combined. Add oats, goji berries, and chocolate and stir until evenly distributed (mixture will be stiff).

3 Divide dough into 24 portions, each about heaping 2 tablespoons. Using damp hands, tightly roll into balls and space 2 inches apart on prepared sheets, 12 balls per sheet. Press balls to ¾-inch thickness.

4 Bake, 1 sheet at a time, until edges are set and centers are soft but not wet, 8 to 10 minutes, rotating sheet halfway through baking. Let cookies cool on sheets for 5 minutes, then transfer to wire rack. Let cookies cool completely before serving.

PER COOKIE
Cal 160; Total Fat 6g, Sat Fat 1.5g; Chol 15mg; Sodium 115mg; Total Carbs 24g, Fiber 2g, Total Sugar 11g, Added Sugar 8g; Protein 3g

EXCELLENT SOURCE OF
Vitamin A

nutritious DELICIOUS

PUMPKIN–CREAM CHEESE BROWNIES

makes 16 brownies

PUMPKIN FILLING

- **4 ounces cream cheese, cut into 4 pieces**
- **¾ cup canned unsweetened pumpkin puree**
- **2 tablespoons sugar**
- **1 tablespoon whole-wheat flour**
- **¼ teaspoon pumpkin pie spice**

BROWNIE BATTER

- **⅔ cup (3⅔ ounces) whole-wheat flour**
- **½ teaspoon baking powder**
- **½ teaspoon salt**
- **4 ounces unsweetened chocolate, chopped fine**
- **1¼ cups (8¾ ounces) sugar**
- **6 tablespoons expeller-pressed canola oil (see page 35)**
- **2 large organic eggs**
- **2 tablespoons organic 1 percent low-fat milk**
- **1 teaspoon vanilla extract**

PER BROWNIE
Cal 210; Total Fat 12g, Sat Fat 4.5g; Chol 30mg; Sodium 120mg; Total Carbs 26g, Fiber 2g, Total Sugar 18g, Added Sugar 17g; Protein 3g

EXCELLENT SOURCE OF
Vitamin A

why this recipe works • *We love a good brownie that boasts a fudgy, ultra-chocolaty interior, but we wondered if we could add nutrients without compromising the brownie's flavor and texture. As vegetables are often mixed into baked goods to provide moisture, we first tried stirring creamy, nutrient-dense pumpkin puree into our batter, but this resulted in brownies that were too light and spongy. We then considered that pumpkin and cream cheese are a delicious pairing in pumpkin cheesecake and wondered: Why not stir the pumpkin into some cream cheese and create pumpkin–cream cheese brownies, which would showcase the vitamin A–rich vegetable in an attractively swirled topping? The test worked. The cream cheese and warm spices mellowed the pumpkin's vegetal flavor and gave it a smooth, creamy texture. We also traded white flour for whole-wheat, and found that the brownies were just as dense and fudgy—and remained so when we scaled back on oil and added some low-fat milk. The result? Perfectly fudgy brownies with pumpkin cheesecake flavor in every bite. To accurately test the doneness of the brownies, be sure to stick the toothpick into the brownie portion, not the pumpkin layer.*

1 Adjust oven rack to middle position and heat oven to 350 degrees. Make foil sling for 8-inch square baking pan by folding 2 long sheets of aluminum foil so each is 8 inches wide. Lay sheets of foil in pan perpendicular to each other, with extra foil hanging over edges of pan. Push foil into corners and up sides of pan, smoothing foil flush to pan. Grease foil.

2 **FOR THE PUMPKIN FILLING** Microwave cream cheese in bowl until soft, 20 to 30 seconds. Whisk in pumpkin puree, sugar, flour, and pumpkin pie spice until combined.

3 **FOR THE BROWNIE BATTER** Whisk flour, baking powder, and salt together in small bowl and set aside. Microwave chocolate in large bowl at 50 percent power, stirring occasionally, until melted, about 2 minutes. Let cool slightly.

4 Whisk sugar, oil, eggs, milk, and vanilla into melted chocolate until incorporated. Using rubber spatula, fold flour mixture into chocolate mixture to combine. Measure out ⅓ cup batter and set aside. Spread remaining batter in prepared pan. Gently spread pumpkin filling evenly over batter.

5 Microwave reserved ⅓ cup batter until warm and fluid, 15 to 30 seconds. Using spoon, dollop softened batter over pumpkin filling, 6 to 8 dollops. Using knife, swirl batter through pumpkin filling, making marbled pattern, 10 to 12 strokes, leaving ½-inch border around edges.

6 Bake until toothpick inserted in center comes out with few moist crumbs attached, 35 to 40 minutes, rotating pan halfway through baking. Let brownies cool in pan on wire rack for 1 hour.

7 Using foil overhang, lift brownies out of pan. Return brownies to wire rack and let cool completely, about 1 hour. Cut into squares and serve.

BEET-CHOCOLATE CUPCAKES

makes 12 cupcakes

- 12 ounces beets, trimmed, peeled, and quartered
- 2 ounces 70 percent dark chocolate, chopped
- ½ cup (1½ ounces) Dutch-processed cocoa powder
- ⅓ cup expeller-pressed canola oil (see page 35)
- ¾ cup (5¼ ounces) sugar
- 2 large organic eggs
- 3 tablespoons organic 1 percent low-fat milk
- 1 teaspoon vanilla extract
- ½ teaspoon baking soda
- ½ teaspoon salt
- ¾ cup (4⅛ ounces) whole-wheat flour
- 1 recipe Yogurt–Cream Cheese Frosting (see page 291)
- 1 recipe Beet "Sprinkles" (recipe follows), optional

PER SERVING
Cal 260; Total Fat 14g, Sat Fat 4.5g; Chol 40mg; Sodium 230mg; Total Carbs 32g, Fiber 3g, Total Sugar 21g, Added Sugar 17g; Protein 5g

EXCELLENT SOURCE OF
Manganese

why this recipe works • *Taking a cue from Victorian-era cakes which sometimes used beets for their natural sweetness and moisture, we turned to the nutrient-packed root vegetable to add a complementary flavor and red hue to our unique red velvet cupcakes—no synthetic dye necessary. Whole-wheat flour underscored the beets' delicate earthiness. Instead of a sugar-laden frosting, we opted for a lightly sweetened Greek yogurt–based frosting, whose cooling tang paired perfectly with the cupcakes' deep chocolate flavor. Do not substitute natural cocoa powder. We prefer the flavor of 70 percent dark chocolate; we tested with higher percentages and found the cupcakes too bitter. These cupcakes are best eaten the day they're made. Once frosted, the cupcakes should be served immediately.*

1 Adjust oven rack to lower-middle position and heat oven to 350 degrees. Line 12-cup muffin tin with paper liners.

2 Working in batches, use food processor fitted with shredding disk to process beets until shredded. Transfer to bowl and microwave, covered, until beets are tender and have released their juices, about 4 minutes, stirring halfway through microwaving. Fit now-empty processor with chopping blade and transfer cooked beets to processor.

3 Microwave chocolate in separate bowl at 50 percent power, stirring occasionally, until melted, about 2 minutes. Whisk in cocoa and oil until smooth and transfer chocolate mixture to food processor with beets; let cool slightly.

4 Process beets and chocolate mixture until smooth, about 45 seconds, scraping down sides of bowl as needed. Add sugar, eggs, milk, vanilla, baking soda, and salt and process until sugar is mostly dissolved and mixture is emulsified, about 15 seconds. Add flour and pulse until just incorporated, about 5 pulses; do not overmix.

5 Divide batter evenly among muffin cups. Bake cupcakes until toothpick inserted in center comes out clean, 20 to 22 minutes, rotating tin halfway through baking. Let cupcakes cool in muffin tin on wire rack for 15 minutes. Remove cupcakes from muffin tin and let cool completely, about 1 hour.

6 Mound 1 tablespoon frosting in center of each cupcake. Using small icing spatula or butter knife, spread frosting to edge of cupcake, leaving slight mound in center. Top with sprinkles, if desired. Serve immediately.

BEET "SPRINKLES"
makes about ¼ cup

These fun 100-percent vegetable sprinkles add a pop of color and concentrated sweetness to top off our Beet-Chocolate Cupcakes.

4 ounces beets, trimmed, peeled, and cut into 1-inch pieces

Adjust oven rack to middle position and heat oven to 200 degrees. Process beets in food processor until finely ground, about 20 seconds, scraping down sides of bowl as needed. Place ground beets in triple layer of cheesecloth and wring out as much liquid as possible. Transfer drained beets to rimmed baking sheet lined with parchment paper and spread into single layer. Bake, stirring occasionally, until dry and crisp, 45 to 55 minutes. Let cool completely before serving. (Beet sprinkles can be stored for up to 2 days.)

CARROT SNACK CAKE

serves 9

- 12 ounces carrots, peeled
- ⅔ cup (4⅔ ounces) sugar
- ¼ cup expeller-pressed canola oil (see page 35)
- ¼ cup organic 1 percent low-fat milk
- 2 large organic eggs
- 2 teaspoons vanilla extract
- 1 teaspoon baking powder
- ½ teaspoon baking soda
- ¾ teaspoon ground cinnamon
- ¼ teaspoon ground nutmeg
- ¼ teaspoon salt
- 1⅓ cups (7⅓ ounces) whole-wheat flour
- 1 recipe Yogurt–Cream Cheese Frosting (recipe follows)

why this recipe works • *Simple, sweet, and satisfying, snack cakes will curb just about any cake craving. Instead of a plain vanilla cake which offers little in the way of nutrition, we wanted a moist, rich carrot snack cake that would offer a boost of vitamin A as well as other nutrients. Carrot cakes typically use oil instead of butter for their fat, another plus. To maximize the nutritional punch of the carrots, we incorporated as many as the batter could handle without making it too difficult to spread or overly vegetal tasting. We tried replacing the standard white flour with whole-wheat and found we preferred whole-wheat flour's earthy, nutty flavor, which complemented the carrots. We included just enough sugar to make our cake pleasantly moist and sweet, but not so much that it overpowered the other flavors. Plenty of fragrant, warm spices complemented the carrots' natural sweetness. To streamline the process, we relied on our food processor to both shred the carrots and mix the batter. Instead of a traditional, super-sweet cream-cheese frosting, we topped our cake with our lightly sweetened, tangy Yogurt–Cream Cheese Frosting.*

1 Adjust oven rack to middle position and heat oven to 350 degrees. Make foil sling for 8-inch square baking pan by folding 2 long sheets of aluminum foil so each is 8 inches wide. Lay sheets of foil in pan perpendicular to each other, with extra foil hanging over edges of pan. Push foil into corners and up sides of pan, smoothing foil flush to pan. Grease foil. Working in batches, use food processor fitted with shredding disk to shred carrots; transfer carrots to bowl.

2 Fit now-empty processor with chopping blade. Process sugar, oil, milk, eggs, vanilla, baking powder, baking soda, cinnamon, nutmeg, and salt until sugar is mostly dissolved and mixture is emulsified, 10 to 12 seconds, scraping down sides of bowl as needed. Add shredded carrots and pulse until combined, about 3 pulses. Add flour and pulse until just incorporated, about 5 pulses; do not overmix.

3 Scrape batter into prepared pan and smooth top. Bake until cake is light golden and toothpick inserted in center comes out clean, 26 to 30 minutes, rotating pan halfway through baking.

4 Let cake cool in pan on wire rack for 10 minutes. Using foil overhang, remove cake from pan and return to wire rack. Discard foil and let cake cool completely on rack, about 2 hours. Spread frosting evenly over top of cake and serve.

PER SERVING
Cal 300; Total Fat 13g, Sat Fat 3.5g; Chol 55mg; Sodium 280mg; Total Carbs 43g, Fiber 4g, Total Sugar 24g, Added Sugar 21g; Protein 7g

EXCELLENT SOURCE OF
Vitamin A, Manganese

YOGURT–CREAM CHEESE FROSTING

makes 1 cup

This silky frosting gets its tang from Greek yogurt. If it becomes too soft to work with, let it chill in the refrigerator until firm.

- ½ cup organic plain 2 percent Greek yogurt
- 4 ounces cream cheese, softened
- ¼ teaspoon vanilla extract
   Pinch salt
- ½ cup (2 ounces) confectioners' sugar

1 Process yogurt, cream cheese, vanilla, and salt in food processor until smooth, about 25 seconds, scraping down sides of bowl as needed. Add sugar and process until incorporated and frosting is creamy and glossy, about 20 seconds.

2 Refrigerate for at least 30 minutes or up to 24 hours until firm but spreadable.

dessert

CRANBERRY-APPLE CRISP

serves 8

TOPPING

- 1 cup (3 ounces) old-fashioned rolled oats
- ½ cup almonds or pecans, chopped coarse
- ¼ cup ground golden flaxseeds
- ¼ cup packed (1¾ ounces) light brown sugar
- ¼ teaspoon ground cinnamon
- ⅛ teaspoon salt
- ¼ cup expeller-pressed canola oil (see page 35)
- 2 tablespoons organic 1 percent low-fat milk or water

FILLING

- 8 ounces fresh or frozen cranberries (2 cups)
- ¼ cup (1¾ ounces) granulated sugar
- 2 tablespoons water
- ½ teaspoon ground ginger
- 1 pound Granny Smith apples, cored and cut into ½-inch pieces
- 1 pound Braeburn apples, cored and cut into ½-inch pieces
- ⅓ cup dried cranberries
- 1 tablespoon instant tapioca

PER SERVING
Cal 320; Total Fat 13g, Sat Fat 1g; Chol 0mg; Sodium 45mg; Total Carbs 49g, Fiber 7g, Total Sugar 31g, Added Sugar 12g; Protein 5g

EXCELLENT SOURCE OF
Fiber, Vitamin E

why this recipe works • *Apple crisp is comfort food at its finest. Its traditional topping of oats and nuts makes for a fairly nutritious starting point as far as desserts go, but we wanted to take it a step further while staying true to its "crisp" name. For the topping, we initially tried incorporating quinoa, which becomes crunchy when baked, but found it bitter; tasters preferred a combination of flaxseed meal, whole and ground oats, and nuts, which provided a boost of fiber, protein, and healthy fats and lots of crunch. No flour was necessary, and instead of butter to keep the topping together, a combination of oil and milk did the trick. To showcase the fruity filling, we combined a mix of tart and sweet apples with vitamin-rich cranberries for beautiful color, tartness, and texture, using both fresh cranberries and dried. We refrained from peeling the apples so they would retain more of their fiber and texture. If you can't find Braeburn apples, Golden Delicious will work. Do not use quick, instant, or thick-cut oats in this recipe. You do not need to thaw frozen cranberries before using.*

1 FOR THE TOPPING Adjust oven rack to middle position and heat oven to 400 degrees. Process ½ cup oats in food processor to fine meal, about 2 minutes. Add almonds, flaxseeds, brown sugar, cinnamon, and salt to processor and pulse until nuts are finely chopped, about 12 pulses. Drizzle oil over oat mixture and pulse until mixture resembles crumbly, wet sand, about 5 pulses, scraping down sides of bowl as needed. Transfer mixture to bowl and stir in remaining ½ cup oats and milk. Cover and refrigerate while preparing filling.

2 FOR THE FILLING Bring fresh or frozen cranberries, granulated sugar, water, and ginger to simmer in Dutch oven over medium-high heat. Cook until cranberries are completely softened and mixture is thickened, 5 to 6 minutes; transfer to bowl. Add apples and dried cranberries to now-empty pot and cook until apples begin to release their juices, about 5 minutes. (You should have about ¼ cup juices; if not add water as needed to equal about ¼ cup.)

3 Off heat, stir cranberry mixture and tapioca into apple mixture in pot until well combined. Transfer to 8-inch square baking dish. Pinch topping into ½-inch clumps and sprinkle evenly over filling.

4 Bake until juices are bubbling and topping is deep golden, 22 to 28 minutes, rotating dish halfway through baking. (If topping is browning too quickly, cover loosely with aluminum foil.) Transfer to wire rack and let cool for 15 minutes before serving.

dessert

SKILLET-ROASTED APPLES WITH DRIED FIGS, WALNUTS, AND MAPLE YOGURT

serves 8

- ½ cup organic plain 2 percent Greek yogurt
- 1 teaspoon maple syrup
- 2 tablespoons expeller-pressed canola oil (see page 35)
- 4 Gala apples, halved and cored
- 1¼ cups dry red wine
- ⅓ cup dried figs, chopped
- 3 tablespoons sugar
- ¼ teaspoon pepper
- ⅛ teaspoon salt
- 1 teaspoon lemon juice
- ⅔ cup walnuts, toasted and chopped

why this recipe works • *We wanted a homey apple dessert that didn't rely on buttery pastry or loads of sugar for flavor. So we turned to roasted apples, which would allow the fruit to shine. Skillet-roasting seemed like the perfect method to get perfectly tender, bronzed apples. Since they contain a lot of liquid, we needed to drive off some moisture before we could achieve any caramelization, so we started the apples on the stovetop to jump-start their cooking. Transferring the skillet to the oven ensured even and consistent browning and fork-tender flesh. To dress up the apples, we took advantage of the flavorful browned bits left in the pan and made a dessert pan sauce; red wine, lemon juice, and pepper offered a simple but decadent profile. A bit of sugar and dried figs added sweetness and a slight chew (plus additional fiber). For more textural contrast, we sprinkled on a handful of walnuts, whose heart-healthy fats provided richness. A dollop of maple-laced Greek yogurt added a pleasant, cooling creaminess in place of traditional ice cream. We prefer Gala apples in this recipe, but Fuji will also work; just make sure to select apples that are firm. Use a medium-bodied dry red wine such as pinot noir here.*

1 Adjust oven rack to middle position and heat oven to 450 degrees. Combine yogurt and maple syrup in small bowl; refrigerate until ready to use.

2 Heat oil in 12-inch ovensafe skillet over medium-high heat until shimmering. Place apples, cut side down, in skillet. Cook, without moving them, until apples are just beginning to brown, 3 to 5 minutes.

3 Transfer skillet to oven and roast apples for 10 minutes. Being careful of hot skillet handle, flip apples and continue to roast until fork easily pierces fruit, 10 to 15 minutes.

4 Remove skillet from oven and carefully transfer apples to serving platter. Add wine, figs, sugar, pepper, and salt to now-empty skillet and bring to simmer over medium-high heat. Cook, whisking to scrape up any browned bits, until sauce is reduced and has consistency of maple syrup, 7 to 10 minutes.

5 Off heat, stir in lemon juice. Pour sauce over apples, dollop with yogurt mixture, and sprinkle with walnuts. Serve.

PER SERVING
Cal 210; Total Fat 9g, Sat Fat 1g; Chol 0mg; Sodium 45mg; Total Carbs 25g, Fiber 3g, Total Sugar 19g, Added Sugar 5g; Protein 3g

EXCELLENT SOURCE OF
Manganese

nutritious DELICIOUS

PEACHES, BLACKBERRIES, AND STRAWBERRIES WITH BASIL AND PEPPER

serves 6

4 teaspoons sugar

2 tablespoons chopped fresh basil

½ teaspoon pepper

3 peaches, halved, pitted, and cut into ½-inch pieces

10 ounces (2 cups) blackberries

10 ounces strawberries, hulled and quartered (2 cups)

1 tablespoon lime juice, plus extra for seasoning

why this recipe works • *Fruit salad is theoretically a healthful alternative to other desserts—but don't expect that from the canned variety, which typically comes heavily processed, packaged in a sugar-laden syrup, and barely recognizable. Fresh fruit makes a much better starting point and just a few simple tweaks dress it up. We chose a combination of peaches, blackberries, and strawberries, which looked beautiful and provided a range of complementary flavors as well as fiber, vitamin C, and vitamin K. A small amount of sugar encouraged the fruit to release its juices, creating a more cohesive salad. For complexity, we mashed the sugar with fragrant, fresh basil before stirring it into the fruit, which ensured even distribution of flavor. To balance the sweetness, we added fresh lime juice. A bit of pepper brought the flavors to life. Nectarines can be substituted for the peaches.*

Combine sugar, basil, and pepper in large bowl. Using rubber spatula, press mixture into side of bowl until sugar becomes damp, about 30 seconds. Add peaches, blackberries, and strawberries and gently toss to combine. Let sit at room temperature, stirring occasionally, until fruit releases its juices, 15 to 30 minutes. Stir in lime juice and season with extra lime juice to taste. Serve.

PER SERVING
Cal 80; Total Fat 0.5g, Sat Fat 0g; Chol 0mg; Sodium 0mg; Total Carbs 20g, Fiber 5g, Total Sugar 14g, Added Sugar 3g; Protein 2g

EXCELLENT SOURCE OF:
Fiber, Vitamin C, Vitamin K, Manganese

CHOCOLATE-AVOCADO PUDDING

serves 6

- 1 cup water
- ¾ cup (5¼ ounces) sugar
- ¼ cup (¾ ounce) unsweetened cocoa powder
- 1 tablespoon vanilla extract
- 1 teaspoon instant espresso powder (optional)
- ¼ teaspoon salt
- 2 large ripe avocados (8 ounces each), halved and pitted
- 3½ ounces 70 percent dark chocolate, chopped

why this recipe works • *Making a luscious chocolate pudding by substituting vitamin-rich, heart-healthy avocados for the cream and eggs has become something of a craze. But more often than not, these puddings are a far cry from the silky-smooth, ultra-chocolaty pudding we want, and yield a grainy texture and lackluster chocolate flavor that doesn't conceal the vegetal notes. We knew we could do better without making the recipe too complicated. Rather than simply blending everything together, we started by creating a simple hot cocoa syrup in a saucepan (with a touch of espresso powder, vanilla, and salt to enhance the chocolate flavor). Meanwhile, we processed the flesh of two large avocados for a full two minutes until they were absolutely smooth. Next, with the food processor running, we carefully streamed in the cocoa syrup until the mixture was velvety and glossy. We finished by blending in a moderate amount of melted dark chocolate to give our pudding a wonderfully full chocolate flavor and additional richness. We prefer the flavor of 70 percent dark chocolate in this recipe, though higher cacao percentages will also work (see page 31).*

1 Combine water, sugar, cocoa, vanilla, espresso powder (if using), and salt in small saucepan. Bring to simmer over medium heat and cook, stirring occasionally, until sugar and cocoa dissolve, about 2 minutes. Remove saucepan from heat and cover to keep warm.

2 Scoop flesh of avocados into food processor bowl and process until smooth, about 2 minutes, scraping down sides of bowl as needed. With processor running, slowly add warm cocoa mixture in steady stream until completely incorporated and mixture is smooth and glossy, about 2 minutes.

3 Microwave chocolate in bowl at 50 percent power, stirring occasionally, until melted, 2 to 4 minutes. Add to avocado mixture and process until well incorporated, about 1 minute. Transfer pudding to bowl, cover, and refrigerate until chilled and set, at least 2 hours or up to 24 hours. Serve.

PER SERVING
Cal 310; Total Fat 19g, Sat Fat 6g; Chol 0mg; Sodium 105mg; Total Carbs 41g, Fiber 8g, Total Sugar 30g, Added Sugar 25g; Protein 4g

EXCELLENT SOURCE OF
Fiber, Vitamin K

CHOCOLATE BARK WITH PEPITAS AND DRIED GOJI BERRIES

serves 16

- 1 pound 70 percent dark chocolate, 12 ounces chopped fine, 4 ounces grated
- 2 teaspoons ground cinnamon
- 1 teaspoon chipotle chile powder
- 2 cups roasted pepitas, 1¾ cups left whole, ¼ cup chopped
- 1 cup goji berries, chopped (see page 34)
- 1 teaspoon coarse sea salt

why this recipe works • *Yes, a small amount of chocolate can be a part of a nutritious diet. The key, apart from portion size, is sticking to a higher cacao chocolate, which contains more antioxidants. A piece of chocolate bark makes the perfect alternative to a candy bar. We filled ours with crunchy roasted pepitas and chewy, tart goji berries; cinnamon and spicy chipotle powder gave it a surprising depth and some heat, while a hit of sea salt brought out all the flavors. Stirring some grated chocolate into melted chocolate proved a simple but effective tempering technique, resulting in chocolate that set up shiny and crisp. We prefer the flavor of 70 percent dark chocolate; higher cacao percentages will also work (see page 31) but the flavor will be less sweet and more intense. To grate the chocolate, use the large holes of a box grater.*

1 Make parchment paper sling for 13 by 9-inch baking pan by folding 2 long sheets of parchment; first sheet should be 13 inches wide and second sheet should be 9 inches wide. Lay sheets in pan perpendicular to each other, with extra parchment hanging over edges of pan. Push parchment into corners and up sides of pan, smoothing parchment flush to pan.

2 Microwave 12 ounces finely chopped chocolate in large bowl at 50 percent power, stirring every 15 seconds, until melted but not much hotter than body temperature (check by holding in the palm of your hand), 2 to 3 minutes. Stir in 4 ounces grated chocolate, cinnamon, and chile powder until smooth and chocolate is completely melted (returning to microwave for no more than 5 seconds at a time to finish melting if necessary).

3 Stir 1¾ cups whole pepitas and ¾ cup goji berries into chocolate mixture. Working quickly, use rubber spatula to spread chocolate mixture evenly into prepared pan. Sprinkle with remaining ¼ cup chopped pepitas and remaining ¼ cup goji berries and gently press topping into chocolate. Sprinkle evenly with salt and refrigerate until chocolate is set, about 30 minutes.

4 Using parchment overhang, lift chocolate out of pan and transfer to cutting board; discard parchment. Using serrated knife and gentle sawing motion, cut chocolate into 16 even pieces. Serve.

PER SERVING
Cal 250; Total Fat 20g, Sat Fat 8g; Chol 0mg; Sodium 150mg; Total Carbs 20g, Fiber 5g, Total Sugar 11g, Added Sugar 0g; Protein 9g

EXCELLENT SOURCE OF
Fiber, Vitamin A, Magnesium, Manganese, Phosphorus

VARIATION
CHOCOLATE BARK WITH ALMONDS AND CHERRIES
Omit cinnamon and chipotle chile powder. Substitute toasted almonds for pepitas and unsweetened dried tart cherries for goji berries.

dessert

CONVERSIONS AND EQUIVALENTS

Baking is a science and an art, but geography has a hand in it, too. Flours and sugars manufactured in the United Kingdom and elsewhere will feel and taste different from those manufactured in the United States. So we cannot promise that a cookie you bake in Canada or England will taste the same as a cookie baked in the States, but we can offer guidelines for converting weights and measures. We also recommend that you rely on your instincts when making our recipes. Refer to the visual cues provided. If the dough hasn't "come together in a ball" as described, you may need to add more flour—even if the recipe doesn't tell you to. You be the judge.

The recipes in this book were developed using standard U.S. measures following U.S. government guidelines. The charts below offer equivalents for U.S. and metric measures. All conversions are approximate and have been rounded up or down to the nearest whole number.

EXAMPLE

1 teaspoon = 4.9292 milliliters, rounded up to 5 milliliters

1 ounce = 28.3495 grams, rounded down to 28 grams

VOLUME CONVERSIONS

U.S.	METRIC
1 teaspoon	5 milliliters
2 teaspoons	10 milliliters
1 tablespoon	15 milliliters
2 tablespoons	30 milliliters
¼ cup	59 milliliters
⅓ cup	79 milliliters
½ cup	118 milliliters
¾ cup	177 milliliters
1 cup	237 milliliters
1¼ cups	296 milliliters
1½ cups	355 milliliters
2 cups (1 pint)	473 milliliters
2½ cups	591 milliliters
3 cups	710 milliliters
4 cups (1 quart)	0.946 liter
1.06 quarts	1 liter
4 quarts (1 gallon)	3.8 liters

WEIGHT CONVERSIONS

OUNCES	GRAMS
½	14
¾	21
1	28
1½	43
2	57
2½	71
3	85
3½	99
4	113
4½	128
5	142
6	170
7	198
8	227
9	255
10	283
12	340
16 (1 pound)	454

CONVERSIONS FOR COMMON BAKING INGREDIENTS

Because measuring by weight is far more accurate than measuring by volume, and thus more likely to produce reliable results, in our recipes we provide ounce measures in addition to cup measures for many ingredients. Refer to the chart below to convert these measures into grams.

INGREDIENT	OUNCES	GRAMS
FLOUR		
1 cup all-purpose flour*	5	142
1 cup cake flour	4	113
1 cup whole-wheat flour	5½	156
SUGAR		
1 cup granulated (white) sugar	7	198
1 cup packed brown sugar (light or dark)	7	198
1 cup confectioners' sugar	4	113
COCOA POWDER		
1 cup cocoa powder	3	85
BUTTER†		
4 tablespoons (½ stick or ¼ cup)	2	57
8 tablespoons (1 stick or ½ cup)	4	113
16 tablespoons (2 sticks or 1 cup)	8	227

* U.S. all-purpose flour, the most frequently used flour in this book, does not contain leaveners, as some European flours do. These leavened flours are called self-rising or self-raising. If you are using self-rising flour, take this into consideration before adding leaveners to a recipe.

† In the United States, butter is sold both salted and unsalted. We recommend unsalted butter. If you are using salted butter, take this into consideration before adding salt to a recipe.

OVEN TEMPERATURE

FAHRENHEIT	CELSIUS	GAS MARK
225	105	¼
250	120	½
275	135	1
300	150	2
325	165	3
350	180	4
375	190	5
400	200	6
425	220	7
450	230	8
475	245	9

CONVERTING TEMPERATURES FROM AN INSTANT-READ THERMOMETER

We include doneness temperatures in many of the recipes in this book. We recommend an instant-read thermometer for the job. Refer to the table above to convert Fahrenheit degrees to Celsius. Or, for temperatures not represented in the chart, use this simple formula:

Subtract 32 degrees from the Fahrenheit reading, then divide the result by 1.8 to find the Celsius reading.

EXAMPLE
"Cook caramel until it registers 160 degrees."

To convert:
160°F − 32 = 128°
128° ÷ 1.8 = 71.11°C, rounded down to 71°C

NUTRITIONAL INFORMATION FOR OUR RECIPES

Analyzing recipes for their nutritional value is a tricky business, and we did our best to be as accurate as possible. To calculate the nutritional values of our recipes, we used The Food Processor SQL by ESHA Research. We entered all the ingredients, using weights for important ingredients such as meat, cheese, and most vegetables. We also used all of our preferred brands. When the recipe called for seasoning with an unspecified amount of salt and pepper, we added ½ teaspoon of salt and ¼ teaspoon of pepper to the analysis. We did not include additional salt or pepper when the food was "seasoned to taste." Note that in ESHA, "added sugar" does not reflect sugar found in some store-bought recipe ingredients; that sugar is, however, captured in the "total sugar" value. Any ingredient listed as "optional" was excluded from the analyses. If a range of an ingredient was provided, our calculations reflect the smaller number.

INDEX

Note: Page references in *italics* indicate photographs.

A

Acorn squash, substituting for butternut squash, 16
Aïoli
Garlic, 152
Sriracha, 152
Allicin, 7
Almond Butter
Raw Beet and Carrot Noodle Salad with Almond-Sesame Dressing, 122, *123*
Sauce, Spicy, Summer Rolls with, *132, 133*
Almond(s)
Anchovy Dip, *266, 267*
-Blueberry Muffins, Whole-Wheat, 58, *59*
Brussels Sprout, Red Cabbage, and Pomegranate Slaw, 214
and Cherries, Chocolate Bark with, 301
Cherry, Chocolate, and Orange Trail Mix, *280, 281*
Chicken and Arugula Salad with Figs and Warm Spices, *126, 127*
and Cranberries, Broccoli Salad with, *210,* 211
Cranberry, Coconut, Chili, and Lime Trail Mix, 281
Cranberry-Apple Crisp, *292, 293*
Flourless Nut and Seed Loaf, 44, *45*
health benefits, 28
Pepita, and Goji Berry Muesli, 40, *41*
and Sunflower Seeds, Quinoa Granola with, *42, 43*
Amaranth
as substitute for quinoa, 29
Three-Grain Breakfast Bowl, *48, 49*
Anchovy(ies)
Dip, *266, 267*
health benefits, 24
Kale Caesar Salad, 108, *109*
Anthocyanin, 7
Antioxidants, 6–7
Apple(s)
-Cranberry Crisp, *292, 293*
and Fennel Salad with Smoked Trout, 130, *131*
health benefits, 10
Skillet Roasted, with Dried Figs, Walnuts, and Maple Yogurt, *294, 295*
skin, vitamins and fiber in, 10
Artichoke(s)
and Cherry Tomatoes, Pesto Farro Salad with, *116,* 117
health benefits, 20
and Mushroom Hash with Parmesan Croutons, 78, *79*
and Navy Bean Dip, *262, 263*
Roasted, with Lemon Vinaigrette, 202, *203*
Arugula
Asparagus, and Cannellini Bean Salad with Walnuts, 114, *115*
and Chicken Salad with Figs and Warm Spices, *126, 127*
Crispy Skillet Turkey Burgers, *158,* 159
Edamame Salad with Arugula and Radishes, 224, *225*

Arugula *(cont.)*
Fennel and Apple Salad with Smoked Trout, 130, *131*
MLTs, 82, *83*
Radicchio, and Fennel Salad, Warm, Parmesan Chicken with, *156, 157*
as substitute for watercress, 13
Super Greens Soup, 92, *93*
Three-Bean Salad with, *118,* 119
Asparagus
Arugula, and Cannellini Bean Salad with Walnuts, 114, *115*
health benefits, 20
and Smoked Salmon, Fluffy Omelet with, 70, *71*
Stir-Fried, with Shiitakes, 204, *205*
Avocado(s)
and Bean Toast, 64, *65*
Black Rice Bowls with Salmon, *142, 143*
Broccoli Salad with Almonds and Cranberries, *210,* 211
Chocolate-, Pudding, 298, *299*
Crema, 152
health benefits, 18
MLTs, 82, *83*
Quinoa Taco Salad, 120, *121*
Salmon, Grapefruit, and Watercress Salad, *128, 129*
Super Cobb Salad, 112, *113*
Super Guacamole, 258, *259*
Tofu Rancheros, 74–75, *75*
Tomato, and Orange, Grilled Flank Steak with, *172, 173*

B

Bacon, healthy swaps for, 3
Baked Stuffed Trout with Red Pepper and Preserved Lemon, *148, 149*
Bananas
Chia Pudding with Fresh Fruit and Coconut, *50,* 51
Barley
Beet Risotto, *188,* 189
and Swiss Chard, Turkey Cutlets with, *162, 163*
Basil
Crispy Skillet Turkey Burgers, *158, 159*
Edamame Salad with Arugula and Radishes, 224, *225*
-Garlic Sauce, Stir-Fried Eggplant with, *226, 227*
Kale and Sunflower Seed Pesto, 153
and Pepper, Peaches, Blackberries, and Strawberries with, *296, 297*
Pesto Farro Salad with Cherry Tomatoes and Artichokes, *116,* 117
Pinto Bean–Beet Burgers, 90, *91*
Summer Rolls with Spicy Almond Butter Sauce, *132, 133*
Thai Red Curry with Lentils and Tofu, *178, 179*
Vegetable Lasagna, 182–83, *183*
BBQ Turkey, Pulled, with Red Cabbage Slaw, 170, *171*

Bean(s)

and Avocado Toast, 64, 65

Black, and Kale Breakfast Burritos, 68, 69

Black, Roasted Tomato Salsa with, 264, 265

Black, Sweet Potato, and Poblano Tacos, 190, 191

Brown Rice Onigiri with Spinach, Edamame, and Sesame, 278, 279

canned, cooking with, 23

Cannellini, Asparagus, and Arugula Salad with Walnuts, 114, 115

Cauliflower-Chickpea Flatbread with Romesco, 198–99, 199

Chicken and Arugula Salad with Figs and Warm Spices, 126, 127

Chickpea Salad Sandwiches, 88, 89

Curried Chickpea Salad Sandwiches, 89

Curried Chickpeas with Garlic and Yogurt, 244, 245

dried, health benefits, 23

Dukkah, 232–33, 233

edamame, health benefits, 22

Edamame Salad with Arugula and Radishes, 224, 225

15- , and Vegetable Soup, Hearty, 102, 103

Green, and Bok Choy, Beef Stir-Fry with, 174, 175

green, health benefits, 22

Green, Sautéed, with Mushroom and Dukkah, 228, 229

green, substitutes for, 22

Mediterranean Chopped Salad, 110, 111

Navy, and Artichoke Dip, 262, 263

Pinto, –Beet Burgers, 90, 91

Pumpkin Turkey Chili, 168, 169

Quinoa Pilaf with Shiitakes, Edamame, and Ginger, 248, 249

Quinoa Taco Salad, 120, 121

Sweet Potato Hummus, 260, 261

Swiss Chard Enchiladas, 192, 193

Three- , Salad with Arugula, 118, 119

Ultimate Nachos, 274, 275

Beef

grass-fed lean, health benefits, 27

Grilled Flank Steak with Tomato, Orange, and Avocado, 172, 173

Stir-Fry with Bok Choy and Green Beans, 174, 175

Thai Grilled-Steak Salad, 176–77, 177

Beet(s)

Barley Risotto, 188, 189

Chips, 270, 271

-Chocolate Cupcakes, 288–89, 289

greens, as substitute for Swiss chard, 13

health benefits, 19

Muhammara, 256, 257

with Orange and Walnuts, 206, 207

–Pinto Bean Burgers, 90, 91

Raw, and Carrot Noodle Salad with Almond-Sesame Dressing, 122, 123

"Sprinkles," 289, 289

Berries. *See* Blackberries; Blueberry(ies); Cranberry(ies); Goji Berry(ies); Raspberries; Strawberries

Beta-carotene, 7, 18

Betalain, 7

Biotin, 4

Black Bean(s)

and Avocado Toast, 64, 65

and Kale Breakfast Burritos, 68, 69

Roasted Tomato Salsa with, 264, 265

Sweet Potato, and Poblano Tacos, 190, 191

Pumpkin Turkey Chili, 168, 169

Quinoa Taco Salad, 120, 121

Ultimate Nachos, 274, 275

Blackberries

Chia Pudding with Fresh Fruit and Coconut, 50, 51

Peaches, and Strawberries with Basil and Pepper, 296, 297

Pepita, Almond, and Goji Berry Muesli, 40, 41

as substitute for blueberries, 8

Sunflower Seed, Hazelnut, and Cherry Muesli, 40

Three-Grain Breakfast Bowl, 48, 49

Black pepper, health benefits, 32

Black Rice

Bowls with Salmon, 142, 143

health benefits, 30

Blender, 36

Blueberry(ies)

-Almond Muffins, Whole-Wheat, 58, 59

buying, 8

Chia Pudding with Fresh Fruit and Coconut, 50, 51

dried, buying, 8

health benefits, 8

-Oat Pancakes, 52, 53

Pepita, Almond, and Goji Berry Muesli, 40, 41

substitutes for, 8

Sunflower Seed, Hazelnut, and Cherry Muesli, 40

Three-Grain Breakfast Bowl, 48, 49

Blue cheese

Super Cobb Salad, 112, 113

Bok Choy

and Green Beans, Beef Stir-Fry with, 174, 175

as substitute for red cabbage, 15

Breads

Avocado and Bean Toast, 64, 65

Flourless Nut and Seed Loaf, 44, 45

100 percent whole-wheat, for recipes, 3

Whole-Wheat Date-Nut, 62, 63

Breakfast

Avocado and Bean Toast, 64, 65

Blueberry-Oat Pancakes, 52, 53

Bowl, Three-Grain, 48, 49

Burritos, Kale and Black Bean, 68, 69

Chia Pudding with Fresh Fruit and Coconut, 50, 51

Cranberry-Orange Oat Muffins, 60, 61

eating vegetables at, 15

Flourless Nut and Seed Loaf, 44, 45

Breakfast (cont.)
    Fluffy Omelet with Smoked Salmon and
        Asparagus, 70, *71*
    Fried Eggs over Garlicky Chard and Bell Pepper, 66, *67*
    Frittata with Broccoli and Turmeric, 72, *73*
    Mushroom and Artichoke Hash with Parmesan
        Croutons, 78, *79*
    100 Percent Whole-Wheat Pancakes, 54, *55*
    Pepita, Almond, and Goji Berry Muesli, 40, *41*
    Pumpkin Spice Waffles, 56, *57*
    Quinoa Granola with Sunflower Seeds and
        Almonds, 42, *43*
    Smoked Trout Hash with Eggs, 76, *77*
    Steel-Cut Oatmeal with Carrots and Cherries, 46, *47*
    Sunflower Seed, Hazelnut, and Cherry Muesli, 40
    Tofu Rancheros, 74–75, *75*
    Whole-Wheat Blueberry-Almond Muffins, 58, *59*
    Whole-Wheat Date-Nut Bread, 62, *63*
Broccoli
    Grilled, with Lemon and Parmesan, 208–9, *209*
    health benefits, 14
    Salad with Almonds and Cranberries, *210*, 211
    stems, cooking with, 15
    Stir-Fried Tempeh with Orange Sauce, *180*, 181
    substitutes for, 14
    and Turmeric, Frittata with, 72, *73*
Broccoli rabe, as substitute for broccoli, 14
Broth, Chicken, 36–37
Broth Base, Vegetable, 37
Brownies, Pumpkin–Cream Cheese, 286–87, *287*
Brown Rice
    health benefits, 30
    Lemony, and Sun-Dried Tomatoes, Turkey Meatballs
        with, *166*, 167
    Onigiri with Spinach, Edamame, and Sesame, 278, *279*
    Pilaf with Dates and Pistachios, 250, *251*
Brussels Sprout(s)
    health benefits, 14
    Red Cabbage, and Pomegranate Slaw, 214
    Roasted, with Walnuts and Lemon, *212*, 213
Bulgur
    Pilaf with Cremini Mushrooms, 252, *253*
    Pilaf with Shiitake Mushrooms, 253
    Pinto Bean–Beet Burgers, 90, *91*
    Tomato, and Red Pepper Soup, Turkish, 94, *95*
Burgers
    Crispy Skillet Turkey, *158*, 159
    Pinto Bean–Beet, 90, *91*
Burritos, Kale and Black Bean Breakfast, 68, 69
Butter, healthy swaps for, 3
Butternut Squash
    health benefits, 16
    and Kale, One-Pan Chicken with, 154, *155*
    Polenta, 246, *247*
    Roasted, with Pistachios and Feta, 234, *235*
    substitutes for, 16
B vitamins, 4, 19

C

Cabbage
    Chinese Chicken Salad, 124, *125*
    Red, Slaw, Pulled BBQ Turkey with, 170, *171*
    Red, Brussels Sprout, and Pomegranate Slaw, 214
    red, health benefits, 15
    substitutes for, 15
    Summer Rolls with Spicy Almond Butter Sauce, *132*, 133
Caesar Salad, Kale, 108, *109*
Cake, Carrot Snack, 290–91, *291*
Calcium, 5
Carrot(s)
    and Cherries, Steel-Cut Oatmeal with, 46, *47*
    Cod in Coconut Broth with Lemon Grass and
        Ginger, 146, *147*
    Garlic-Chicken and Wild Rice Soup, 96, *97*
    health benefits, 17
    Raw, and Beet Noodle Salad with Almond-Sesame
        Dressing, 122, *123*
    Snack Cake, 290–91, *291*
    Summer Rolls with Spicy Almond Butter Sauce, *132*, 133
    "Tabbouleh" with Fennel, Orange, and Hazelnuts, 216
    "Tabbouleh" with Mint, Pistachios, and Pomegranate
        Seeds, 216, *217*
    Turkey Shepherd's Pie, 164–65, *165*
    Whole, Slow-Cooked, 218
    Whole, Slow-Cooked, with Pine Nut Relish, 218, *219*
Cauliflower
    -Chickpea Flatbread with Romesco, 198–99, *199*
    health benefits, 14
    Puree, 220, *221*
    Rice, 222, *223*
    Steaks, 194, *195*
    Turkey Shepherd's Pie, 164–65, *165*
Cayenne, health benefits, 32
Chard (Swiss)
    and Barley, Turkey Cutlets with, 162, *163*
    Enchiladas, *192*, 193
    Garlicky, and Bell Pepper, Fried Eggs over, 66, *67*
    health benefits, 13
    Hearty 15-Bean and Vegetable Soup, *102*, 103
    and Lentils, Pomegranate Roasted Salmon with, 140, *141*
    Macaroni and Cheese, *184*, 185
    stems, cooking with, 15
    substitutes for, 13
    Super Greens Soup, 92, *93*
    and Sweet Potato Gratin, 238, *239*
    Ultimate Nachos, 274, *275*
Cheese
    Butternut Squash Polenta, 246, *247*
    Cauliflower-Chickpea Flatbread with Romesco, 198–99, *199*
    Cream, –Pumpkin Brownies, 286–87, *287*
    Cream, –Yogurt Frosting, 291, *291*
    Crispy Skillet Turkey Burgers, *158*, 159
    Fluffy Omelet with Smoked Salmon and
        Asparagus, 70, *71*

Cheese *(cont.)*
    Frittata with Broccoli and Turmeric, *72, 73*
    Grilled Broccoli with Lemon and Parmesan, *208–9, 209*
    Kale Caesar Salad, 108, *109*
    Mediterranean Chopped Salad, *110*, 111
    Mushroom and Artichoke Hash with Parmesan
        Croutons, *78, 79*
    Parmesan Chicken with Warm Arugula, Radicchio,
        and Fennel Salad, *156, 157*
    Pesto Farro Salad with Cherry Tomatoes and
        Artichokes, *116, 117*
    Quinoa Taco Salad, 120, *121*
    Roasted Butternut Squash with Pistachios and
        Feta, *234, 235*
    Roasted Spiralized Sweet Potatoes with Walnuts
        and Feta, 240, *241*
    Super Cobb Salad, 112, *113*
    Sweet Potato and Swiss Chard Gratin, *238, 239*
    Swiss Chard Enchiladas, *192*, 193
    Swiss Chard Macaroni and, *184*, 185
    Turkey Cutlets with Barley and Swiss Chard, *162, 163*
    Ultimate Nachos, *274, 275*
    Vegetable Lasagna, *182–83, 183*
    Whole-Wheat Pizza with Kale and Sunflower Seed
        Pesto, *196–97, 197*
Chermoula Sauce, 153, *194*
Cherry(ies)
    and Almonds, Chocolate Bark with, 301
    and Carrots, Steel-Cut Oatmeal with, 46, *47*
    Chocolate, and Orange Trail Mix, *280, 281*
    dried, buying, 9
    health benefits, 9
    Quinoa Granola with Sunflower Seeds and
        Almonds, *42, 43*
    Sunflower Seed, and Hazelnut Muesli, 40
    Turmeric Chicken Salad Sandwiches, *84, 85*
Chia (seeds)
    health benefits, 34
    Pudding with Fresh Fruit and Coconut, *50, 51*
    Whole-Wheat Seeded Crackers, *272, 273*
Chicken
    and Arugula Salad with Figs and Warm Spices, *126, 127*
    Broth, 36–37
    Garlic-, and Wild Rice Soup, *96, 97*
    lean white, health benefits, 27
    One-Pan, with Kale and Butternut Squash, 154, *155*
    Parmesan, with Warm Arugula, Radicchio, and Fennel
        Salad, *156, 157*
    Poached, with Warm Tomato-Ginger Vinaigrette, 150, *151*
    Salad, Chinese, 124, *125*
    Salad Sandwiches, Turmeric, *84, 85*
    Super Cobb Salad, 112, *113*
Chickpea(s)
    -Cauliflower Flatbread with Romesco, *198–99, 199*
    Chicken and Arugula Salad with Figs and Warm
        Spices, *126, 127*

Chickpea(s) *(cont.)*
    Curried, with Garlic and Yogurt, 244, *245*
    Dukkah, 232–33, *233*
    Mediterranean Chopped Salad, *110*, 111
    Salad Sandwiches, *88, 89*
    Salad Sandwiches, Curried, 89
    Sweet Potato Hummus, *260, 261*
    Three-Bean Salad with Arugula, *118, 119*
Chiles
    Kale and Black Bean Breakfast Burritos, *68, 69*
    Pumpkin Turkey Chili, *168, 169*
    Quick Sweet-and-Spicy Pickled Red Onions, 64, *65*
    Roasted Tomato Salsa with Black Beans, *264, 265*
    Super Guacamole, *258, 259*
    Sweet Potato, Poblano, and Black Bean Tacos, *190, 191*
    Thai Grilled-Steak Salad, *176–77, 177*
    Tofu Rancheros, *74–75, 75*
    Tomato Salsa, *274, 275*
    Ultimate Nachos, *274, 275*
Chili, Pumpkin Turkey, *168, 169*
Chimichurri Sauce, 153
Chinese broccoli, as substitute for broccoli, 14
Chinese cabbage, as substitute for red cabbage, 15
Chinese Chicken Salad, 124, *125*
Chocolate
    -Avocado Pudding, *298, 299*
    Bark with Almonds and Cherries, 301
    Bark with Pepitas and Dried Goji Berries, *300, 301*
    -Beet Cupcakes, 288–89, *289*
    Cherry, and Orange Trail Mix, *280, 281*
    dark, health benefits, 31
    and Goji Berries, Oatmeal Cookies with, 284, *285*
    Pumpkin–Cream Cheese Brownies, 286–87, *287*
Cilantro
    Avocado and Bean Toast, 64, *65*
    Avocado Crema, 152
    Chermoula Sauce, 153
    Chinese Chicken Salad, 124, *125*
    Quinoa Taco Salad, 120, *121*
    Super Guacamole, *258, 259*
    Thai Grilled-Steak Salad, *176–77, 177*
    Tofu Rancheros, *74–75, 75*
    Tomato Salsa, *274, 275*
Cinnamon
    health benefits, 33
    Pumpkin Spice Waffles, *56, 57*
Clementines, as substitute for oranges, 10
Cobb Salad, Super, 112, *113*
Coconut
    Broth, Cod in, with Lemon Grass and Ginger, 146, *147*
    Cranberry, Chili, and Lime Trail Mix, 281
    and Fresh Fruit, Chia Pudding with, *50, 51*
    Quinoa Granola with Sunflower Seeds and
        Almonds, *42, 43*
Cod
    in Coconut Broth with Lemon Grass and Ginger, 146, *147*
    Fillets, Nut-Crusted, 144, *145*

Collard greens
Salmon Tacos with Super Slaw, *138, 139*
as substitute for kale, 12
Cookies, Oatmeal, with Chocolate and Goji Berries, 284, 285
Copper, 5
Coriander seeds
Dukkah, 232–33, *233*
Crackers, Whole-Wheat Seeded, 272, 273
Cranberry(ies)
and Almonds, Broccoli Salad with, *210,* 211
-Apple Crisp, *292, 293*
Coconut, Chili, and Lime Trail Mix, 281
health benefits, 8
One-Pan Chicken with Kale and Butternut Squash, 154, *155*
-Orange Oat Muffins, 60, *61*
Cream Cheese
–Pumpkin Brownies, 286–87, *287*
-Yogurt Frosting, 291, *291*
Crema, Avocado, 152
Crisp, Cranberry-Apple, 292, 293
Crispy Skillet Turkey Burgers, 158, 159
Croutons, Parmesan, Mushroom and Artichoke Hash with, 78, 79
Cucumbers
Black Rice Bowls with Salmon, 142, 143
Mediterranean Chopped Salad, *110,* 111
Summer Rolls with Spicy Almond Butter Sauce, *132, 133*
Thai Grilled-Steak Salad, 176–77, *177*
Cumin, health benefits, 32
Cupcakes, Beet-Chocolate, 288–89, 289
Curried Chickpea Salad Sandwiches, 89
Curried Chickpeas with Garlic and Yogurt, 244, 245
Curry, Thai Red, with Lentils and Tofu, 178, 179

D

Dandelion greens, as substitute for watercress, 13
Date(s)
health benefits, 11
-Nut Bread, Whole-Wheat, 62, *63*
and Pistachios, Brown Rice Pilaf with, 250, *251*
Delicata squash, substituting for butternut squash, 16
Dessert
Beet-Chocolate Cupcakes, 288–89, *289*
Carrot Snack Cake, 290–91, *291*
Chocolate-Avocado Pudding, 298, *299*
Chocolate Bark with Almonds and Cherries, 301
Chocolate Bark with Pepitas and Dried Goji Berries, *300,* 301
Cranberry-Apple Crisp, 292, *293*
eating vegetables at, 15
Oatmeal Cookies with Chocolate and Goji Berries, 284, *285*
Peaches, Blackberries, and Strawberries with Basil and Pepper, *296,* 297
Pumpkin–Cream Cheese Brownies, 286–87, *287*
Skillet Roasted Apples with Dried Figs, Walnuts, and Maple Yogurt, 294, *295*

Dips and spreads
Anchovy Dip, 266, *267*
Beet Muhammara, *256, 257*
Navy Bean and Artichoke Dip, *262, 263*
Roasted Tomato Salsa with Black Beans, *264, 265*
Super Guacamole, *258, 259*
Sweet Potato Hummus, *260, 261*
Tomato Salsa, *274, 275*
Dukkah, 232–33, 233

E

Easy Sauces, 152–53
Edamame
health benefits, 22
Salad with Arugula and Radishes, *224, 225*
Shiitakes, and Ginger, Quinoa Pilaf with, *248, 249*
Spinach, and Sesame, Brown Rice Onigiri with, *278, 279*
Eggplant
health benefits, 17
Stir-Fried, with Garlic-Basil Sauce, *226, 227*
Vegetable Lasagna, 182–83, *183*
Egg(s)
Fluffy Omelet with Smoked Salmon and Asparagus, 70, *71*
Fried, over Garlicky Chard and Bell Pepper, 66, *67*
Frittata with Broccoli and Turmeric, 72, *73*
health benefits, 26
Kale and Black Bean Breakfast Burritos, 68, *69*
organic, buying, 26
Salad Sandwiches with Radishes and Watercress, 86, *87*
Smoked Salmon Deviled, 276
Smoked Trout Deviled, *276, 277*
Smoked Trout Hash with, 76, *77*
Super Cobb Salad, 112, *113*
Enchiladas, Swiss Chard, 192, 193
Escarole
Mediterranean Chopped Salad, *110,* 111
Quinoa Taco Salad, 120, *121*
as substitute for watercress, 13

F

Farro
and Kale, Italian Wedding Soup with, *106, 107*
Pesto Salad with Cherry Tomatoes and Artichokes, *116,* 117
Fats, healthy
for absorption of vitamins and antioxidants, 18, 35
in avocados, 18
benefits of, 35
choosing, 35
Fennel
and Apple Salad with Smoked Trout, 130, *131*
Arugula, and Radicchio Salad, Warm, Parmesan Chicken with, *156, 157*
Orange, and Hazelnuts, Carrot "Tabbouleh" with, 216

Feta

    Mediterranean Chopped Salad, *110*, 111

    and Pistachios, Roasted Butternut Squash with, *234, 235*

    and Walnuts, Roasted Spiralized Sweet Potatoes
        with, 240, *241*

Figs

    Dried, Walnuts, and Maple Yogurt, Skillet Roasted Apples
        with, 294, *295*

    health benefits, 11

    and Warm Spices, Chicken and Arugula Salad
        with, *126,* 127

Fish

    Baked Stuffed Trout with Red Pepper and Preserved
        Lemon, *148,* 149

    Black Rice Bowls with Salmon, *142, 143*

    Cod in Coconut Broth with Lemon Grass and
        Ginger, 146, *147*

    Fennel and Apple Salad with Smoked Trout, 130, *131*

    Fluffy Omelet with Smoked Salmon and Asparagus, 70, *71*

    mackerel, as substitute for trout, 25

    Nut-Crusted Cod Fillets, 144, *145*

    Oven-Roasted Salmon with Miso-Sesame Sauce, 137

    Oven-Roasted Salmon with Tangerine and Ginger
        Relish, *136,* 137

    Pomegranate Roasted Salmon with Lentils and
        Chard, 140, *141*

    Salmon, Avocado, Grapefruit, and Watercress
        Salad, *128,* 129

    Salmon Tacos with Super Slaw, *138, 139*

    sardines, health benefits, 24

    Smoked Salmon Deviled Eggs, 276

    Smoked Trout Deviled Eggs, 276, *277*

    Smoked Trout Hash with Eggs, 76, *77*

    trout, health benefits, 25

    white, health benefits, 25

    white, types of, 25

    wild salmon, health benefits, 24

    see also Anchovy(ies)

Flaxseeds

    Cranberry-Apple Crisp, 292, 293

    Flourless Nut and Seed Loaf, 44, 45

    health benefits, 34

    Whole-Wheat Seeded Crackers, *272, 273*

Flourless Nut and Seed Loaf, 44, 45

Flours, whole-grain, health benefits, 35

Fluffy Omelet with Smoked Salmon and Asparagus, 70, 71

Folic acid/folate, 4

Food processor, 36

Fried Eggs over Garlicky Chard and Bell Pepper, 66, 67

Frittata with Broccoli and Turmeric, 72, 73

Frosting, Yogurt–Cream Cheese, 291, 291

Fruit

    "clean fifteen," 20

    at dessert time, 15

    "dirty dozen," 20

    Fresh, and Coconut, Chia Pudding with, *50, 51*

    see also specific fruits

G

Garlic

    Aïoli, 152

    -Basil Sauce, Stir-Fried Eggplant with, 226, 227

    -Chicken and Wild Rice Soup, 96, 97

    Chips and Spinach, Lentils with, 242, 243

    health benefits, 33

    and Yogurt, Curried Chickpeas with, 244, 245

Garlicky Braised Kale, 230, 231

Ginger

    Brown Rice Onigiri with Spinach, Edamame, and
        Sesame, 278, 279

    Chinese Chicken Salad, 124, 125

    health benefits, 32

    and Lemon Grass, Cod in Coconut Broth with, 146, *147*

    Pumpkin Spice Waffles, 56, 57

    Shiitake, Tofu, and Mustard Greens Soup, 104, 105

    Shiitakes, and Edamame, Quinoa Pilaf with, 248, 249

    Stir-Fried Eggplant with Garlic-Basil Sauce, 226, 227

    and Tangerine Relish, Oven-Roasted Salmon with, *136,* 137

    -Tomato Vinaigrette, Warm, Poached Chicken with, 150, *151*

Glucosinolates, 7

Goji Berry(ies)

    and Chocolate, Oatmeal Cookies with, 284, *285*

    Dried, and Pepitas, Chocolate Bark with, 300, 301

    health benefits, 34

    Pepita, and Almond Muesli, 40, *41*

Grain(s)

    Beet Barley Risotto, 188, 189

    Butternut Squash Polenta, 246, 247

    Italian Wedding Soup with Kale and Farro, 106, 107

    Mushroom and Wheat Berry Soup, 98, 99

    Pesto Farro Salad with Cherry Tomatoes and
        Artichokes, *116,* 117

    quinoa, health benefits, 29

    Quinoa Granola with Sunflower Seeds and Almonds, 42, 43

    Quinoa Pilaf with Shiitakes, Edamame, and Ginger, 248, 249

    Quinoa Taco Salad, 120, *121*

    Three- , Breakfast Bowl, 48, 49

    Turkey Cutlets with Barley and Swiss Chard, 162, *163*

    whole, health benefits, 30

    see also Bulgur; Oat(s); Rice

Granola, Quinoa, with Sunflower Seeds and Almonds, 42, 43

Grapefruit

    red and pink, health benefits, 11

    Salmon, Avocado, and Watercress Salad, *128,* 129

    white, as substitute for red and pink, 11

Gratin, Sweet Potato and Swiss Chard, 238, 239

Green Beans

    and Bok Choy, Beef Stir-Fry with, *174, 175*

    health benefits, 22

    Sautéed, with Mushroom and Dukkah, 228, 229

    Three-Bean Salad with Arugula, *118,* 119

Greens

    beet, health benefits, 19

    collard, as substitute for kale, 12

Greens (cont.)

dandelion, as substitute for watercress, 13

Egg Salad Sandwiches with Radishes and
Watercress, 86, 87

escarole, as substitute for watercress, 13

Mediterranean Chopped Salad, 110, 111

Mushroom and Wheat Berry Soup, 98, 99

mustard, as substitute for Swiss chard, 13

Mustard, Shiitake, and Tofu Soup, 104, 105

nutrient-dense, for salads, 13

Parmesan Chicken with Warm Arugula, Radicchio, and
Fennel Salad, 156, 157

Quinoa Taco Salad, 120, 121

Salmon, Avocado, Grapefruit, and Watercress
Salad, 128, 129

Salmon Tacos with Super Slaw, 138, 139

Smoked Trout Hash with Eggs, 76, 77

Super, Soup, 92, 93

Super Cobb Salad, 112, 113

turnip, as substitute for Swiss chard, 13

watercress, health benefits, 13

see also Arugula; Chard; Kale; Spinach

Grilled Broccoli with Lemon and Parmesan, 208–9, 209

**Grilled Flank Steak with Tomato, Orange, and
Avocado, 172, 173**

Gruyère cheese

Swiss Chard Macaroni and Cheese, 184, 185

Guacamole, Super, 258, 259

H

Hash

Mushroom and Artichoke, with Parmesan Croutons, 78, 79

Smoked Trout, with Eggs, 76, 77

Hazelnut(s)

Fennel, and Orange, Carrot "Tabbouleh" with, 216

Salmon, Avocado, Grapefruit, and Watercress
Salad, 128, 129

Sunflower Seed, and Cherry Muesli, 40

Twice-Baked Sweet Potatoes with, 236, 237

Hearty 15-Bean and Vegetable Soup, 102, 103

Hemp seeds, health benefits, 34

Herbs

adding to recipes, 15

health benefits of, 33

see also Basil; Cilantro; Mint; Parsley

Hummus, Sweet Potato, 260, 261

I

Iron, 5

Isoflavones, 7

Italian Wedding Soup with Kale and Farro, 106, 107

J

Jícama

Salmon Tacos with Super Slaw, 138, 139

K

Kale

and Black Bean Breakfast Burritos, 68, 69

Braised, 230, 231

and Butternut Squash, One-Pan Chicken with, 154, 155

Caesar Salad, 108, 109

Chips, 268, 269

and Farro, Italian Wedding Soup with, 106, 107

health benefits, 12

substitute for, 12

and Sunflower Seed Pesto, 153

and Sunflower Seed Pesto, Whole-Wheat Pizza with,
196–97, 197

Super Cobb Salad, 112, 113

Super Greens Soup, 92, 93

L

Lasagna, Vegetable, 182–83, 183

Lemon Grass and Ginger, Cod in Coconut Broth with, 146, 147

Lemon(s)

health benefits, 34

and Parmesan, Grilled Broccoli with, 208–9, 209

Preserved, and Red Pepper, Baked Stuffed Trout
with, 148, 149

Vinaigrette, Roasted Artichokes with, 202, 203

-Yogurt Sauce, 152–53

Lentil(s)

and Chard, Pomegranate Roasted Salmon with, 140, 141

health benefits, 23

Red, Soup with North African Spices, 100, 101

with Spinach and Garlic Chips, 242, 243

and Tofu, Thai Red Curry with, 178, 179

Lettuce, iceberg, healthy swaps for, 3

Lignans, 7

Lime(s)

Cranberry, Coconut, and Chili Trail Mix, 281

health benefits, 34

Lunch

Asparagus, Arugula, and Cannellini Bean Salad
with Walnuts, 114, 115

Chicken and Arugula Salad with Figs and
Warm Spices, 126, 127

Chickpea Salad Sandwiches, 88, 89

Chinese Chicken Salad, 124, 125

Curried Chickpea Salad Sandwiches, 89

Egg Salad Sandwiches with Radishes and
Watercress, 86, 87

Fennel and Apple Salad with Smoked Trout, 130, 131

Garlic-Chicken and Wild Rice Soup, 96, 97

Hearty 15-Bean and Vegetable Soup, 102, 103

Lunch *(cont.)*

Italian Wedding Soup with Kale and Farro, *106, 107*

Kale Caesar Salad, 108, *109*

Mediterranean Chopped Salad, *110,* 111

MLTs, 82, 83

Mushroom and Wheat Berry Soup, 98, 99

Pesto Farro Salad with Cherry Tomatoes and
Artichokes, *116, 117*

Pinto Bean–Beet Burgers, 90, *91*

Quinoa Taco Salad, 120, *121*

Raw Beet and Carrot Noodle Salad with Almond-Sesame
Dressing, 122, *123*

Red Lentil Soup with North African Spices, *100,* 101

Salmon, Avocado, Grapefruit, and Watercress
Salad, *128, 129*

Shiitake, Tofu, and Mustard Greens Soup, 104, *105*

Summer Rolls with Spicy Almond Butter Sauce, *132,* 133

Super Cobb Salad, 112, *113*

Super Greens Soup, 92, *93*

Three-Bean Salad with Arugula, *118,* 119

Turkish Tomato, Bulgur, and Red Pepper Soup, 94, *95*

Turmeric Chicken Salad Sandwiches, 84, *85*

Lutein, 7

Lycopene, 7, 18

M

Macaroni and Cheese, Swiss Chard, 184, *185*

Mackerel, as substitute for trout, 25

Magnesium, 5

Main dishes

Baked Stuffed Trout with Red Pepper and Preserved
Lemon, *148, 149*

Beef Stir-Fry with Bok Choy and Green Beans, *174, 175*

Beet Barley Risotto, *188, 189*

Black Rice Bowls with Salmon, *142, 143*

Cauliflower-Chickpea Flatbread with Romesco, 198–99, *199*

Cauliflower Steaks, 194, *195*

Cod in Coconut Broth with Lemon Grass and
Ginger, 146, *147*

Crispy Skillet Turkey Burgers, *158,* 159

Grilled Flank Steak with Tomato, Orange,
and Avocado, 172, *173*

Mushroom Bourguignon, 186–87, *187*

Nut-Crusted Cod Fillets, 144, *145*

One-Pan Chicken with Kale and Butternut Squash, 154, *155*

Oven-Roasted Salmon with Miso-Sesame Sauce, 137

Oven-Roasted Salmon with Tangerine and Ginger
Relish, *136,* 137

Parmesan Chicken with Warm Arugula, Radicchio,
and Fennel Salad, *156,* 157

Poached Chicken with Warm Tomato-Ginger
Vinaigrette, 150, *151*

Pomegranate Roasted Salmon with Lentils and
Chard, 140, *141*

Pulled BBQ Turkey with Red Cabbage Slaw, 170, *171*

Main dishes *(cont.)*

Pumpkin Turkey Chili, *168, 169*

Salmon Tacos with Super Slaw, *138, 139*

Spice-Rubbed Turkey Breast with Sour Orange
Sauce, *160, 161*

Stir-Fried Tempeh with Orange Sauce, *180, 181*

Sweet Potato, Poblano, and Black Bean Tacos, *190, 191*

Swiss Chard Enchiladas, *192, 193*

Swiss Chard Macaroni and Cheese, *184, 185*

Thai Grilled-Steak Salad, 176–77, *177*

Thai Red Curry with Lentils and Tofu, 178, *179*

Turkey Cutlets with Barley and Swiss Chard, 162, *163*

Turkey Meatballs with Lemony Brown Rice and
Sun-Dried Tomatoes, *166, 167*

Turkey Shepherd's Pie, 164–65, *165*

Vegetable Lasagna, 182–83, *183*

Whole-Wheat Pizza with Kale and Sunflower Seed
Pesto, 196–97, *197*

Mandoline, 36

Manganese, 5

Maple Yogurt, Dried Figs, and Walnuts, Skillet Roasted
Apples with, *294, 295*

Mayonnaise, healthy swaps for, 3

Meat. *See* Beef

Meatballs, Turkey, with Lemony Brown Rice and
Sun-Dried Tomatoes, *166, 167*

Mediterranean Chopped Salad, *110,* 111

Millet

Three-Grain Breakfast Bowl, 48, *49*

Minerals

best food sources for, 5

key functions and benefits, 5

Mint

Brown Rice Pilaf with Dates and Pistachios, 250, *251*

Edamame Salad with Arugula and Radishes, 224, 225

Pistachios, and Pomegranate Seeds, Carrot "Tabbouleh"
with, 216, *217*

Salmon, Avocado, Grapefruit, and Watercress
Salad, *128, 129*

Thai Grilled-Steak Salad, 176–77, *177*

Miso-Sesame Sauce, Oven-Roasted Salmon with, 137

MLTs, 82, 83

Monterey Jack cheese

Crispy Skillet Turkey Burgers, *158, 159*

Swiss Chard Enchiladas, *192, 193*

Ultimate Nachos, 274, *275*

Mozzarella cheese

Vegetable Lasagna, 182–83, *183*

Muesli

Pepita, Almond, and Goji Berry, 40, *41*

Sunflower Seed, Hazelnut, and Cherry, 40

Muffins

Cranberry-Orange Oat, 60, *61*

Whole-Wheat Blueberry-Almond, 58, *59*

Muhammara, Beet, 256, *257*

Mushroom(s)
and Artichoke Hash with Parmesan Croutons, 78, 79
Bourguignon, 186–87, 187
Cremini, Bulgur Pilaf with, 252, 253
and Dukkah, Sautéed Green Beans with, 228, 229
health benefits, 21
Hearty 15-Bean and Vegetable Soup, 102, 103
MLTs, 82, 83
Quinoa Pilaf with Shiitakes, Edamame, and
  Ginger, 248, 249
Shiitake, Bulgur Pilaf with, 253
Shiitake, Tofu, and Mustard Greens Soup, 104, 105
Stir-Fried Asparagus with Shiitakes, 204, 205
Super Cobb Salad, 112, 113
Turkey Shepherd's Pie, 164–65, 165
Vegetable Lasagna, 182–83, 183
and Wheat Berry Soup, 98, 99
Mustard Greens
Mushroom and Wheat Berry Soup, 98, 99
Shiitake, and Tofu Soup, 104, 105
Smoked Trout Hash with Eggs, 76, 77
as substitute for Swiss chard, 13

N

Nachos, Ultimate, 274, 275
Navy Bean and Artichoke Dip, 262, 263
Niacin, 4
Nutrient-dense eating
benefits of, 1
building recipes for, 1–3
flavor boosters, 32–34
homemade broths, 36–37
key vitamins and minerals, 4–5
recipe nutrition information, 2
simple ingredient swaps for, 3
spices and herbs for, 32–33
tools of the trade, 36
50 superfoods to turbocharge everyday cooking, 8–31
Nut(s)
Carrot "Tabbouleh" with Fennel, Orange,
  and Hazelnuts, 216
Cranberry-Apple Crisp, 292, 293
-Crusted Cod Fillets, 144, 145
Pine Nut, Relish, Slow-Cooked Whole Carrots
  with, 218, 219
Salmon, Avocado, Grapefruit, and Watercress
  Salad, 128, 129
Steel-Cut Oatmeal with Carrots and Cherries, 46, 47
Sunflower Seed, Hazelnut, and Cherry Muesli, 40
Twice-Baked Sweet Potatoes with
  Hazelnuts, 236, 237
see also Almond(s); Pistachios; Walnuts

O

Oat flour
Blueberry-Oat Pancakes, 52, 53
Cranberry-Orange Oat Muffins, 60, 61
health benefits, 28
Pumpkin Spice Waffles, 56, 57
Oatmeal, Steel-Cut, with Carrots and Cherries, 46, 47
Oatmeal Cookies with Chocolate and Goji
  Berries, 284, 285
Oat(s)
-Blueberry Pancakes, 52, 53
Cranberry-Apple Crisp, 292, 293
Flourless Nut and Seed Loaf, 44, 45
health benefits, 28
Oatmeal Cookies with Chocolate and Goji
  Berries, 284, 285
Pepita, Almond, and Goji Berry Muesli, 40, 41
Steel-Cut Oatmeal with Carrots and Cherries, 46, 47
Sunflower Seed, Hazelnut, and Cherry Muesli, 40
Oils
canola, expeller-pressed, 35
canola, replacing butter with, 3
extra-virgin olive, cold-pressed, 35
healthy, choosing, 35
high in unsaturated fats, 35
vegetable, avoiding, 35
Olives
Baked Stuffed Trout with Red Pepper and Preserved
  Lemon, 148, 149
Mediterranean Chopped Salad, 110, 111
Omelet, Fluffy, with Smoked Salmon and Asparagus, 70, 71
100 Percent Whole-Wheat Pancakes, 54, 55
One-Pan Chicken with Kale and Butternut Squash, 154, 155
Onigiri, Brown Rice, with Spinach, Edamame, and
  Sesame, 278, 279
Onions
health benefits, 21
Mushroom Bourguignon, 186–87, 187
Red, Quick Sweet-and-Spicy Pickled, 64, 65
Orange(s)
Chinese Chicken Salad, 124, 125
Chocolate, and Cherry Trail Mix, 280, 281
-Cranberry Oat Muffins, 60, 61
health benefits, 10
Sauce, Sour, Spice-Rubbed Turkey Breast with, 160, 161
Sauce, Stir-Fried Tempeh with, 180, 181
substitutes for, 10
Tomato, and Avocado, Grilled Flank Steak with, 172, 173
and Walnuts, Beets with, 206, 207
Organic food, 20
Oven-Roasted Salmon with Miso-Sesame Sauce, 137
Oven-Roasted Salmon with Tangerine and Ginger
  Relish, 136, 137

P

Pancakes
   Blueberry-Oat, 52, *53*
   100 Percent Whole-Wheat, *54, 55*
Pantothenic acid, 4
Parmesan
   Butternut Squash Polenta, *246, 247*
   Cauliflower-Chickpea Flatbread with Romesco, 198–99, *199*
   Chicken with Warm Arugula, Radicchio, and Fennel
      Salad, *156, 157*
   Croutons, Mushroom and Artichoke Hash with, *78, 79*
   Fluffy Omelet with Smoked Salmon and
      Asparagus, 70, *71*
   Frittata with Broccoli and Turmeric, *72, 73*
   Kale Caesar Salad, 108, *109*
   and Lemon, Grilled Broccoli with, 208–9, *209*
   Pesto Farro Salad with Cherry Tomatoes and
      Artichokes, *116, 117*
   Sweet Potato and Swiss Chard Gratin, 238, *239*
   Turkey Cutlets with Barley and Swiss Chard, 162, *163*
   Vegetable Lasagna, 182–83, *183*
   Whole-Wheat Pizza with Kale and Sunflower Seed
      Pesto, 196–97, *197*
Parsley
   Cauliflower-Chickpea Flatbread with Romesco, 198–99, *199*
   Chimichurri Sauce, 153
Pasta
   healthy swaps for, 3
   Swiss Chard Macaroni and Cheese, *184,* 185
   Vegetable Lasagna, 182–83, *183*
   whole-wheat, for recipes, 3
**Peaches, Blackberries, and Strawberries with Basil
   and Pepper, 296, 297**
Peas
   as substitute for green beans, 22
   Thai Red Curry with Lentils and Tofu, 178, *179*
Pecans
   Cranberry-Apple Crisp, 292, *293*
   Steel-Cut Oatmeal with Carrots and Cherries, 46, *47*
Pepita(s)
   Almond, and Goji Berry Muesli, 40, *41*
   Cherry, Chocolate, and Orange Trail Mix, 280, *281*
   Cranberry, Coconut, Chili, and Lime Trail Mix, 281
   Cranberry-Orange Oat Muffins, 60, *61*
   and Dried Goji Berries, Chocolate Bark with, *300,* 301
   Flourless Nut and Seed Loaf, *44, 45*
   health benefits, 29
   Super Guacamole, 258, *259*
Pepper(s)
   Beet Muhammara, 256, *257*
   Bell, and Garlicky Chard, Fried Eggs over, 66, *67*
   Cauliflower-Chickpea Flatbread with Romesco, 198–99, *199*
   Chinese Chicken Salad, 124, *125*
   Pumpkin Turkey Chili, 168, *169*
   Red, and Preserved Lemon, Baked Stuffed Trout
      with, *148, 149*

Pepper(s) *(cont.)*
   Red, Tomato, and Bulgur Soup, Turkish, 94, *95*
   red bell, health benefits, 19
   red bell, substitutes for, 19
   Stir-Fried Eggplant with Garlic-Basil Sauce, 226, *227*
   Stir-Fried Tempeh with Orange Sauce, *180,* 181
   Summer Rolls with Spicy Almond Butter Sauce, *132, 133*
   Swiss Chard Enchiladas, *192, 193*
   Thai Red Curry with Lentils and Tofu, 178, *179*
   see also Chiles
Pesto
   Farro Salad with Cherry Tomatoes and
      Artichokes, *116, 117*
   Kale and Sunflower Seed, 153
   Kale and Sunflower Seed, Whole-Wheat Pizza
      with, 196–97, *197*
Phenolic acids, 7
Phosphorus, 5
Phytonutrients
   acting as antioxidants, 6–7
   benefits of, 6, 7
   best food sources for, 7
   classes of, 6
Pickled Red Onions, Quick Sweet-and-Spicy, 64, 65
Pine Nut Relish, Slow-Cooked Whole Carrots with, 218, 219
Pinto Bean(s)
   –Beet Burgers, 90, *91*
   Swiss Chard Enchiladas, *192, 193*
Pistachios
   and Dates, Brown Rice Pilaf with, *250, 251*
   Dukkah, 232–33, *233*
   and Feta, Roasted Butternut Squash with, *234, 235*
   Mint, and Pomegranate Seeds, Carrot "Tabbouleh"
      with, 216, *217*
   Nut-Crusted Cod Fillets, 144, *145*
Pizza
   Cauliflower-Chickpea Flatbread with
      Romesco, 198–99, *199*
   Whole-Wheat, with Kale and Sunflower Seed
      Pesto, 196–97, *197*
**Poached Chicken with Warm Tomato-Ginger
   Vinaigrette, 150, *151***
Polenta, Butternut Squash, 246, 247
Pomegranate (Seeds)
   Brussels Sprout, and Red Cabbage Slaw, 214
   health benefits, 9
   juice, buying, 9
   Mint, and Pistachios, Carrot "Tabbouleh" with, 216, *217*
   Roasted Salmon with Lentils and Chard, 140, *141*
   Super Guacamole, 258, *259*
Potassium, 5
Potato(es)
   Smoked Trout Hash with Eggs, 76, *77*
   Sweet, and Swiss Chard Gratin, 238, *239*
   sweet, health benefits, 16
   Sweet, Hummus, 260, *261*

Potato(es) *(cont.)*
   Sweet, Poblano, and Black Bean Tacos, *190, 191*
   Sweet, Roasted Spiralized, with Walnuts and Feta, 240, *241*
   Sweet, Twice-Baked, with Hazelnuts, *236, 237*
Poultry
   lean white, health benefits, 27
   see also Chicken; Turkey
Probiotics, in yogurt, 31
Pudding
   Chia, with Fresh Fruit and Coconut, 50, 51
   Chocolate-Avocado, 298, 299
Pumpkin
   –Cream Cheese Brownies, 286–87, *287*
   Spice Waffles, *56, 57*
   Turkey Chili, *168, 169*

Q

Queso fresco
   Quinoa Taco Salad, 120, *121*
Quick Sweet-and-Spicy Pickled Red Onions, 64, 65
Quinoa
   Granola with Sunflower Seeds and Almonds, *42, 43*
   health benefits, 29
   Pilaf with Shiitakes, Edamame, and Ginger, *248, 249*
   substitute for, 29
   Taco Salad, 120, *121*
   Three-Grain Breakfast Bowl, *48, 49*

R

Radicchio
   Arugula, and Fennel Salad, Warm, Parmesan Chicken
      with, *156, 157*
   Super Cobb Salad, 112, *113*
Radishes
   Black Rice Bowls with Salmon, *142, 143*
   Edamame Salad with Arugula and Radishes, *224, 225*
   Salmon Tacos with Super Slaw, *138, 139*
   and Watercress, Egg Salad Sandwiches with, 86, *87*
Raisins
   Anchovy Dip, 266, 267
   Curried Chickpea Salad Sandwiches, 89
   Curried Chickpeas with Garlic and Yogurt, 244, 245
   Pepita, Almond, and Goji Berry Muesli, *40, 41*
   Sunflower Seed, Hazelnut, and Cherry Muesli, 40
Raspberries
   Chia Pudding with Fresh Fruit and Coconut, 50, 51
   Pepita, Almond, and Goji Berry Muesli, 40, *41*
   as substitute for blueberries, 8
   Sunflower Seed, Hazelnut, and Cherry Muesli, 40
   Three-Grain Breakfast Bowl, *48, 49*
**Raw Beet and Carrot Noodle Salad with Almond-Sesame
   Dressing, 122, *123***
Red Lentil Soup with North African Spices, *100, 101*

Red rice, health benefits, 30
Relish, Tangerine and Ginger, *136*, 137
Resveratrol, 7
Riboflavin, 4
Rice
   Black, Bowls with Salmon, *142, 143*
   Brown, Lemony, and Sun-Dried Tomatoes, Turkey
      Meatballs with, *166, 167*
   Brown, Onigiri with Spinach, Edamame,
      and Sesame, *278, 279*
   Brown, Pilaf with Dates and Pistachios, 250, *251*
   health benefits, 30
   Super Greens Soup, 92, 93
   Wild, and Garlic-Chicken Soup, *96, 97*
Ricotta cheese
   Cauliflower-Chickpea Flatbread with Romesco, 198–99, *199*
   Vegetable Lasagna, 182–83, *183*
Risotto, Beet Barley, *188*, 189
Roasted Artichokes with Lemon Vinaigrette, 202, 203
Roasted Brussels Sprouts with Walnuts and Lemon, 212, 213
Roasted Butternut Squash with Pistachios and Feta, 234, 235
**Roasted Spiralized Sweet Potatoes with Walnuts
   and Feta, 240, *241***
Roasted Tomato Salsa with Black Beans, 264, 265
Romesco, Cauliflower-Chickpea Flatbread with, 198–99, *199*

S

Salads
   Arugula, Radicchio, and Fennel, Warm, Parmesan
      Chicken with, *156, 157*
   Asparagus, Arugula, and Cannellini Bean,
      with Walnuts, 114, *115*
   Broccoli, with Almonds and Cranberries, *210, 211*
   Brussels Sprout, Red Cabbage, and Pomegranate
      Slaw, 214
   Carrot "Tabbouleh" with Fennel, Orange, and
      Hazelnuts, 216
   Carrot "Tabbouleh" with Mint, Pistachios, and
      Pomegranate Seeds, 216, *217*
   Chicken, Chinese, 124, *125*
   Chicken and Arugula, with Figs and Warm Spices, *126, 127*
   Edamame, with Arugula and Radishes, *224, 225*
   Fennel and Apple, with Smoked Trout, 130, *131*
   Kale Caesar, 108, *109*
   Mediterranean Chopped, *110, 111*
   nutrient-dense greens for, 13
   Pesto Farro, with Cherry Tomatoes and Artichokes, *116, 117*
   Quinoa Taco, 120, *121*
   Raw Beet and Carrot Noodle, with Almond-Sesame
      Dressing, 122, *123*
   Salmon, Avocado, Grapefruit, and Watercress, *128, 129*
   Super Cobb, 112, *113*
   Thai Grilled-Steak, 176–77, *177*
   Three-Bean, with Arugula, *118*, 119

Salmon
Avocado, Grapefruit, and Watercress Salad, *128, 129*
Black Rice Bowls with, *142, 143*
Oven-Roasted, with Miso-Sesame Sauce, 137
Oven-Roasted, with Tangerine and Ginger Relish, *136, 137*
Pomegranate Roasted, with Lentils and Chard, 140, *141*
Smoked, and Asparagus, Fluffy Omelet with, 70, *71*
Smoked, Deviled Eggs, 276
Tacos with Super Slaw, *138, 139*
wild, health benefits, 24

Salsa
Roasted Tomato, with Black Beans, 264, *265*
Tomato, *274, 275*

Sandwiches
Chickpea Salad, *88, 89*
Curried Chickpea Salad, 89
Egg Salad, with Radishes and Watercress, 86, *87*
MLTs, *82, 83*
Turmeric Chicken Salad, *84, 85*

Sardines, health benefits, 24

Sauces
Avocado Crema, 152
Beet Muhammara, 256, *257*
Chermoula, 153
Chimichurri, 153
Garlic Aïoli, 152
Kale and Sunflower Seed Pesto, 153
Lemon-Yogurt, 152–53
Miso-Sesame, 137
Orange, Sour, *160, 161*
Sriracha Aïoli, 152
Tahini Yogurt, 153

Sautéed Green Beans with Mushroom and Dukkah, 228, 229

Sautéed Spinach with Yogurt and Dukkah, 232, 233

Seeds. *See* Chia (seeds); Flaxseeds; Pepita(s); Sesame seeds; Sunflower seed(s)

Selenium, 5

Sesame seeds
Brown Rice Onigiri with Spinach, Edamame, and Sesame, *278, 279*
Dukkah, 232–33, *233*
health benefits, 34
Oven-Roasted Salmon with Miso-Sesame Sauce, 137
Whole-Wheat Seeded Crackers, *272, 273*

Shepherd's Pie, Turkey, 164–65, *165*

Shiitake, Tofu, and Mustard Greens Soup, 104, *105*

Sides
Beets with Orange and Walnuts, 206, *207*
Broccoli Salad with Almonds and Cranberries, *210, 211*
Brown Rice Pilaf with Dates and Pistachios, 250, *251*
Brussels Sprout, Red Cabbage, and Pomegranate Slaw, 214
Bulgur Pilaf with Cremini Mushrooms, *252, 253*
Bulgur Pilaf with Shiitake Mushrooms, 253
Butternut Squash Polenta, 246, *247*

Sides *(cont.)*
Carrot "Tabbouleh" with Fennel, Orange, and Hazelnuts, 216
Carrot "Tabbouleh" with Mint, Pistachios, and Pomegranate Seeds, 216, *217*
Cauliflower Puree, 220, *221*
Cauliflower Rice, 222, *223*
Curried Chickpeas with Garlic and Yogurt, 244, *245*
Edamame Salad with Arugula and Radishes, 224, *225*
Garlicky Braised Kale, 230, 231
Grilled Broccoli with Lemon and Parmesan, 208–9, *209*
Lentils with Spinach and Garlic Chips, 242, *243*
Quinoa Pilaf with Shiitakes, Edamame, and Ginger, 248, *249*
Roasted Artichokes with Lemon Vinaigrette, 202, *203*
Roasted Brussels Sprouts with Walnuts and Lemon, *212, 213*
Roasted Butternut Squash with Pistachios and Feta, *234, 235*
Roasted Spiralized Sweet Potatoes with Walnuts and Feta, 240, *241*
Sautéed Green Beans with Mushroom and Dukkah, 228, *229*
Sautéed Spinach with Yogurt and Dukkah, 232, *233*
Slow-Cooked Whole Carrots with Pine Nut Relish, 218, *219*
Stir-Fried Asparagus with Shiitakes, 204, *205*
Stir-Fried Eggplant with Garlic-Basil Sauce, 226, *227*
Sweet Potato and Swiss Chard Gratin, 238, *239*
Twice-Baked Sweet Potatoes with Hazelnuts, 236, *237*

Skillet Roasted Apples with Dried Figs, Walnuts, and Maple Yogurt, 294, 295

Slaws
Red Cabbage, Pulled BBQ Turkey with, 170, *171*
Super, Salmon Tacos with, *138, 139*

Slow-Cooked Whole Carrots with Pine Nut Relish, 218, *219*

Smoked Salmon
and Asparagus, Fluffy Omelet with, 70, *71*
Deviled Eggs, 276

Smoked Trout
Deviled Eggs, 276, *277*
Fennel and Apple Salad with, 130, *131*
Hash with Eggs, 76, *77*

Snacks
Anchovy Dip, 266, *267*
Beet Chips, 270, *271*
Beet Muhammara, 256, *257*
Brown Rice Onigiri with Spinach, Edamame, and Sesame, *278, 279*
Cherry, Chocolate, and Orange Trail Mix, 280, *281*
Cranberry, Coconut, Chili, and Lime Trail Mix, 281
Kale Chips, 268, *269*
Navy Bean and Artichoke Dip, 262, *263*
Roasted Tomato Salsa with Black Beans, 264, *265*
Smoked Salmon Deviled Eggs, 276

index

Snacks *(cont.)*

Smoked Trout Deviled Eggs, *276, 277*
Super Guacamole, *258, 259*
Sweet Potato Hummus, *260, 261*
Ultimate Nachos, *274, 275*
Whole-Wheat Seeded Crackers, *272, 273*

Soups

15-Bean and Vegetable, *102, 103*
Garlic-Chicken and Wild Rice, *96, 97*
Italian Wedding, with Kale and Farro, *106, 107*
Mushroom and Wheat Berry, *98, 99*
Red Lentil, with North African Spices, *100, 101*
Shiitake, Tofu, and Mustard Greens, *104, 105*
Super Greens, *92, 93*
Tomato, Bulgur, and Red Pepper, Turkish, *94, 95*

Soybeans. *See* Edamame

Spice grinder, 36

Spice-Rubbed Turkey Breast with Sour Orange Sauce, *160, 161*

Spices

adding to recipes, 15
health benefits of, 32–33

Spinach

baby, cooking with, 12
Chickpea Salad Sandwiches, *88, 89*
cooking, note about, 12
curly-leaf, cooking with, 12
Curried Chickpea Salad Sandwiches, 89
Edamame, and Sesame, Brown Rice Onigiri with, *278, 279*
Garlic-Chicken and Wild Rice Soup, *96, 97*
and Garlic Chips, Lentils with, *242, 243*
health benefits, 12
Kale and Sunflower Seed Pesto, 153
Pesto Farro Salad with Cherry Tomatoes and Artichokes, *116, 117*
Sautéed, with Yogurt and Dukkah, *232, 233*
Turmeric Chicken Salad Sandwiches, *84, 85*
Vegetable Lasagna, *182–83, 183*

Spiralizer, 36

Squash

acorn, substituting for butternut squash, 16
Butternut, and Kale, One-Pan Chicken with, *154, 155*
butternut, health benefits, 16
Butternut, Polenta, *246, 247*
Butternut, Roasted, with Pistachios and Feta, *234, 235*
butternut, substitutes for, 16
delicata, substituting for butternut squash, 16
Pumpkin–Cream Cheese Brownies, *286–87, 287*
Pumpkin Spice Waffles, *56, 57*
Pumpkin Turkey Chili, *168, 169*

Sriracha Aïoli, 152

Steel-Cut Oatmeal with Carrots and Cherries, *46, 47*

Stir-Fried Asparagus with Shiitakes, *204, 205*

Stir-Fried Eggplant with Garlic-Basil Sauce, *226, 227*

Stir-Fried Tempeh with Orange Sauce, *180, 181*

Strawberries

Chia Pudding with Fresh Fruit and Coconut, *50, 51*
Peaches, and Blackberries with Basil and Pepper, *296, 297*
as substitute for blueberries, 8

Sugar, note on, 35

Summer Rolls with Spicy Almond Butter Sauce, *132, 133*

Sunflower seed(s)

and Almonds, Quinoa Granola with, *42, 43*
Edamame Salad with Arugula and Radishes, *224, 225*
Flourless Nut and Seed Loaf, *44, 45*
Hazelnut, and Cherry Muesli, 40
health benefits, 29
and Kale Pesto, 153
and Kale Pesto, Whole-Wheat Pizza with, *196–97, 197*
Pesto Farro Salad with Cherry Tomatoes and Artichokes, *116, 117*

Super Cobb Salad, 112, *113*

Superfoods

almonds, 28
anchovies & sardines, 24
apples, 10
artichokes, 20
asparagus, 20
avocados, 18
beets, 19
blueberries, 8
broccoli, 14
Brussels sprouts, 14
butternut squash, 16
carrots, 17
cauliflower, 14
cherries, 9
cranberries, 8
dark chocolate, 31
dates, 11
dried beans, 23
edamame, 22
eggplant, 17
eggs, 26
figs, 11
grapefruit, 11
grass-fed lean red meat, 27
green beans, 22
kale, 12
lean white poultry, 27
lentils, 23
mushrooms, 21
oats, 29
onions, 21
oranges, 10
plain yogurt, 31
pomegranates, 9

Superfoods *(cont.)*
quinoa, 29
red bell peppers, 19
red cabbage, 15
salmon (wild), 24
spinach, 12
sunflower seeds & pepitas, 28
sweet potatoes, 16
Swiss chard, 13
tofu & tempeh, 26
tomatoes, 18
trout, 25
walnuts, 28
watercress, 13
white fish, 25
whole grains, 30
wild rice, black rice, red rice, and brown rice, 30
Super Greens Soup, 92, 93
Super Guacamole, 258, 259
Sweet Potato(es)
health benefits, 16
Hummus, 260, 261
Poblano, and Black Bean Tacos, 190, 191
Roasted Spiralized, with Walnuts and Feta, 240, 241
and Swiss Chard Gratin, 238, 239
Twice-Baked, with Hazelnuts, 236, 237
Swiss chard. *See* Chard (Swiss)

T

"Tabbouleh"
Carrot, with Fennel, Orange, and Hazelnuts, 216
Carrot, with Mint, Pistachios, and Pomegranate
Seeds, 216, 217
Tacos
Salmon, with Super Slaw, 138, 139
Sweet Potato, Poblano, and Black Bean, 190, 191
Taco Salad, Quinoa, 120, 121
Tahini
Sweet Potato Hummus, 260, 261
Yogurt Sauce, 153
**Tangerine and Ginger Relish, Oven-Roasted Salmon
with, 136, 137**
Tangerines, as substitute for oranges, 10
Tempeh
health benefits, 26
Stir-Fried, with Orange Sauce, 180, 181
Thai Grilled-Steak Salad, 176–77, 177
Thai Red Curry with Lentils and Tofu, 178, 179
Thiamine, 4
Three-Bean Salad with Arugula, 118, 119
Three-Grain Breakfast Bowl, 48, 49
Toast, Avocado and Bean, 64, 65
Tofu
health benefits, 26
and Lentils, Thai Red Curry with, 178, 179

Tofu *(cont.)*
Rancheros, 74–75, 75
Shiitake, and Mustard Greens Soup, 104, 105
Summer Rolls with Spicy Almond Butter Sauce, 132, 133
Tomato(es)
Avocado and Bean Toast, 64, 65
Bulgur, and Red Pepper Soup, Turkish, 94, 95
canned, buying, 18
Cherry, and Artichokes, Pesto Farro Salad with, 116, 117
Crispy Skillet Turkey Burgers, 158, 159
-Ginger Vinaigrette, Warm, Poached Chicken with, 150, 151
health benefits, 18
Mediterranean Chopped Salad, 110, 111
MLTs, 82, 83
Orange, and Avocado, Grilled Flank Steak with, 172, 173
Pumpkin Turkey Chili, 168, 169
Quinoa Taco Salad, 120, 121
Roasted, Salsa with Black Beans, 264, 265
Salsa, 274, 275
Sun-Dried, and Lemony Brown Rice, Turkey Meatballs
with, 166, 167
Super Cobb Salad, 112, 113
Super Guacamole, 258, 259
Tofu Rancheros, 74–75, 75
Vegetable Lasagna, 182–83, 183
Whole-Wheat Pizza with Kale and Sunflower Seed
Pesto, 196–97, 197
Tortillas and tortilla chips
Kale and Black Bean Breakfast Burritos, 68, 69
Salmon Tacos with Super Slaw, 138, 139
Sweet Potato, Poblano, and Black Bean Tacos, 190, 191
Swiss Chard Enchiladas, 192, 193
Tofu Rancheros, 74–75, 75
Ultimate Nachos, 274, 275
Trail Mix
Cherry, Chocolate, and Orange, 280, 281
Cranberry, Coconut, Chili, and Lime, 281
Trout
Baked Stuffed, with Red Pepper and Preserved
Lemon, 148, 149
health benefits, 25
Smoked, Deviled Eggs, 276, 277
Smoked, Fennel and Apple Salad with, 130, 131
Smoked, Hash with Eggs, 76, 77
substitutes for, 25
Turkey
Breast, Spice-Rubbed, with Sour Orange Sauce, 160, 161
Burgers, Crispy Skillet, 158, 159
Chili, Pumpkin, 168, 169
Cutlets with Barley and Swiss Chard, 162, 163
Italian Wedding Soup with Kale and Farro, 106, 107
lean white, health benefits, 27
Meatballs with Lemony Brown Rice and Sun-Dried
Tomatoes, 166, 167
Pulled BBQ, with Red Cabbage Slaw, 170, 171
Shepherd's Pie, 164–65, 165

Turkish Tomato, Bulgur, and Red Pepper Soup, 94, 95
Turmeric
  and Broccoli, Frittata with, 72, 73
  Chicken Salad Sandwiches, 84, 85
  health benefits, 32
  Whole-Wheat Seeded Crackers, 272, 273
Turnip greens, as substitute for Swiss chard, 13
Twice-Baked Sweet Potatoes with Hazelnuts, 236, 237

U

Ultimate Nachos, 274, 275

V

Vegetable(s)
  at breakfast, 15
  Broth Base, 37
  "clean fifteen," 20
  at dessert time, 15
  "dirty dozen," 20
  Lasagna, 182–83, 183
  see also specific vegetables
Vinaigrette, Warm Tomato-Ginger, 150, 151
Vinegar, health benefits, 34
Vitamin A, 4
Vitamin B1, 4
Vitamin B2, 4
Vitamin B3, 4
Vitamin B5, 4
Vitamin B6, 4
Vitamin B7, 4
Vitamin B9, 4
Vitamin B12, 4
Vitamin C, 4, 19
Vitamin D, 5
Vitamin E, 5
Vitamin K, 5
Vitamins
  best food sources for, 4–5
  heat-sensitive, 19
  key functions and benefits, 4–5

W

Waffles, Pumpkin Spice, 56, 57
Walnuts
  Asparagus, Arugula, and Cannellini Bean Salad
    with, 114, 115
  Beet Muhammara, 256, 257
  Cauliflower-Chickpea Flatbread with Romesco, 198–99, 199
  Cherry, Chocolate, and Orange Trail Mix, 280, 281

Walnuts (cont.)
  Cranberry, Coconut, Chili, and Lime Trail Mix, 281
  Dried Figs, and Maple Yogurt, Skillet Roasted Apples
    with, 294, 295
  and Feta, Roasted Spiralized Sweet Potatoes with, 240, 241
  health benefits, 28
  and Lemon, Roasted Brussels Sprouts with, 212, 213
  Mediterranean Chopped Salad, 110, 111
  and Orange, Beets with, 206, 207
  Pinto Bean–Beet Burgers, 90, 91
  Turmeric Chicken Salad Sandwiches, 84, 85
  Whole-Wheat Date-Nut Bread, 62, 63
Watercress
  health benefits, 13
  and Radishes, Egg Salad Sandwiches with, 86, 87
  Salmon, Avocado, and Grapefruit Salad, 128, 129
Wheat Berry and Mushroom Soup, 98, 99
White beans
  Asparagus, Arugula, and Cannellini Bean Salad
    with Walnuts, 114, 115
  Navy Bean and Artichoke Dip, 262, 263
Whole-wheat flour
  Carrot Snack Cake, 290–91, 291
  earthy flavors, for recipes, 35
  100 Percent Whole-Wheat Pancakes, 54, 55
  Pumpkin–Cream Cheese Brownies, 286–87, 287
  Whole-Wheat Blueberry-Almond Muffins, 58, 59
  Whole-Wheat Date-Nut Bread, 62, 63
  Whole-Wheat Pizza with Kale and Sunflower Seed
    Pesto, 196–97, 197
  Whole-Wheat Seeded Crackers, 272, 273
Wild Rice
  and Garlic-Chicken Soup, 96, 97
  health benefits, 30

Y

Yogurt
  –Cream Cheese Frosting, 291, 291
  and Dukkah, Sautéed Spinach with, 232, 233
  and Garlic, Curried Chickpeas with, 244, 245
  Greek, about, 31
  -Lemon Sauce, 152–53
  Maple, Dried Figs, and Walnuts, Skillet Roasted Apples
    with, 294, 295
  plain, health benefits, 31
  swapping mayonnaise for, 3
  Tahini Sauce, 153

Z

Zeaxanthin, 7
Zinc, 5

31901063028171